THE BLUE GUIDES

James Boswell, in the costume of a Corsica chief

BLUE GUIDE

Corsica

Roland Gant

A & C Black
London

WW Norton
New York

Second edition 1992

Published by A & C Black (Publishers) Limited
35 Bedford Row, London WC1R 4JH

A CIP catalogue record of this book
is available from the British Library.

ISBN   0–7136–3589–4

Published in the United States of America by
WW Norton and Company, Inc
500 Fifth Avenue, New York, NY 10110

Published simultaneously in Canada by
Penguin Books Canada Limited
2801 John Street, Markham, Ontario L3R 1B4

ISBN   0–393–30967–3   USA

The author and the publishers have done their best to ensure the accuracy
of all the information in Blue Guide Corsica; however, they can accept no
responsibility for any loss, injury or inconvenience sustained by any
traveller as a result of information or advice contained in the guide.

Maps and plans drawn by András Bereznay.
Atlas section by Thames Cartographic.

Roland Gant has always written and travelled. In publishing he was in turn
Editorial Director of Michael Joseph and Literary Director of William
Heinemann. He has contributed to and/or reviewed for *The Daily
Telegraph, The Times, The Evening Standard, The Guardian*, etc. and many
periodicals. His relationship with Corsica, visited many times during the
past forty years, is one of both heart and mind.

Printed and bound in Great Britain by
Butler & Tanner Ltd, Frome and London

PREFACE

Corsica is one of the 22 *Régions* of France and is divided into two *départements*, Corse-du-Sud and Haute-Corse. It differs in many ways—geographical, historical, cultural, in climate, economy and vegetation—from mainland France, presenting a variety that is specially attractive to visitors. Why is the island so different and special?

Corsica's 1000km coastline, unpolluted and uncongested, has everything to offer: extensive and clean sandy beaches, spectacular cliffs and rocky coves, *ports de plaisance* and six car-ferry harbours, hotels and motels in all categories, camping sites and gîtes. Bathing, windsurfing, sea-angling, underwater fishing and exploration can all be enjoyed and for those aquatic sports where equipment is needed it can be hired easily.

Pearly clichés form around grains of truth and those applied to Corsica are all accurate—l'Ile de Beauté, the scented isle, a mountain in the sea. Its beauty is exceptional, the smell of the *maquis*, the flowering undergrowth that exists nowhere on the mainland, is unforgettable, and within a few kilometres of the shore are soaring peaks, some snow-topped for most of the year. Much of the interior consists of mountain ranges with tumbling torrents and magnificent forests of Corsican pine, the *laricio* that can reach 50m in height and over 700 years in age. Activities in these inland regions include mountain walks (see Rte 16) of varied duration and challenge on paths that are well-marked, some with overnight shelters on the more remote stretches; organised pony-trekking; river exploration by canoe and kayak; spelaeology; rock climbing; downhill and cross-country skiing in winter; hang-gliding and parapente (see Practical Information: Sport).

Man has been in Corsica for some 10,000 years. In the last 50 years archaeological research has increased and developed rapidly, originally at sites first recorded by Prosper Mérimée during his visit to the island in 1839 as Inspecteur Général des Monuments Historiques and at many others since, and still being, discovered. Together with Pisan churches, Genoese fortresses and shoreline watchtowers, baroque chapels which are sometimes in unexpected and half-forgotten places, the many museums devoted to every aspect of Corsican life, traditions, arts and crafts—the richness of Corsica's history is present everywhere throughout the island.

The pleasant climate enjoyed by Corsica is described on p 11 but reaction to weather is partly conditioned by environment. Mountains, beaches, farmlands, forests, vineyards, hilltop villages and fishing ports, the colourful and extensive variety of landscape is present in one relatively small island and yet everywhere one is conscious of space. A few comparisons will help to show why.

Corsica at its longest and broadest is 183km by 83km, with an area of 8681 sq km and a population of 250,000. Cyprus, 925 sq km, pop. 698,300; Jamaica, 10,991 sq km, pop. 2,392,300; Puerto Rico, 8860 sq km, pop. 3,346,000. Of roughly the same area as Corsica: Lincolnshire with Leicestershire, pop. 1,468,100; Connecticut, pop. 3,107,576; Grampian Region of Scotland, pop. 499,580; Delaware, smaller with 5,003 sq km, pop. 594,338.

Further to plenty of space in which to breathe and move around, Corsica, although an integral part of France, has a unique history of centuries of occupation by a series of foreign powers, opposed with resolute courage, and a strong sense of identity as a people with its own language, still spoken and written with pride. Here there are obvious similarities between Corsica, Wales and Quebec. In 1990–1991 there was controversial discussion at French parliamentary level as to whether '*le peuple corse*' should receive official recognition within the framework of the French nation. An initial decision to do so was shortly after reversed. The existence of '*un peuple corse*' is self-evident without benefit of statute. Nothing, either, can alter the important contribution of Corsicans in many areas of French government service such as the police, in the former colonies and in the army. Forty thousand Corsican soldiers died in the First World War, a higher proportion of the population than that in any other French *département*.

Given this evidence of Corsicans as patriotic Frenchmen, where does Corsican separatism stand? There are a number of separatist movements which from time to time regroup with consequent changes of name and the initials by which they are generally known and which, spray-painted on walls, may be noticed by visitors. Demands range from increased administrative devolution (the Corsican Assembly has fewer powers than has the Scottish Office, by the way) through autonomy such as the 17 regions including Catalunya, the Canaries and Aragon, were granted in Spain under the 1978 Constitution, to secession from France and total independence, action similar to that taken in 1990–1991 by a number of republics in the USSR.

Without speculating on the nature of an eventual *modus vivendi*, a comment on the present position for the information of visitors to Corsica is appropriate here because media reporting, in Anglophone countries as well as in France, on violence committed in the name of separatism, is invariably sensational. There is nothing in common with what happens in, for example, Northern Ireland or the Middle East. Tourists are never put at risk in these attempts, regrettable but sometimes understandable, to exert an influence on or draw attention to issues of importance to the life and future of Corsica, such as job-creation and ecology. Tourists are never drawn into discussion of these questions and it is courteous not to raise them.

Seldom reported outside the Corsican press are the many positive achievements resulting from the islanders' determination to keep their country untainted by industrial and financial pollution, to further the development of the University, museums, craft and music centres, archaeology, the restoration of ancient buildings and the vigorous revival of an agricultural and pastoral economy that was withering.

The Parc Naturel Régional de la Corse is a triumph of creative imagination and enterprising co-operation which merits world-wide attention and is an example of ecological planning which could be followed in many other countries. Its success has been achieved by the will and efforts of the entire Corsican population.

Since I was in Corsica to prepare the first edition of this Blue Guide in 1983–1985 the progress in these and many other fields has been steady and impressive. So, too, has been the widespread acceptance of tourism as an essential part of the island's economy. Corsicans have applied themselves to the efficient growth of tourism with energetic professionalism but that does not mean that visitors are processed as mere money-producing units along a conveyor belt of hotels, camping sites, tours and restaurants. Visitors are welcomed, with very rare exceptions, with courteous dignity and generosity. Corsicans are proud of their island and of ensuring that visitors enjoy to the full its beauty and unique character.

Roland Gant, Au Vieux Pont

A Note on Blue Guides

The Blue Guide series began in 1915 when Muirhead Guide-Books Limited published 'Blue Guide London and its Environs'. Finlay and James Muirhead already had extensive experience of guidebook publishing: before the First World War they had been the editors of the English editions of the German Baedekers, and by 1915 they had acquired the copyright of most of the famous 'Red' Handbooks from John Murray.

An agreement made with the French publishing house Hachette et Cie in 1917 led to the translation of Muirhead's London guide, which became the first 'Guide Bleu'—Hachette had previously published the blue-covered 'Guides Joannes'. Subsequently, Hachette's 'Guide Bleu Paris et ses Environs' was adapted and published in London by Muirhead. The collaboration between the two publishing houses continued until 1933.

In 1933 Ernest Benn Limited took over the Blue Guides, appointing Russell Muirhead, Finlay Muirhead's son, editor in 1934. The Muirhead's connection with the Blue Guides ended in 1963 when Stuart Rossiter, who had been working on the Guides since 1954, became house editor, revising and compiling several of the books himself.

The Blue Guides are now published by A & C Black, who acquired Ernest Benn in 1984, so continuing the tradition of guidebook publishing which began in 1826 with 'Black's Economical Tourist of Scotland'. The Blue Guide series continues to grow: there are now almost 50 titles in print with revised editions appearing regularly and many new Blue Guides in preparation.

'Blue Guides' is a registered trade mark.

Acknowledgements

I am for ever grateful to those who helped me when I was preparing the first edition of this Guide and whose names I listed on its acknowledgements page. Some of them extended their assistance and advice to me while I was working on this new edition so my thanks to them is renewed. I cannot give the names of the many men and women who gave information, practical aid when travelling, and generous hospitality. Heartfelt thanks to them all.

I am particularly grateful to the following: l'Association des Amis du Parc Naturel Régional de la Corse, its Secrétaire Générale, Mme R. Judais, and Dominique Farellacci, Chargé d'Information; La Société Nationale Corse-Méditerranée—SNCM Ferryterranée, Mme Deshusse and Commandant Gérard Boursaus, captain 'Napoleon'; Le Musée Fesch and Mme Biass-Fabiani, Conservateur; Le Musée de la Préhistoire Corse, Sartène and Paul Nebbia, Conservateur; Dorothy Carrington, La Casa Musicale de Pigna, and Toni and Jérome Casalonga; Dr François Mancini; Michel Mohrt de l'Académie Française; Polly and Frank Muir; Dr Francis Neri; Jean Olhagaray; Françoise Thibault; Daniel Vidoni.

Nadia Legrand I thank again for encouragement, companionship, photographs and advice, and Blue Guides and Gemma Davies for patience and understanding in working with a sometimes elusive author at long distance.

CONTENTS

Maps and Plans

Maps

Plans

BACKGROUND INFORMATION

Geography

Corsica is the fourth largest island in the Mediterranean, after Sicily, Sardinia and Cyprus, with an area of 8681 sq km. From the tip of Cap Corse in the north to the Straits of Bonifacio in the south its greatest length is 183km and at its widest, a little north of the centre, it is 83km (see also Preface).

The island has a backbone range of mountains composed of granite which varies in both the constituent combination and in colour. The highest are Monte Cinto (2710m), Monte Rotondo (2622m), Paglia Orba (2525m), Monte d'Oro (2389m), Monte Renoso (2352m) and Monte Incudine (2128m). The granite ranges are separated from the schist mountains in east Corsica, more recent in formation, by a central depression running north-west to south-east with no peaks over 700m. Through the centuries before roads were built and transport was by hoof and foot there were virtually two Corsicas. The En-Deça-des-Monts was 'this side of the mountains', that is to say the east side which was colonised from Italy and consisted of the Eastern Plain, Cap Corse, Castagniccia, Casinca, the lowlands of the central depression and the Balagne. The Au-Delà-des-Monts was 'beyond the mountains' and consisted of the jaggedly picturesque west coast, the Ajaccio region, the south-west and south of the island and the east coast as far north as Solenzara. When in 1975 Corsica was divided into two départements of France which together comprise the Région of Corsica the ancient partition was broadly reflected. There are geographical similarities with Scotland where the Highland Line marks the great subsidence of the Central Lowlands and divides the Highlands from the Southern Uplands.

The west coastline is indented with gulfs where rivers rising on the central watershed reach the sea, such as the Prunelli at the Gulf of Ajaccio and the Porto at the Gulf to which it gives its name. The shoreline of red rocks is studded with coves and long beaches of fine sand and there are ports and harbours, large and small.

Rivers flowing to the east coast are slowed by their passage through the alluvial plain. In the past, marshlands were formed near the sea and it was here that the anopheles mosquito flourished and spread malaria which, together with repeated invasions by Vandals and Barbary pirates, depopulated the Eastern Plain after the Romans left in the mid 5C and the irrigation systems which they had established became derelict. It was not until the Second World War that the US Army's DDT banished the mosquito from what Baedeker in 1907 called 'the malarious plain of Aléria'. This formerly uninhabitable region of Corsica has been transformed in the last half century into a rich agricultural area producing many new as well as traditional crops and with an energetic growth of tourism on the coast. Visitors attracted by the long stretches of safe sandy beaches ideal for bathing, sailing and all marine sports, are now catered for by hotels in a wide price and comfort range, *villages de vacances*, châlets or 'bungalows', and self-catering *gîtes*. The same amenities are present on the rockier Cap Corse and Bonifacio region shores.

In the central mountains roads are continually being improved and accommodation developed for those who want either to walk in this magnificent area on the GR 20, Between Sea and Mountain, From Sea to Sea and other long-distance paths or, without moving around much, to enjoy the scenery and invigorating air.

Climate

Corsica's individuality, strongly evident in geology, vegetation, history, human endeavour and character, is also apparent in its climate which is obviously Mediterranean but has specific features such as being hotter in the north than in the south and with an east coast rainfall higher than that of the west coast. Corsica on the whole gets more rain than south mainland France and it is this that keeps the island so green. Rainfall is heaviest in November–December followed by that in March–April. Snow can be heavy in the mountains and some passes may be blocked for weeks at a time in late winter and early spring. Yet it should be remembered that Ajaccio, on the same latitude as Rome, has a higher total of hours of sunshine—almost 3000 hours annually—than anywhere in continental France.

Above 1500m altitude the climate is Alpine. It is warm throughout the island in summer and it can be very hot on the coast but there is nearly always a breeze, the *mezzogiorno* from around 09.00 which dies out in the afternoon to be replaced by land breezes in the evening which last through the night. While evenings are fresh by the sea they can be cool to cold in the mountains, even in mid-summer.

Prevailing winds from the south-west, west and north-west are called *libeccio* and *mistral*, the *sirocco* blows on the east coast from the south-west, the *levante* from the east, the *grecale* from the north-east and the *tramontane* from the north, with the strongest winds at the two extremities, the most exposed, of the island, Cap Corse in the north and Bonifacio in the south.

To sum up, the Corsican climate offers a variety at all times and one rarely feels trapped or frustrated for long by rainy or dull weather. Days of endless rain are practically unknown and when mid-summer beaches are too hot to stay on all day the cooler mountains and lakes are well within an hour's drive from nearly everywhere on the coast.

Average temperatures at sea level

MONTH	Min.	Max.
April	8.9	18.5
May	11.7	22.2
June	15.7	28.1
July	17.8	29.4
August	17.8	29.4
September	16.1	27.2
October	12.2	22.2

Average sea temperatures

MONTH	
April	13.9
May	16.3

June	19.3
July	22.3
August	23.4
September	22.0
October	19.7

Average number of hours of sunshine in the year

Corse du Sud: more than 2750
Haute Corse: 2500–2750

Average number of days in the month on which rain falls

MONTH	DAYS
April	6–8
May	6
June	4
July	2
August	4
September	4
October	6

Historical Introduction

There were human beings in Corsica some 10,000 years ago and they probably came from Sardinia or Tuscany. A female skeleton was found at Araguina, near Bonifacio, in the course of archaeological excavation in 1972, and has been dated to c 6570 BC and the evidence of ritual burial of some complexity points to the existence of an established and organised community (see Rte 9, Levie). Discoveries at other sites, including Filitosa, Currachiaghju, Strette, Cucuruzzu, Cauria and Torre show that there has been continuous occupation by people who kept domestic beasts, cultivated cereals, fashioned tools for tilling, harvesting, shelter construction, and weapons for hunting and defence.

With the advance in boatbuilding skills and navigation Corsica's importance in the Mediterranean became obvious as a staging place on trade lanes and therefore of strategic significance. It was an island with plentiful fresh water, very fertile in parts, possessing a number of good harbours and a central mountain system that could protect the backs of inhabitants defending themselves from predatory invasion of the coast.

Greeks, naming the island Kyrnos, from the Asia Minor maritime state of Phocaea, founded a colony at Alalia (Aléria) c 565 BC. In the battle of Alalia c 540 BC fought at sea against a large Carthaginian-Etruscan fleet, the Phocaeans won a narrow victory but soon left Alalia to strengthen and develop their colony of Massilia (Marseille) on the coast of Gaul.

The Greeks provided Corsica's first major contact with the outside world and they also brought and cultivated vines, olive trees and cereals. After they abandoned Alalia as a colony the Greeks continued to use it as an intermediary port between their colony of Velia on the coast of Southern Italy and Massilia. Alalia was made use of in the same way by the Etruscans and by the Carthaginians who captured and occupied the port 278–259 BC.

It was always this east coast of Corsica that was chosen by invaders, partly because landings were easier than on the rocky west and south coasts and also because of the relative closeness (average 82km) of the long Italian mainland compared with sailing distances to Nice (180km), Marseille (360km) and the Spanish coast (450km). In 260 BC the Romans drove out the Carthaginians from the Eastern Plain and replaced Alalia with Aléria, not merely as a trading port but as a military base for the conquest and subjection of the whole island which, due to stubborn Corsican resistance, took a century to complete. From 163 BC Corsica enyoyed nearly six centuries of relative peace and acquired Latin speech and Christianity. With the crumbling of the Roman Empire Corsica fell prey to Vandals, a Germanic people who controlled the island from 460 until they were defeated by Justinian's general, Belisarius, in 534, thus incorporating Corsica in the Byzantine Empire from which control was taken temporarily (549–53) by another invading Germanic people, the Ostrogoths. After repeated attacks by the Lombards from c 581 Corsica was annexed to the Kingdom of Lombardy in 725.

In 755 the King of the Franks, Pépin le Bref (son of Charles Martel and father of Charlemagne) promised Corsica to the Pacacy once it was liberated from the Lombards. Charlemagne confirmed this donation in 774 but the Papacy was incapable of protecting the island from Saracen raids during the next three centuries. In 1077 Pope Gregory VII sent Landolfe, Bishop of Pisa, to assert Papal authority over the island, above all to bring to heel the turbulent Corsican nobles and bishops. During the two centuries of Pisan rule some of the most beautiful churches in Corsica were built, such as the Cathedral of the Nebbio, la Canonica, San Michele di Murato and La Trinité d'Aregno.

During that period there was strife between the forces of Pisa and Genoa between whom Pope Innocent II in 1133 had divided the Corsican bishoprics. Genoese ambition was even more territorial than ecclesiastical and they established themselves in Bonifacio in 1187, in Calvi in 1268, and defeated the Pisans in the naval battle of Meloria in 1284. This struggle in Corsica between Pisa and Genoa was turned to his own advantage by Sinucello della Rocca of the noble house of Cinarca. He gained control over the whole island by supporting first one side and then the other through half a century and because of the justice which he administered earned from Corsicans the sobriquet Giudice—the Judge. He was supported by the people but the nobility resented his curbs on their greed. The Genoese sided with the nobles and once they had defeated Pisa they captured Giudice, through the treacherous connivance of one of his own bastards, and sent him to the mainland to die in prison, blind and nearly a hundred years old, in 1306 (see Rte 6, Cinarca).

Apart from their troubles with the Corsicans the Genoese were threatened by the Aragonese whose kings had been invested in 1297 with the sovereignty of Corsica by Pope Boniface VIII to replace the domination of Pisa. The Cinarchesi *seigneurs* now sided with Aragon the better to oppose Genoa and for a quarter of a century Arrigo della Rocca, helped by Aragon, waged endless war from 1376 against Genoa and at times had more of the island under his control than Genoa did. It was through his defeat of them at Aléria in 1380 that the Genoese began to develop and fortify Bastia.

While Pisa left its mark on Corsica in its churches Genoa built the fortifications which can still be seen—the great bastions of Bastia, Bonifacio, Calvi, and a ring of watch-towers around the coast. The Genoese, like some 19C and 20C governments, believed that business organisation could be applied to running a country. At the end of the 14C the administration of Corsica was conferred on the Maona, an association of Genoese merchants. They were unsuccessful in quelling resistance by the Cinarchesi. In 1453 Genoa made a second attempt along the same lines by appointing the Office or Bank of St George to implement Genoese rule in Corsica. The Office was a powerful business corporation with its own military force and administrative organisation—there are some similarities with the East India Company in British India 18–19C. Under the Office's harshly efficient rule the fortresses and towers were built, the town of Ajaccio was founded in 1492, and relentless pressure brought about the collapse of rebellions led by the Cinarchesi *seigneurs*, the last of whom, Rinuccio della Rocca, deserted and powerless, was hunted to his death in 1511.

Corsica has had many figures of Shakespearean stature. Rinuccio was one and Sampiero Corso was another. He had served in the French army where he had attained the rank of colonel, before leading rebellion against Genoa, later to be betrayed and killed in an ambush in 1567 (see Rte 2, Bastelica). Sampiero had received covert support from the French who had administered Corsica 1557–59 before handing it back to Genoa by whom it was ruled directly until 1729 when widespread rebellion broke out, national independence declared and a constitution adopted by a national congress at Corte. There was a lull in 1732 but the revolt was renewed and a measure of how desperately Corsica sought an alternative to Genoa was the crowning of a German adventurer, Theodor von Neuhof, King of Corsica in April 1736 (see Rte 12, Alesani). His seven-month reign ended when he quit Corsica in November, leaving little but some coins minted as hastily as were the orders he created and bestowed on his supporters. He paid a fleeting visit to Corsica in April 1738 but nobody was interested in either him or a Restoration.

During the 18C Genoa's grip on Corsica weakened and the influence of France increased. There was a period of Corsican independence 1755–69 when Pasquale Paoli was the elected General of the Nation. During those years Corte was the capital, a constitution was drafted and adopted at the National Assembly in November 1755 and in 1765 the university was founded with the aim of forming among its 300 students graduates in the liberal professions such as medicine and the law needed by the nascent Corsican state. Paoli's administration was firm and just and his organisation of military and naval resistance to the Genoese blockade and attempt to crush independence directly or with the help of Corsican dissidents and French military intervention, was as effective as it could be against powerful odds. Genoa ceded Corsica to France by the Treaty of Versailles (15 May 1768), the French army was opposed by Paoli's troops but their resistance was crushed at the battle of Ponte Nuovo on 8 May 1769. Paoli went into exile in England and the four-year-old university was closed and had to wait until 1980 before it was reopened.

Twenty years later Corsicans welcomed the French Revolution, many believing that it would alleviate or even end their troubles. The French Assembly voted in November 1789 that Corsica be integrated into the French nation. The ban on political exiles was lifted and Paoli returned in triumph, landing at Bastia on 17 July 1790. He was elected Commander-in-Chief of the Corsican National Guards and then President of the Conseil Général of the département of Corsica. There were intrigues against him, helped along by the Bonaparte family which was now in the ascendant. When an attempt was made to arrest him the National Assembly at Corte proclaimed Paoli Father of the Nation at the end of May 1793, defying orders from Paris. In July of that year Paoli and Charles-André Pozzo di Borgo, both of them outlawed by the French Government, appealed to the British for help and in January 1794 Sir Gilbert Elliot arrived in Corsica and discussed a constitution with Paoli. There was more than talk because during that spring and summer the British besieged and took Saint-Florent, Bastia and Calvi. The defenders of Calvi, outnumbered by 40 to 1, and the starving civilian population, suffered heavy casualties during the incessant artillery bombardment. It was on the heights above Calvi that Captain Horatio Nelson was wounded by a rock splinter and lost the sight of his right eye (see Rte 5, Calvi).

In June 1794 the establishment of the Anglo-Corsican kingdom was announced at the National Assembly in Corte and a constitution was formulated and adopted. Paoli remained head of the provisional government until 1 October when, to his and Corsica's humiliation, Sir Gilbert was named Viceroy. French-inspired riots broke out in mid-1795 and this kingdom, which had lasted only twenty months longer than that of Théodore, came to an end when Sir Gilbert and the British forces left Corsica in early October 1796 and on 15 October French soldiers arrived from Italy and landed without meeting any resistance. From then on Corsica was part of France and subject to French laws, to certain sections of which some of the population, particularly priests, objected, such as the Civil Constitution of the Clergy.

In 1811 Napoleon signed the Décret Impérial by which Corsica became a single French département with its administrative capital at Ajaccio. He never exerted himself unduly on behalf of his homeland and Corsicans tried to do more for Napoleon than he did for them. On 4 March 1815 some Bonapartist agents landed and organised a successful rising in support of the ex-Emperor who was about to embark on his last desperate adventure of the Hundred Days. His partisans defeated the Royalist garrisons and until Waterloo the island was governed by Arrighi de Casanova, a general created Duc de Padoue by Napoleon (see Rte 14, Corte). Corsica had provided Napoleon with some 10,000 soldiers, including 43 generals.

During the 19C progress in the island economy continued steadily although there was some resistance to new methods introduced to replace traditional farming. Communications improved and the east and west of Corsica, for so long virtually two countries separated by mountains, were brought into closer touch with each other by the building of new roads and the railway on which work began in 1887. The First World War halted plans announced in 1908 by Clemenceau, then Minister of the Interior, for further improvements in Corsican economy. But emigration increased with islanders taking up occupations on the mainland, chiefly in government service, which provided dependable salaries during working life and pensions on retirement whether they returned to their native isle or remained on the continent.

Many Corsicans emigrated to North Africa and to the Americas. Numerous place-names in the USA include Paoli—'the heart of Hoosier hospitality' in Indiana, Corsica and Morosaglia in Pennsylvania, Corsica in South Dakota and Colorado, and Corsicana near Dallas, Texas. The Monticellos in some twenty States are more likely to have been inspired by the name of President Jefferson's Virginian residence than by a score of Balanins following a wandering star. A Corsican community of over 400,000 thrives

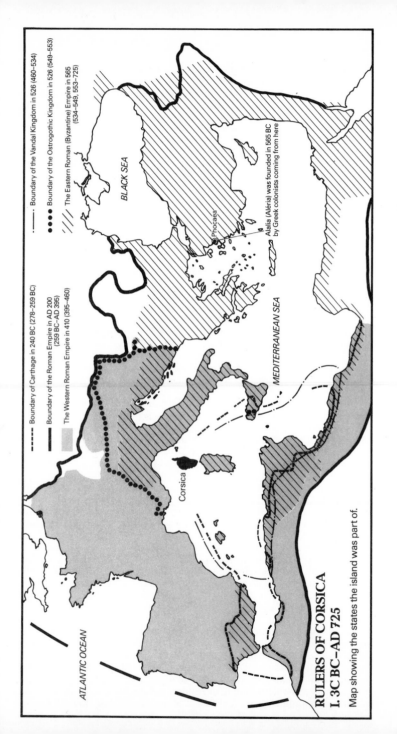

RULERS OF CORSICA
I. 3C BC–AD 725

Map showing the states the island was part of.

Boundary of Carthage in 240 BC (278–259 BC)

Boundary of the Roman Empire in AD 200 (259 BC–AD 395)

The Western Roman Empire in 410 (395–460)

Boundary of the Vandal Kingdom in 526 (460–534)

Boundary of the Ostrogothic Kingdom in 526 (549–553)

The Eastern Roman (Byzantine) Empire in 565 (534–549, 553–725)

Alalia (Aléria) was founded in 565 BC by Greek colonists coming from here

ATLANTIC OCEAN

BLACK SEA

MEDITERRANEAN SEA

Phocaea

Corsica

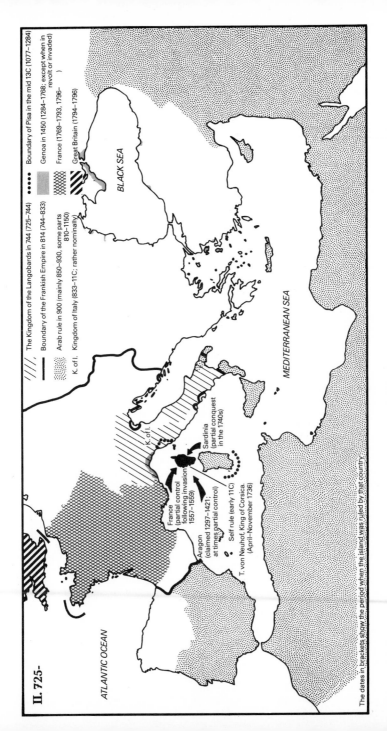

II. 725-

Legend:

- ///// The Kingdom of the Langobards in 744 (725–744)
- —— Boundary of the Frankish Empire in 814 (744–833)
- (dotted) Arab rule in 900 (mainly 850–930, some parts 810–1150)
- K. of I. Kingdom of Italy (833–11C; rather nominally)

- •••• Boundary of Pisa in the mid 13C (1077–1284)
- (shaded) Genoa in 1450 (1284–1768; except when in revolt or invaded)
- (cross-hatch) France (1769–1793, 1796–)
- (diagonal hatch) Great Britain (1794–1796)

ATLANTIC OCEAN

BLACK SEA

MEDITERRANEAN SEA

K. of I.

K. of

Sardinia (partial conquest in the 1740s)

France (partial control following invasion 1557–1559)

Aragon (claimed 1297–1421; at times partial control)

Self rule (early 11C)

T. von Neuhof, King of Corsica. (April–November 1736)

The dates in brackets show the period when the island was ruled by that country.

in Puerto Rico and Raoul Léoni, from a Murato family in the Nebbio, was a progressive President of Venezuela 1964–1969.

During the Second World War first Italian and later German occupation forces found Corsicans more than a match for them. The term Maquis came to be applied to any French resistance group but it originated in Corsica where anti-Axis fighters hid in and operated from the dense *maquis* undergrowth. It took one Axis soldier to watch two islanders, including women and children. Corsica was the first French département to be liberated through Corsican efforts and Allied help in late 1943. It was then that the US Army liberated the east coast from the centuries-old scourge of mosquito and malaria by massive application of DDT (dichlor-diphenyl-trichlorethane).

Since 1945 Corsica's development and progress has been swift and impressive. In 1957 plans were made by the French Government to revitalise Corsican agriculture and SOMIVAC (*Société de mise en valeur agricole de la Corse*) was set up to further these aims. Again there was reluctance by farmers and shepherds to change ancient working methods and living habits but intelligent persuasion, practical instruction in how to improve quality and increase yield, extensive help with money, machines, irrigation, the selling and transport of produce, triumphed in the end. Another organisation, SETCO (*Société d'équipement touristique de la Corse*) was created to promote tourism but also met with some initial opposition by those who feared that large seasonal invasions by 'Continentals' could lead to erosion of habits, manners and language. But Corsicans have adapted to and made a success of tourism in the island (see Preface).

Any impression, both within and beyond the island, that Corsica was an underprivileged offshore appendix of the Provence-Côte d'Azur Région of which, administratively, it had formed part since 1956, was dispelled in 1970 by the creation of the Région Corse in its own right with Ajaccio as Régional chef-lieu or 'capital'. In 1975 the island was divided into two French départements, Corse-du-Sud and Haute-Corse, the departmental and postal codes being 2A and 2B respectively. The geographical approximation of the division to that of En Deça des Monts and Au Delà des Monts, the hallowed partition through the centuries, with the old communication problems now resolved by roads, railway and telephone, satisfied traditionalists. The Parc Naturel Régional lies across territory of both départements and is an enduring unifying force.

Administrative centralisation which for so long was felt to be the stranglehold of Paris not only in Corsica but throughout provincial France has been steadily and yet quite rapidly reduced by a deliberate policy of devolution which has been to the benefit of the Régions. Yet this progress in the delegation of many powers to local authorities has coincided with the growth of an articulate and active separatism in Corsica. I have said as much on this subject as I think is needed in the Preface.

The Corsican language plays a large part in island life and politics. Does it present problems for English-speaking visitors? Provided one has a basic working knowledge of French, which is the language taught in schools and spoken by everybody, there are no greater difficulties encountered than in, for example, Provence, Brittany, Alsace or Quebec. In the mountain districts of Corsica many old people are more at home talking in their own tongue than in French. It is spoken in shops, in the street, in bars and cafés throughout the island with a wide range of inflection and pronunciation. In the larger towns there are many, mostly young people, who understand English and are delighted to exercise it in conversation. Tourists, on the other hand, can enjoy the intellectual effort of learning a few Corsican words and phrases and the use of them will be much appreciated as a courteous example of interest.

The origins of Corsican as spoken and written today are neither clear nor free of controversy. The language spoken by the first inhabitants of the island has left no trace except some faint pre-Indo-European echoes in a few place-names similar to those evoking physical aspects of landscape or seashore which are to be found in other parts of the Mediterranean. Although the Roman conquest was complete by 111 BC Seneca, exiled to Corsica c 40–49 AD, described the natives as ferocious and their language incomprehensible. This may tell us more about Seneca than it does about the Corsican tongue. Latinisation progressed slowly, with fluctuations in accent, pronunciation and variety of meaning. This Latin basis was then subjected to Tuscanisation, particularly in the east, during the Pisan occupation. Genoa used Tuscan as its official language during 500 years of occupation and Tuscan was retained by the French for all state and legal documents in Corsica until the middle of the 19C. Up to the early years of the 20C Church business was conducted not in Latin or French but in Italian. Osmosis between Corsican and French is minimal because the two languages are used side by side and there is therefore no phenomenon of 'Francorse' similar to 'Franglais'. Largely thanks to a determined campaign by Scola Corsa, the island's cultural federation, the French Government recognised Corsican as a 'regional language' in 1974.

Songs have been transmitted orally in Corsican from generation to generation, such as the *chiama rispondi*, a dialogue improvised in 16-syllable lines, and the *voceri*, lamentations composed and sung by a woman for the recently dead who, in the past, were often vendetta victims. Ancient Corsican hymns may be heard on Saint's Days and at other religious processions such as the Catenacciu (see Rte 3, Sartène). During the 19C songs were collected and published but it is particularly from the middle of the 20C that Corsican syntax, spelling and vocabulary have become the subject of detailed study and that a vigorous vernacular literature has developed. Recordings of Corsican songs, music performed on traditional instruments, poetry and prose readings are available in bookshops and music stores in the larger towns.

Instruction and market-place conversation apart, how does the Corsican language impinge on the tourist's everyday experience? Very little and then mostly in road signs which tend more and more to be in Corsican and vary from the spelling on all but the most recent maps. During many visits to Corsica over the years I became used to the kind of spray-can corrections that one used to see in Wales but, as happened in Wales, local authorities could take the multi-coloured hints that often obliterated completely the signposts and had new road-signs made with changed spelling. But, unlike many alterations from English to Welsh where a baffling new identity faces the motorist, French into Corsican remains recognisable in both appearance and sound (and the information is often given in the two languages), e.g. Vergio-Verghio-Verghju, Propriano-Prupria, l'Ile Rousse-Isula Rossa, Saint-Florent-San Fiurenzu. Many changes consist only of o into u, e.g. Borgo-Burgu, Murato-Muratu.

These inconsistencies will, unfortunately, continue until cartographers catch up with the '*corsisation*' of place-names (see Corsican Toponomy at end of Bibliography). Until there is standardisation it is simpler, and less muddling, to continue to present many places in their most familiar forms and in which they appear on the majority of maps still in use. This is what

I have done while at the same time making many changes from the first edition of the Guide, and where inconsistencies occur I trust that they are preferable to the possible bewilderment and irritation that readers might otherwise experience.

A Chronology of Corsican History

3rd millennium BC	Archaeological discoveries (e.g. menhirs, dolmens) record megalithic civilisation in Corsica, Mediterranean Bronze Age.
2nd and 1st millennium BC	End of Bronze Age. Torréen ('tower builders') civilisation in south-east of island. Name derived from circular tower monuments of death rites significance. Examples Torre, Cucuruzzu. The *torre* similar to Sardinian *nuraghi*.
c 565 BC	Alalia (now Aléria) founded by Phocaeans (Greeks from west coast Asia Minor) on east coast, later same century taken by Etruscans and Carthaginians.
259–162 BC	Romans conquer east coastal plain, first building Aléria on site of former Alalia, then founding colony of Mariana. Central mountainous region unconquered.
2–4C AD	Growth of Christianity in Corsica. Martyrs include Restitute, Julie, Devote, later canonised.
5–6C	Invasions by Vandals and Ostrogoths. Vandals hold Corsica until defeated by Byzantine force, commanded by Belisarius, in 534.
522	Corsica and Sardinia incorporated in Byzantine Empire.
8–10C	Frequent Saracen invasions.
c 725	Corsica annexed to Kingdom of Lombardy.
774	Charlemagne confirmed gift of Corsica by his father Pépin le Bref to the Papacy in 754. Thenceforth the Pope titular sovereign of the island.
1014	Pisa and Genoa join forces to eject Moors from Corsica.
1077	Pope grants rule of Corsica to Bishop of Pisa.
1133	Pope divides Corsica between Pisa and Genoa.
1264	Sinucello della Rocca, nobleman of Cinarca, gains control of Corsica by favouring Pisa and Genoa turn and turn about and becomes known as Judge, Giudice di Cinarca.
1284	Definitive victory by Genoa over Pisa in naval battle of Meloria.
1296	Pope hands Corsica and Sardinia to Kingdom of Aragon.
1306	Giudice di Cinarca dies in Genoese prison.
1347	Genoa supplants Aragon as ruler of Corsica but hindered by ravages of Black Death which kills two-thirds of population.
1358	Rising under Sambucuccio d'Alando. Creation of Terre des Communes, agreement between Corsican people and landowners. Latter support Aragon against Genoa.
1378	Arrigo della Rocca, Aragon partisan, lands in Corsica. Genoa assigns control of island to a Genoese financial organisation, the Maona.

1404	Arrigo's nephew, Vincentello d'Istria, named Lieutenant in Corsica by Aragon. Gains control of most of island, notable exception Bonifacio. Captured and executed by Genoa 1434.
1453	Genoa assigns Corsica to another financial organisation, the Office or Bank of St George. The Bank had its private army, rebuilt fortresses, set watch-towers around the coast, founded the present town of Ajaccio and ruled Corsica with iron hand for a century.
1553	Henri II of France, at war with Charles V of Holy Roman Empire, invades Corsica with help of Turkish fleet and support of Corsicans under Sampiero Corso, Corsican patriot and colonel in French army. Calvi and Bastia hold out against France who hand Corsica back to Genoa in 1559.
1564–67	Sampiero Corso raises rebellion against Genoa. Controlled island for a while. Betrayed and assassinated in ambush 1567.
1571	Amnesty accorded by Genoese Governor and publication of *Statuti civili et criminali di Corsica*.
17C	Known as the Century of Misery, Corsicans chafe helplessly at harsh administration by Genoa's officials.
1676	Genoa gives permission for 700 Greeks, in flight from Turks, to settle in Corsica, first at Paomia near Sagone and then at Cargèse.
1729	Beginning of armed revolt throughout the island—Corsican War of Independence.
1731	First National Constitution adopted at a National Assembly at Corte.—Genoa asks Austria for help in crushing insurrection; four battalions of Imperial troops land in Corsica.
1736	Theodor von Neuhof, Westphalian adventurer, lands from English ship at Aléria on 11 March with money and munitions provided by Greek and Jewish merchants in Tunis. Crowned King Théodore I of Corsica at Alesani 15 April, achieves nothing, leaves Corsica 11 November.
1739	French suppress, at request of Genoa, revolt led by Gaffori and Giacinto Paoli (Pasquale's father).
1741	French troops withdraw.
1743	Corsicans supported by Sardinia and Britain, who planned to occupy and divide the island, during Austrian War of Succession. British warships twice bombarded Bastia in 1745 and 1748.
1747	Successful landing by French.
1753	Genoa succeeds in assassinating Gaffori.
1755	Pasquale Paoli elected General of the Nation on 15 July. His Constitution for Corsica adopted by National Assembly November, university founded at Corte from 1765, l'Ile Rousse created as rival port to Genoa's Calvi.
1764	France occupies Corsican fortresses in name of her ally Genoa. Paoli refuses to serve France.
1765	James Boswell meets Paoli at Sollacaro in October.
1768	Genoa cedes Corsica to France.
1769	Corsicans, under Paoli, defeated by French forces at Ponte Nuovo, 8 May. Paoli leaves for England. Napoleon

	Bonaparte born Ajaccio 15 August.
1789	Corsican Constituent Assembly votes 30 November that 'The island of Corsica is hereby declared to be part of the French Empire and its inhabitants subject to the same constitution as all other French…'.
1790	Paoli lands at Bastia in triumph 17 July. At Congress of Orezza in September elected Commander in Chief of the Corsican National Guards. Later appointed President of the départemental Conseil General.
1790	Corsica accorded, as a département of France, same administrative, judiciary and religious organisations.
1793	Failure of expedition against Sardinia. Paoli and Pozzo di Borgo indicted and order for their arrest issued. Corsican National Assembly opposes French Government and proclaims Paoli Father of the Nation. Paolists enter Ajaccio, loot houses of pro-French families, including that of the Bonapartes. Napoleon, serving with French military and naval forces who fail to take the town, gets his mother, sisters and uncle Fesch away by sea to Toulon on 11 June. Paoli and Pozzo di Borgo declared outlaws by French Government on 17 July and they appeal to Britain for help.
1794	In January British envoy Sir Gilbert Elliot arrives in Corsica and discusses with Paoli the creation of an Anglo-Corsican kingdom which is proclaimed at National Assembly at Corte in June. Paoli head of government until October when Sir Gilbert appointed Viceroy. British besiege and capture Saint-Florent, Bastia and Calvi where Nelson loses an eye.
1796	At end of September British withdraw from Corsica. Paoli returns to London. In October French forces re-occupy Corsica unopposed. In December Corsica divided into two départements on advice of Napoleon.
1807	Paoli dies in London, buried in St Pancras. On 3 September 1889 his ashes buried in private chapel at his birthplace, Morosaglia. Bust of Paoli in Westminster Abbey.
1811	Corsica declared a single département with Ajaccio as centre of administration for whole island.
1814	Bastia appeals to British for protection against French severity. Troops landed but withdrawn when Napoleon abdicates.
1839–40	Prosper Mérimée visits Corsica as Inspector of Historic Monuments. His discoveries stimulated interest in Corsican archaeology and 'Colomba', his novel set in Corsica, brought to the attention of readers outside the island the Corsican phenomenon of the *vendetta*.
1850	In the mid 19C emigration increases.
c 1860	British discover Corsica (e.g. Edward Lear, Thomasina Campbell).
1882	Introduction of compulsory education. Schools built.
1883	Work begins on Corsican railway.
1914–18	Corsica loses some 40,000 men in the Great War.

1920–40	Mussolini reiterates Italian claims to 'Nizza, Corsica, Tunisia'.
1940–43	Corsica occupied by Italian and German troops—one soldier to two Corsicans, men, women, children.
1943	Italians surrender 8 September. Germans continue to fight the Partisans—the original Maquis. End of 1943 Corsica first French département to be liberated. US troops stationed in Corsica clear east coast of mosquitoes and resultant malaria, opening the way for post-war agricultural development.
1957	Plans for Corsican economic growth in two domains, agriculture and tourism. Formation of SOMIVAC (Société de mise en valeur agricole de la Corse) and SETCO (Société d'équipement touristique de la Corse).
1970	Corsica separated from 'Provence-Côte d'Azur Région' and made a Région in its own right.
1972	Creation of the Parc Naturel Régional de la Corse.
1975	Corsica becomes two départements of France, 2A Corse-du-Sud and 2B Haute-Corse.
1981	The University of Corsica reopens at Corte.
1982	In accordance with French intention to decentralise government Corsica becomes first Région to elect a Regional Assembly.

Bibliography

Some books in English

Two centuries separate two important books on Corsica: James Boswell's *Journal* (1768) and Dorothy Carrington's *Granite Island* (1971). Midway between them is Edward Lear's *Journal* (1870).

Boswell, James, *An Account of Corsica: the Journal of a Tour to that Island, and Memoirs of Pascal Paoli.* Included in *Boswell on the Grand Tour: Italy, Corsica and France 1765–1766*, edited by Frank Brady and Frederick A. Pottle (Yale Editions of the Private Papers of James Boswell, McGraw-Hill, New York, and Heinemann, London, 1955). Boswell's heart was in that often rigorous journey and his first meeting with Paoli, to whom he bore a letter of introduction from Rousseau, was unforgettable (see Rte 2, Sollacaro). 'Having resolved to pass some years abroad for my instruction and entertainment, I conceived a design of visiting the island of Corsica...I should find what was to be seen nowhere else, a people actually fighting for liberty'. On his return to England Boswell worked hard for the cause of Corsican liberty, his efforts included persistent requests to the elder Pitt for an interview, courteously granted, to talk about Paoli, raising £700 in Scotland by private subscription to send a shipload of cannon to Corsica and even haranguing on the subject—'dressed as a Corsican chief'—those gathered at Stratford in 1769 for the Shakespeare Jubilee. When Paoli was an exile in London Boswell introduced him to Samuel Johnson, an action which made him feel like 'an isthmus that joins two great continents'.

Carrington, Dorothy. *Granite Island: a Portrait of Corsica* (Longman, London, 1971, and Penguin, London and New York, 1984). The reissue in paperback of this invaluable book, which received the Heinemann Award in 1971, is both welcome and easy to carry. It is 'based on the observations of a visit to Corsica in 1948, interwoven with experiences and researches spaced through the next 20 years'. Dorothy Carrington (Frederica, Lady Rose) read English at Lady Margaret Hall, Oxford, and in 1986 was created Chevalier de l'Ordre des Arts et des Lettres by Jack Lang, French Minister of Culture, and in the same year was one of three historians to represent Corsica at the XVI Consortium on Revolutionary Europe at the State University of Florida, Talahassee. She has lived in Corsica for 30 years and in 1991 the University of Corsica conferred a Doctorat Honoris Causa on her. Her latest book, *Napoleon and his Parents on the Threshold of History,* was published by Viking in 1987.

Lear, Edward. *Journal of a Landscape Painter in Corsica* (London, 1870 and 1966). It was Lear who first gave the outside world an idea of what Corsica's fortresses, mountains and laricio pines looked like, through his dramatic and romantic drawings (see Rtes 11, 14 and 16).

Campbell, Thomasina. *Notes on the island of Corsica* (London, 1868), (another ed. published as *Southward Ho!*). A friend of Lear, this energetic spinster 'of Moniack Castle, Scotland' refers often to her native land in her lively accounts of travels in the island (see Rte 1, Ajaccio).

Although this and many other books in English are now out of print they may still be found in libraries. For those whose interest in Corsica is aroused by the prospect, or memories, of a visit the following is a short selection of books worth looking for.

Thrasher, Peter Adam, *Pasquale Paoli: an Enlightened Hero* (London, 1970).

Pirie, Valerie, *His Majesty of Corsica* (London, 1939). A biography of Neuhof, King Théodore I (see Rte 12, Alesani).

Vallance, Aylmer, *The Summer King* (London, 1956). Another life of Neuhof.

Elliot, Emma Eleanor, Countess of Minto. *Life and Letters of Sir Gilbert Elliot* (3 vols, London, 1874). This humane and liberal Scot, whose education was supervised by David Hume in Paris where he was befriended by Mirabeau, loved Corsica which he likened to Scotland 'with a fine climate'. Created Baron Minto in 1797 he had the Corsican Moor's head incorporated in his arms.

Chiari, Joseph, *The Scented Isle; a parallel between Corsica and Scotland* (Glasgow, 1945). The comparison made by a Corsican who served France in the UK during the Second World War and after. Equally persuasive is Chiari's *Corsica: Columbus' Isle* (London, 1960) an examination of Calvi's claim to be the explorer's birthplace (see Rte 5, Calvi).

Some books in French

The History of Corsica

Arrighi, Paul and Olivesi, Antoine, and eight other contributors, *Histoire de la Corse* (Toulouse, Privat, new ed. 1990).

Antonetti, P. *Histoire de la Corse* (Paris, Laffont, 1983).

Carrington, Dorothy, *Sources de l'histoire corse du Public Record Office de*

Londres, avec 38 lettres inédites de Pasquale Paoli (Ajaccio, La Marge, 1985).
Pomponi, F, *Histoire de la Corse* (Paris, Hachette, 1979).
Renucci, Janine. *La Corse. (Paris, Presses Universitaires de France, 1982); Corse traditionnelle et Corse nouvelle. (Lyon, Audun, 1974).*

Archaeology
Acquaviva, Lucien and Cesari, Jean-Dominique. *Lumières de granite: la Corse à l'aube de son histoire. (Filitosa, Edicorse, 1990).*
Jehasse, Jean and Laurence, *Aléria Antique* (Aléria, new ed. 1991).
Grosjean, Roger, *La Corse avant l'histoire* (Paris, Klincksieck, new ed. 1981). *Filitosa, haut-lieu de la Corse préhistorique* (Centre de préhistoire corse, 1975). *Torre et Torréens* (Centre de préhistoire corse, 1975).
Mérimée, Prosper, *Notes d'un voyage en Corse* (1840, new ed. Paris Adam Biro, 1989)

Architecture and Art
Lorgues-Lapouge, C., *Corse baroque* (Nice, Editions Serre 1988).
Moracchini-Mazel, G., *Corse romane* (Paris, Zodiaque, 1972), and Carrington, D., *Les trésors oubliés des églises de Corse* (Paris, Klincksieck, 1967).

Literature
Benoit, P., *Les Agriates*, Novel (Paris, Albin Michel, 1950).
Daudet, A., *Lettres de mon moulin* (Paris, Livres de Poche Classiques, 1984).
Maupassant, G., *Chroniques insulaires* (Bastia, Marzocchi, 1987).
Mérimée, Prosper., *Colomba*. Novel (Paris, Livres de Poche Classiques, 1973).
Orsini-Marzoppi, M.-F., *Récits et contes populaires de la Corse* (Ajaccio, Cyrnos et Méditerranée, 1988).
Yvia-Croce, H., *Anthologie des écrivains corses* (Paris, Gallimard, 1978).
   English translations of some of the above have been published, e.g. Daudet and Mérimée, but may not be in print.

Guide Books
Corse (Paris, Hachette-Guides Bleus, 1990). This new larger-format, 400 pp edition conforms to the high standard of the Guides Bleus series. There is no connection whatsoever between Guides Bleus published by Hachette and Blue Guides published by A & C Black. A mutual agreement between the respective original publishers of the two series was in operation between 1917 and 1933 but lapsed completely at this latter date and has never been revived in any form (see p 7 A Note on Blue Guides).
Guide Michelin: Corse (Clermont-Ferrand, Michelin 1988). The layout and presentation of the latest edition of this volume in the well-known Michelin series has been made more attractive and includes some colour photographs.
Le Guide du Routard: Provence, Côte d'Azur, Corse (Paris, Hachette, annually). Brisk, lively commentary plus information on mainly lower-priced hotels, auberges, restaurants, campsites etc.
Le Parc Naturel Régional de la Corse
The following guides, well illustrated in black and white and colour, on the wildlife, geology, etc. of the Parc are published by the PNRC.
Civilisations perdues en Alta Rocca
Plantes et Fleurs rencontrées
Oiseaux de Corse

Poissons de Corse
Roches et paysages de Corse
Scandola (courrier spécial)
Lacs (Courrier du Parc)
Requins (Courrier du Parc)
Oiseaux de Corse (more extensive than that listed above)
Arburi, arbe, arbigliule
Mammifères de Corse
L'art de la Fresque en Corse (1450–1520)
Catalogue des Plantes Vasculaires de la Corse
Bandes dessinées: 'Mouflon de Corse', 'Cerf de Corse', 'Balbuzard pêcheur', 'Gypaete barbu'

Walking in Corsica

GR 20: Topo-Guide du Sentier de Grande Randonnée GR 20: à travers la Montagne Corse, de Calenzana à Conca (FFRP-CNSGR 10th ed. 1992).
Corse entre Mer et Montagne: Mare e Monti; Mare a Mare (PNRC-FFRP 1st ed. 1991).
Walks in Corsica: a guide to 600km of footpaths in Corsica; the famous GR 20 and including four new walks. Translated by Harry Pretty and Helen McPhail (London, Robertson McCarta, 1st ed. 1991). One of the Footpaths of Europe series produced by Robertson McCarta in association with the FFRP. The 'four new walks' are Mare e Monti and the three Mare a Mare walks—Nord, Centre and Sud.
Haute Route à Ski (provisional guide prepared and published by PNRC, 1990).
Les Sentiers de Pays: l'Alta Rocca, le Boziu, le Fiumorbu, le Venachese, le Taravu, le Niolu (PNRC, latest eds in print 1991).
Les 100 plus belles courses. Agresti et Quilici. (Paris, Denoël 1986)
Guides des Montagnes Corses: Randonnées pédestres et escalades. Michel Fabrikant (Grenoble, Didier et Richard, 1982).

Maps

Maps are not sold by the FFRP-CNSGR but are obtainable from bookshops and newsagents in Corsica and throughout France. All IGN maps may be ordered, either direct or through bookshops and map centres in English-speaking countries, from l'Institut Géographique National, 107 rue La Boétie, 75008 Paris, tel. 42-25-87-90.

The Topo-Guides listed above, both French and English editions, are provided with IGN 1:50,000 maps divided into sections covering the stages of the walks described on the facing page. The complete maps covering the area of the Parc are as follows:

Editions Didier et Richard IGN 1:50,000
20 Corse Nord: de Calvi à Vizzavona.
23 Corse Sud: de Vizzavona à la Montagne de Cagna.
IGN cartes touristiques locales 1:25,000 TOP 25
GR 20: 4149 AT, 4150 OT, 4251 OT, 4252 OT, 4253 OT, 4254 OT
Mare e Monti: 4149 OT, 4150 OT, 4151 OT
Mare a Mare Nord and alternative: 4150 OT, 4151 OT, 4251 OT
Mare a Mare Centre: 4153 OT, 4252 OT, 4253 OT, 4253 ET

Mare a Mare Sud: 4154 OT, 4253 OT, 4254 OT, 4254 ET
IGN serie verte 1:100,000
73 Bastia Corte: Parc Naturel Régional de la Corse (Nord), Français,
English, Deutsch (Key)
74 Ajaccio Bonifacio: Parc Naturel Régional de la Corse (Sud), Français,
English, Deutsch (Key)
Michelin Carte Routière et Touristique 1:200,000
90: avec index touristique.

Corsican toponomy
The *corsisation* of place-names progresses steadily but more rapidly on
road-signs than on maps because of the lapse of time between printings.
Often the changes amount to no more than a few letters and the alteration
in orthography does not affect pronunciation, e.g. Verghju, Vergio, Verghio,
Verghiu sound the same to the ear. Sometimes the change to Corsican of a
place-name gives something totally different, e.g. Bocca di l'Acchedu/Col
de l'Oiseau. It is useful, particularly when walking, to know what physical
features are described by a name. Here are a few of those most likely to be
seen on signs and maps:

BOCCA: mountain pass, generally interchangeable with Col, e.g. Bocca a
Mela/Col de Mela
CALANCA: ravine, gorge, canyon, creek enclosed by rocky cliffs
CAPU: mountain summit, cape on a coast
FIUME: river
FIUMICELLU: stream
FOCE: high, narrow mountain pass, mouth of river
FRANGHJU: olive mill
FUNTANA: fountain, spring
GULFU: gulf
LAU, LAVU: lake
PADULE: marsh, swamp
PIANA: plateau
PISCIA, SPISCIA: waterfall
SERRA: mountain chain, summit, ridge
STAGNU: pond, pool, mere
SURGENTE: spring
TEPPA: short and steep climb, mound, hillock

PRACTICAL INFORMATION

Approaches to Corsica

When you have decided to go to Corsica get in touch with your nearest French Government Tourist Office at once. Being an island is one of Corsica's great attractions but bookings, especially if car-ferry transport is involved, should be made as far ahead as possible. The following Tourist Offices in English-speaking countries will give information and advice.

Great Britain

French Government Tourist Office, 178 Piccadilly, London W1V 0A1. Tel. 071-491 7622

French Railways Limited (SNCF), 179 Piccadilly, London W1V 0BA. Tel. 071-495 3055

Ireland

French Government Tourist Office, 35 Lower Abbey Street, Dublin 1. Tel. 31-77-1871

United States of America

French Government Tourist Office, 610 Fifth Avenue Suite 222, New York, NY 10020. Tel. 212-757-1125

French Government Tourist Office, 645 North Michigan Avenue, Chicago, Illinois 60611 2836. Tel. 312-751-7804

French Government Tourist Office, 9454 Wilshire Boulevard, Beverly Hills, California 90212. Tel. 213-271-7838

French Government Tourist Office, Cedar Maple Plaza, 2306 Cedar Springs Road Suite 205, Dallas, Texas 75201. Tel. 214-720-0250

Canada

French Government Tourist Office, 1 Dundas Street West Suite 205, Box 8 Toronto, Ont M5G 1Z3. Tel. 514-288-4264

Australia

French Tourist Bureau, BNP Building 12th Floor, 12 Castlereagh Street, Sydney, NSW 2000. Tel. 231-5244

South Africa

French Tourist Office, PO Box 41022, Craighall 2024. Tel. 880-8062

Hong Kong

Representation française de Tourisme, c/o Air France, Alexandra House, 21st Floor, Chater Road, Hong Kong. Tel. 524-7584

As in any other business, travel agents come and go, in all sections of the leisure and vacation field, from ski to Corsica. Wherever you plan to go it pays to deal with experienced tour operators specialising in the place of your choice. They have built up durable relationships with regular and charter airlines, railways and ferries, hotels, directors of self-catering accommodation and campsites. Among such specialist companies of whom holiday-makers I talked with in Corsica spoke with satisfaction are France Voyages Limited, Castle Yard, 22a Hill Street, Richmond, Surrey, TW9 1TW, tel. 081-332 0909, and Falcon Holidays, 33 Notting Hill Gate, London W11 3JQ, tel. 071-221 6298. Other companies include Corsican Affair, 34 Lillie Road, London SW6 1TN, tel. 071-385 8138 and Simply Corsica, tel. 081-747 3580.

I have written in the Historical Introduction of the presence and achievements of Corsicans in North and South America and the Corsican names of towns in the United States. There is a society in London—ACRU, l'Association des Corses au Royaume-Uni—whose aim is to develop cultural, economic and historical links between Britain and Corsica. Corsicans have long memories and I have often admired their knowledge of island history and connections with the UK and how often Boswell is recalled, together with Paoli's periods of exile in London and, or course, the Anglo-Corsican kingdom which I have been told 'could have been made to work to the benefit of both sides'. The vice-president of ACRU, incidentally, is the managing director of France Voyages, a Corsican who has made his home in England.

To Corsica by Air. Offices of the the French Goverment Tourist service and those of Air France will give information. From the UK to Corsica there are both regular and charter flights, direct or with connections in Paris, Nice or Marseille, going to Ajaccio, Bastia, Calvi and Figari. There is little point in giving detailed information here because routes, connections, destinations and participating airlines may be subject to change under EEC legislation in the near future.

To Corsica by Rail and Sea. Again, all information is available from French Government Tourist Offices or from offices of French Railways Limited (SNCF). At the time of going to press the sole ferry service from mainland France to Corsica is by the State-owned SNCM whose fleet of spotless, comfortable and well-appointed Ferryterranée car-ferries ply day and night between Marseille, Toulon, Nice and Ajaccio, Bastia, Calvi, l'Ile Rousse and Propriano.

SNCM Ferryterranée. The car-ferry 'Napoleon' at Bastia

Travel in Corsica

Motoring. Even allowing for the difficult mountainous terrain of so much of the island the Corsican road network is very good, with extensive constant improvement and a high standard of maintenance. To the two main arterial highways, the N 198 Bastia–Porto Vecchio–Bonifacio that follows the east coast, and the N 193 Bastia–Corte–Ajaccio through the centre of the island and continuing as the N 196 to Bonifacio, was added the D 8 in 1990. This is a fast route from just N of Ponte Leccia to the west coast 20km north-east of l'Ile Rousse, an alternative to the more sinuous and picturesque N 197 between Ponte Leccia and Lozari, 8km north-west of l'Ile Rouse, that goes by way of Belgodère.

In the more remote areas of the mountains roads are often narrow with many tight bends and a sharp lookout for both oncoming traffic and passing places needs to be kept.

Car hire can be arranged in most towns, at airports and seaports or in advance through international agencies such as Avis, Budget, Godfrey Davis, Hertz etc.

Railway. The Corsican railway merits a brief history. The greater and most difficult part of the system is a triumph of 19C engineering. On plans approved in 1883 the first part of the line was constructed between Bastia and Casamozza and opened in 1988. The main line from the junction at Casamozza went west along the Golo valley to Ponte Leccia while another line pushed south through the east coastal plain to Ghisonaccia. In 1890 the Ponte Leccia–Calvi section was opened and by 1894 the link between Corte and Ajaccio through the mountains was completed. Further work was delayed by the First World War but the Ghisonaccia–Solenzara section was opened in 1930 and further extended to Porto Vecchio in 1935, bringing the total railway network to 365km of 1m gauge track. Plans for extensions from Porto Vecchio to Bonifacio and from Ajaccio to Propriano were shelved at the outbreak of the Second World War in 1939 and by the end of the war the length of track remaining had been reduced to 232km and remains so today. In autumn 1943 the retreating Germans destroyed bridges, tunnels, galleries in the mountainside and systematically demolished control systems, locomotives, rolling stock and stations. The east coast section has never been brought back into use and the southernmost station before the track turns west and inland is Casamozza. A suburban service for the 15 min. journey between Bastia and Biguglia runs for the benefit of commuters and others who live south of the town. There are 4–6 trains daily between Bastia and Ajaccio, according to season and taking on average 3½–4 hours. Bastia–Calvi is served by two trains daily, with connections at Ponte Leccia, taking on average 3 hrs 20 mins. Ajaccio-Port (all trains start and leave from here, subtract 15 mins on journeys to and from Ajaccio-Gare) to and from Calvi, 2 trains daily taking approximately 5 hours. Again, frequency and travel time are subject to seasonal changes but the above gives an idea of the service from early June to early September.

The administration of the railway has been chequered and there were several periods when it was threatened with closure. Originally run by the SNCF it was conceded to private operation in 1965, but in 1983 its continuation was ensured by it becoming an integral part of SNCF, Chemins de Fer de la Corse, in which the Ile Rousse-Calvi section is designated Trains–Tramways de la Balagne.

A ride on the railway, called affectionately in Corsican 'Trinichellu'—The Trembler—should not be missed, if possible. From the diesel railcar which usually hauls a second carriage there are views on the Bastia–Ajaccio section of ravines and peaks more dramatic than can be seen from the road. A folklore, including songs, has grown up around both track and train and looking out from it one marvels at the triumph of human muscle aided only

'Trinichellu' to passengers and friends, the 1metre gauge Chemins de Fer de la Corse

by draught animals and unsophisticated machinery over such daunting terrain more than a century ago. Gustave Eiffel (1832–1923) who gave his name to the 1887–1889 Paris landmark was also, among his engineering feats such as the Garabit viaduct and the bridge across the Douro, responsible for the Vivario metal viaduct by which Trinichellu rumbles staidly 100m above the River Vecchio.

Sport

The Sea. Around the 1000km coastline of Corsica there are creeks, bays, estuaries and harbours. The island is ideal for sailing and a wide variety of boats may be hired. Information from l'Union des ports de plaisance de Haute-Corse, port de Campoloro, 20232 Santa Maria Poggia, tel. 95-38-07-61 and from l'Union des ports de plaisance de la Corse-du-Sud, Capitainerie du port, 20000 Ajaccio, tel. 95-22-31-98. Windsurfing is possible almost everywhere and boards and equipment are for hire in most places where the sport is practised.

Sea Fishing. General information from La Fédération Régionale de Pêche et de Pisciculture, 7 boulevard Paoli, 20200 Bastia, tel. 95-31-47-31. For underwater fishing, apply to Quartier des Affaires Maritimes d'Ajaccio, 1 rue St Roch BP 19, 20185 Ajaccio or to Quartier des Affaires Maritimes de Bastia, le Vieux Port, 20289 Bastia.

The Rivers. Information about fishing in rivers and lakes from Muntagne Corse in Liberta, Imm. Girolata, parc Billelo, 20090 Ajaccio, tel. 95-20-53-14.

There being no heavy industry in Corsica the rivers are free of pollution and apart from the pleasures of swimming, sunbathing and picnics on the banks, there are sections of some rivers, such as the Asco, Taravo, Rizzanese, Travo, Liamone, Gravone, Vecchio and Fium'Orbo, which are navigable by canoe or kayak. The best time is spring when the rivers are fed by the melting snow on the mountains but the conditions can vary from year to year. Information from Errances, Villa Floralie, Chemin de Loreto, 20000 Ajaccio, tel. 95-22-73-81.

Pony Trekking. There are many centres for la Randonnée Equestre and the central and local tourist information offices can give addresses. A useful booklet, giving addresses of *centres equestres* in all the French *départements* is available from l'Association Nationale pour le Tourisme Equestre (ANTE), 15 rue de Bruxelles, 75009 Paris.

Parapente and Hang-Gliding. *Vol libre* in Corsica is somewhat restricted because of the rugged nature of so much of the terrain and the widespread *maquis*. Information from Les Ailes Insulaires, Occapièces, ZI Baleone, 20167 Sarrola Carcopino, tel. 95-20-71-40.

The Mountains. The Corsican long-distance paths and the shorter *sentiers de pays* and information about them are given in 16 Le Parc Naturel Régional de la Corse and the publications relating to them are listed in the Bibliography under the same heading. The address of the Fédération Française de la Randonnée Pédestre (FFRP), Comité National des Sentiers de Grande Randonnée (CNSGR) is 9 avenue George V, 75008 Paris, tel. 47-23-62-32. The British representative of this organisation is Robertson McCarta Ltd, 15 Highbury Place, London N5 1QP, tel. 071-354 1616, who publish the Footpaths of Europe series of walking guides based on translations of the FFRP Topo-Guides with the addition of maps in full colour.

For information on rock climbing in the mountains and gorges— I Muntagnoli Corsi, 20122 Quenza, tel. 95-78-64-05.

Skiing. Alpine ski centres:
Asco (1480–1820m) 76km from Bastia, 120km from Ajaccio. Ecole Internationale Ski, 20276 Asco, tel. 95-47-82-02.
Bastelica (1600m) 41km from Ajaccio. Ecole de Ski français, 20119 Bastelica, tel. 95-20-90-66.
Ghisoni (1580–1450m) 37km from Ghisonaccia. Station de Ski Renoso, 20227 Ghisoni, tel. 95-57-01-45.
Vergio (1400–1600m) 100km from Bastia, 80km from Ajaccio. Hôtel Castel Vergio, 20224 Albertacce, tel. 95-48-00-01.

Cross-country, *ski de fond* centres:
Evisa (835m) 70km from Ajaccio, 20km from Porto. Foyer ski de fond, 20126 Evisa, tel. 95-26-23-79.
Quenza (805m) 50km from Porto Vecchio, 45km from Sartène. Centre Ecole de ski de fond, 20122 Quenza, tel. 95-78-64-79.
Zicavo (1600m) 60km from Ajaccio, 80km from Corte. Association de ski de fond du Coscione, 20132 Zicavo, tel. 95-24-44-73.

Information on skiing in general from: Le Comité corse de ski, 1 boulevard Auguste Gaudin, 20200 Bastia, tel. 95-32-01-94.

General information on the above sports and also on bicycling, golf, spelaeology, tennis, motor sports, carnivals, concerts and all other leisure occupations and on accommodation from:
Loisirs Accueil Corse, 24 boulevard Dominique Paoli, 20090 Ajaccio, tel. 95-22-70-79.
l'Office de Tourisme, Place Foch, 20000 Ajaccio, tel. 95-21-40-87.
Tourisme Office Municipal, Place St Nicolas, 20200 Bastia, tel. 95-31-00-89.

THE WEST COAST

1 Ajaccio

Ajaccio (Aiacciu; 58,315 inhab.) is situated in the *Golfe d'Ajaccio*, the biggest gulf on the Corsican coast, measuring some 20km north to south and about 20km at its widest extent west to east. The town of Ajaccio is set along the shore in a wide south-facing bay on the north shore of the Golfe and is protected by a crescent of mountains on the landward side. To this position it owes its exceptionally pleasant climate, mild in winter and warm in summer, the heat alleviated by sea breezes. Ajaccio's old town is at sea level, the streets of the business and office districts extend north while the mainly residential areas climb the slopes of the hills and have expanded west along the coast road to the Iles Sanguinaires. With its white buildings, palms and plane trees, it is the most French Mediterranean of Corsican towns, just as Bastia reflects the atmosphere and style of the west coast Italian ports. As the greatest distance in sightseeing is under 2km it is preferable to visit on foot.

In 1970, under the French Government's programme of de-centralisation, Corsica was designated Région Corse with its administrative centre at Ajaccio. The Région was then divided in 1975 into two départements of France: Corse-du-Sud (2A) with its Préfecture at Ajaccio; Haute-Corse (2B) with its Préfecture at Bastia.

According to legend the name of the town is derived from Ajax but more probably it comes from *adjacium*, meaning a place where shepherds stopped on the way to the mountains with their flocks during the transhumance. The Romans came here and so, in the 10C, did the Saracens who destroyed it. Ajaccio subsequently passed under control of several of the warring clans including, in the late 14C, the Lords of Cinarca (the Cinarchesi), their enemies the Lecas, the Kings of Aragon, and Genoa. Unable to keep the Corsicans under control, Genoa ceded the island to the Bank or Office of St George, a powerful financial corporation with its own tough army. The Bank was responsible for fortifying the ports and setting up watch-towers.

Its rule ended in 1463 and, after Genoa again took control, Ajaccio passed to France in 1553 and then back to Genoa in 1559. The French began building the citadel which was completed by the Genoese who established firm authority over both the harbour which the citadel dominated and over Ajaccio itself from which Corsicans were banned. Genoa ruled despotically from 1562 until 1729 and the outbreak of the National Corsican Rebellion. There followed 40 years of confusion and fighting in the island, with repeated French intervention. In 1735 Paoli was elected General of the Nation and, after the defeat of his troops at Ponte Nuovo on 8 May 1769 by the French, he retired to England. Since that time Corsica has been French except for a brief period (1790–96) when Paoli returned in triumph and presided over the formation of the Anglo-Corsican Kingdom, with Sir Gilbert Elliot as Viceroy. In 1795 Paoli went into a second and final exile in England and in October 1796 the British left Corsica and the French returned.

In June 1793 Napoleon Bonaparte, a 24-year-old army officer, fled Ajaccio, sending his mother, Letizia (née Ramolino) and her younger children to Toulon. Their house was looted by the Paolists and by an ironical coincidence, on the arrival of the British troops, Hudson Lowe, who was later to be in charge of the Emperor in exile on Saint Helena, was billeted in the Bonaparte house. In 1796, on the advice of Napoleon, the Convention divided Corsica into two regions. No longer known as the En Deçà des Monts and l'Au delà des Monts (meaning the areas to the east and west of the central mountains) they were re-named the Départements of the Golo and the Liamone. Ajaccio was capital of the latter. In 1811 the two were reunited into one département,

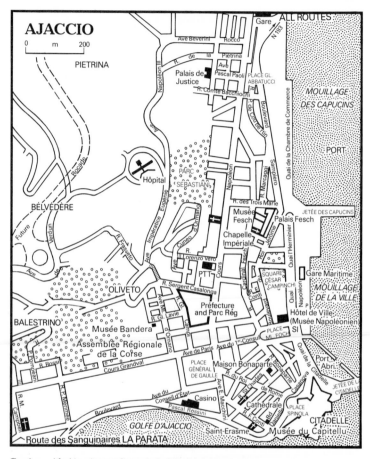

Corsica, with Ajaccio as sole capital of the island, and remained so until the creation of two départements in 1975, Haute-Corse and Corse-du-Sud.

Ajaccio's history is very much that of Corsica as a whole: a succession of colonisations, occupations and foreign military intervention. The town is uniquely distinguished in two ways. Firstly as the birthplace of Napoleon Bonaparte (15 August 1769) and secondly the first French town to be liberated from Axis occupation in the Second World War (9 September 1943) by the local Resistance forces. These were joined on 13 September by the 1st Bataillon de Choc, the first France Libre unit to set foot on French soil. The unit of 109 men had been brought from Algiers by the submarine *Casabianca* commanded by Captain l'Herminier, which had made many earlier voyages to bring arms and supplies to the Corsican Resistance forces.

The PLACE GENERAL DE GAULLE is a good starting point with the Old Town to the south-east and the modern parts of the town to the north. This large square, was called until 1945 the Place du Diamant (the Diamanti family property was here). It is a favourite spot for those Ajacciens who linger over a drink on a café terrace or sit on the public benches and look out to the Golfe or inland towards the rising strata of the suburbs. The square contains

Square César-Campinchi, opposite the Ferry Port, the Ajaccio Market of Corsican produce every morning

a *statue of Napoleon*, one of the town's many monuments to its most famous son.

Here he is depicted in Roman dress, on horseback, surrounded by his four be-togaed brothers: Lucien (1775–1840), Prince of Canino; Joseph (1768–1844), King of Spain; Louis (1778–1846), King of Holland; and Jérôme (1784–1860), King of Westphalia. The monument was cast in bronze by Barye in 1865 from plans by Viollet-le-Duc. According to the eye of the beholder it is magnificent, pompous, grandiose, majestic, or comic, in the vein of 'A funny thing happened on the way to the Forum'. Sometimes referred to as 'The Inkstand', by Ajacciens.

The Old Town extends to the east and south of the Place de Gaulle. From the Place follow the Avenue E Macchini to the sea and the Boulevard Pascal Rossini where to the right is the Casino (car park under the Place de Gaulle). Follow the quay into the Boulevard Danielle Casanova.

On the seaward side stands the **Citadel** (begun by the French in 1554 and finished by the Genoese when the French left in 1559), built as one with the base of the rocky peninsula. Occupied by the army, it is not open to the public. Opposite the Citadel is the privately-owned Musée du Capitellu (10.00–12.00, 14.00–16.00, closed 12.00 Sun, 14.00 Mon, April–Oct) History of Ajaccio from a family collection, including a painting by a nephew of J.M.W. Turner. Next to entrance No. 18, is a plaque marking the birthplace of D. Casanova (1909–43), the Resistance heroine who died in Auschwitz. Follow the Boulevard Casanova to the Quai de la Citadelle and turn right to follow the *Jetée de la Citadelle* (200m long) from which there are fine views of the port, the town and the mountains to the north and north-east.

Alternatively, on leaving the Place de Gaulle take the Av. E. Macchini until the second turn left into Rue Forcioli Conti, then again second left into the Rue St Charles, at the corner of which is the **Cathedral of Ajaccio**, dedicated to Notre-Dame de Miséricorde, *la Madonuccia*. It was built in Venetian Renaissance style (1554–93) to the plans of Pope Gregory XIII's architect, Giacomo della Porta. The proportions were reduced by Joseph Moscardi, the bishop of the time, who thought the building work would take too long. Reference to this is made (in Latin) in a frieze inscription above the entrance to the cathedral which records that the bishop in 1593, Joseph Giustiniani (whose arms were set above the plaque), laid the last stone. 'What wouldn't he have given to have laid the first'.

INTERIOR. Above the altar of the 1st chapel to the left, a Delacroix *Vierge du Sacré Cœur*. The chapel is decorated with stuccoes attributed to Tintoretto. To the right of the main door is the white marble font which served at the baptism of Napoleon Bonaparte on 21 July 1771 (he was 23 months old). The first pillar on the left of the nave has a plaque in red marble bearing Napoleon's wish expressed shortly before his death: *'Si on proscrit mon cadavre comme on a proscrit ma personne, je souhaite qu'on m'inhume auprès de mes ancêtres dans la Cathédrale d'Ajaccio en Corse'* (If my corpse is exiled [from Paris] as my living body has been I would wish to be buried beside my forebears in the Cathedral of Ajaccio in Corsica). The Bonapartes had traditionally been buried in their family vault in the cathedral and this continued until the Imperial Chapel (see Palais Fesch) was completed in 1858 on the orders of Napoleon III. In the 2nd chapel to the left are sculptures (1739) by the Genoese architect Garibaldi Solari, and three 17C frescoes. The 3rd chapel on the left contains 15 small 17C paintings on the theme of the mystery of the Rosary. In 1811 Napoleon's sister, Elisa Bacciochi, Princess of Lucca and Piombino, Grand Duchess of Tuscany, presented to the cathedral the white marble high altar surmounted by four columns of Italian black marble veined with yellow. An 18C marble statue, the Immaculate Conception, can be found in the 2nd chapel to the right.

On the right in the Rue Forcioli Conti, just before it joins the Rue Casanova, is the church of *St Erasme*. Built in 1602, it was the chapel of the Jesuit college until the expulsion of the Order. During the Revolution it was used as offices, was subsequently returned to being a chapel and was restored in 1932 and 1978. Erasmus is the patron saint of sailors and the chapel contains models of sailing ships as well as three Christs on the Cross which are carried in a religious procession on 2 June of each year.

The Rue Saint Charles, north-east from the cathedral, leads (200m) to the Maison Bonaparte or, as it was called when Napoleon was born there on 15 August 1769, the Casa Buonaparte. Built late 17C–early 18C, it became the family home in 1743 and carries the Bonaparte arms on the façade. Facing the house is a small tree-shaded square, the *Place Letizia*, named for Napoleon's mother, in the middle of which is a bust of Napoleon's son as a child by Vézin (1936).

The **Maison Bonaparte** has since 1923 been a museum. (Open 1 May–30 Sept every day, except Sun pm and Mon am, 09.00–12.00 and 14.00–18.00; 1 Oct–30 April, every day except Sun pm and Mon am, 10.00–12.00 and 14.00–17.00. There is a charge for the partly-guided visit which lasts about 40 minutes.)

On the ground floor a sedan chair in which, it is believed, Napoleon's mother, feeling the pains of oncoming childbirth, was brought back from the service in the cathedral to the house for the future emperor to be born. On the first floor is the salon which Madame Letizia had enlarged and refurbished in Louis XVI style, upholstered in red damask (now reproduction), paid for by 97,500f compensation, awarded to her by the Directoire in 1798 for the damage done by Paolist and British troops in 1794. Next to it is Madame Mère's bedroom with a big Louis XV bed. In the *'chambre natale'* is the couch on which Napoleon was born. The 12m-long gallery with Italian inlaid wardrobes and looking-glasses give the room an air which it is unlikely to have had at the end of the 18C. Two small rooms with white walls contrast with the general décor. One of them is said to have been Napoleon's bedroom. Far from the atmosphere of his childhood and youth is his death mask, made at St Helena on his death in 1821. A number of copies were made but this is believed to be the original, in private hands for many years and brought here early in 1991.

On the second floor are four rooms. In the first of these are genealogical trees, portraits of the Bonaparte parents, personal possessions of Napoleon

Bust of Napoleon's son, l'Aiglon, roi de Rome, by Vezin, in the Place Letizia opposite the Maison Bonaparte

and of his father and, in facsimile, the *acte de reconnaissance de noblesse* of the Bonaparte family, which was approved by the Conseil Supérieur de la Corse, 13 September 1771. In another room are portraits of Napoleon's siblings and the third opens to an alcove where Napoleon may have slept on his return from the Egyptian campaign. A fourth room is given over to Napoleon III, the Empress Eugénie and their voyage to Corsica (1860).

Continue along the Rue St Charles to where it meets the Rue Bonaparte, the *carrugio dritto* which divided the old Genoese city into the east district of Macello, a poor area mainly occupied by butchers, and the Petite Vendée to the west where the rich tradespeople lived. The Rue Bonaparte leads to the PLACE MARÉCHAL FOCH, formerly called the Piazza Porta because it was the site of the only gate (demolished in 1813) leading into the Genoese city. The square, well-shaded by palms and planes, is open on the east side to the port (many restaurants specialising in lobster and fish). In the centre of the square is a fountain (1827; by Maglioli, Ajaccien painter and sculptor) surrounded by four lions with woollen-toy expressions, and a statue of Bonaparte as First Consul, toga-wrapped, by Laboureur. A small statue, set in the niche of a house on the south side of the square, of *La Madunnuccia*, Notre Dame de Miséricorde, patron of Ajaccio, bears an inscription in Latin: 'They have placed me here as guardian'. It recalls the appeal for protection from the plague of 1656 then raging in Genoa. The feast of the Miséricorde, 18 March, is celebrated each year by the citizens of Ajaccio.

On the north side of the square the *Hôtel de Ville* (1826) has the Syndicat d'Initiative office for Ajaccio and Corsica and the **Musée Napoléonien** (open summer 09.00–12.00 and 14.30–18.00, closed Sun, winter 09.00–12.00 and 14.00–17.00, closed Sun). The museum is on the first floor of the Hôtel de Ville and contains portraits of the Bonaparte family, including a Winterhalter of Napoleon III with the Empress Eugénie and the Prince Imperial (son of Napoleon III, killed by Zulus in South Africa in 1879 while serving with the British Army). The baptism certificate dated 21 July 1771 shows that Napoleon was baptised at the same time as his sister Marianne, born on 1 July that year. Collection of medals and coins, the latter commemorating outstanding events from 1797–1876.

Leaving the Place Foch from the same side but other end from the Hôtel de Ville, turn right into the Rue Cardinal Fesch. Plaques on two houses recall Napoleon's brief visits to his native town; No. 28 where he hid for three days in May 1793 before escaping to the mainland from his Anglo-Paolist pursuers; No. 44 where the young artillery lieutenant Bonaparte on 23 January 1791 addressed the Patriotic (Jacobin) Club. A plaque on no. 41 marks the birthplace of the singer Tino Rossi (1907–83). Half-way along the Rue Fesch and impossible to miss is the **Palais Fesch**, on the right, built 1827–37 on the orders of Cardinal Fesch (1763–1839), half-brother of Napoleon's mother. In 1796 Napoleon appointed him Commissioner of Supplies to the Army of Italy. In 1802 nominated Archbishop of Lyon, Primate of the Gauls and Cardinal, he became in the following year Minister Plenipotentiary to the Holy See. Throughout his life an ardent collector, first of French, Flemish and Dutch pictures with the intention of creating a collection illustrating the history of European painting, later, retiring to Rome after Waterloo, he bought in large numbers the Italian works of 14–18C which rank in importance second only to those in the Louvre. A bronze statue of him (1855–56) by Vital Debray stands in the central courtyard.

The Cardinal's books, together with later donations by, among others, Prince Roland Bonaparte and Louis Campi (works on Corsica) formed the basis of what is now the Municipal Library housed on the ground floor of the left wing of the Palais.

The Museum was reopened in mid-1990 after many years of rebuilding and repair. Of the 800 paintings it owns, some 300, including those skilfully restored at Versailles and the Louvre, are displayed to maximum effect against the white walls of the spacious galleries on the upper floors of the Palais. Lack of space does not permit details here but among innumerable masterpieces are the Rimini triptych, 14C, Tura's Virgin and Child, 15C, Botticelli's Virgin and Child, supported by an angel beneath a garland, 15C, Titian's Man with glove, 16C. Detailed specialist information and viewing directions are generously provided by the dedicated and enthusiastic staff. No visitor to Corsica should miss the unique aesthetic experience of a visit to the Musée Fesch (09.00–12.00 and 14.30–16.00 daily except public holidays).

Behind the Préfecture, 1 Rue Général Levie, A Bandera: **Musée d'histoire Corse-Méditerranée** (May–Sept 10.00–12.00, 15.00–19.00 daily except Sun, rest of year Wed, 14.00–18.00, Thurs, Fri 10.00–12.00 and 14.00–18.00). Attractively arranged display: 'Corsican history through 10,000 years'. Dioramas, models, armour, weapons, documents etc. Room 1 Prehistoric–Middle Ages; Room 2 Barbarian invasions; Room 3 Wars of independence 1729–1769; Room 4 1st and 2nd Empires, vendetta, bandits; Room 5 First and Second World Wars. South of and parallel to the Rue Levie is the Rue du Général Fiorella, on the corner of which with Rue Campi (behind the Préfecture) is the information office of the Parc Naturel Régional de Corse—centre of friendly, helpful information on everything to do with the Parc, GR 20 and all walking, cycling, pony, river etc. expeditions.

The south wing of the Palais, the CHAPELLE IMPERIALE, was built (1855–58) in Renaissance style on the orders of Napoleon III. It fulfilled a stated wish by Cardinal Fesch (1763–1839) that the remains of the Bonapartes be brought together in one place. The Imperial Chapel was left to the French nation in 1923 by Prince Victor Napoleon.

Nine members of the family are buried there: Napoleon's mother, born Letizia Ramolino (1750–1836); Charles (formerly Carlo), Napoleon's father (1746–85); Charles-Lucien (1803–57), son of Lucien and nephew of Napoleon; Napoleon-Charles (1839–99), grandson of Lucien and son of Charles-Lucien; two of Napoleon-Charles's daughters, Zenaïde (1861–63) and Eugénie (1872–1949); Cardinal Fesch (1763–1839), Napoleon's half-uncle.

At the top of the vault stairway are the tombs of Prince Victor (uncle of the present prince, descended from Jérôme Bonaparte) and Princess Clémentine. The remains of Napoleon's father were brought from Montpellier in 1951.

Above the main altar hangs the Coptic Crucifix which General Bonaparte brought back from Egypt, he had 'borrowed' it, as he put it. After the campaign he gave the crucifix to his mother. The interior of the dome, the walls of the choir and the pendentives are decorated in *trompe l'oeil* by the Ajaccio artist Jérôme Maglioli who also designed the fountain of the four lions in the Place Foch.

The Rue Fesch joins to the north the Cours Napoleon, the 800m-long principal street of the town running from the Place de Gaulle in the south to the Palais de Justice (1873) and the railway station in the north. This avenue, shaded by orange trees and bordered with elegant shops and smart cafés is the fashionable centre of Ajaccio. About half-way along the Cours the church of *St Roch* (1895) has good stained glass (1956) by Gabriel Loire.

The *Préfecture*, south of the Post Office at the lower end of the Cours, has in the entrance hall a 3C sarcophagus.

The main avenue east from the Place de Gaulle going west to the Place d'Austerlitz begins as the Cours Grandval and then becomes the Avenue Général Leclerc. It has none of the commercial bustle of the Cours Napoleon and apart from the ochre Assemblée de Corse with its palms and leafy garden, consists mostly of apartment blocks, offices, clinics and villas. 250m along on the right the brown, pebbly *Anglican Church*, now deconsecrated and a school of dancing, built in the 1860s largely at the instigation of Scottish Thomasina Campbell (Rue Miss Campbell leads off the other side of the Avenue).

The British colony could stroll, top-hatted and be-bonneted, to divine service from their Balestrino hillside villas which they, in British upper middle class tradition, referred to as 'cottages'.

Miss Campbell's 'Notes on the island of Corsica', and the 'Journal of a Landscape Painter in Corsica' by her friend Edward Lear, attracted other English. Few emulated Thomasina's travels throughout the island. More interested in botanising than bandits, she dedicated her book to 'those in search of health and enjoyment', writing 'So pleasant and fertile does this valley [of the Ortolu that rises on the Vacca Morta in the south-west] appear, it is hardly possible to believe malaria *can* exist there; probably the imagination predisposes the system for the disease, for every ailment, from indigestion to a cold in the head, is here called 'the fever'. Porridge, cod liver oil and no nonsense carried Thomasina through.

On the Boulevard Leclerc is the monument to Fred Scamaroni, Corsican Resistance fighter, sent from London by General de Gaulle, head of the Free French opposition to Nazi-occupied Pétainist France, in 1941. Scamaroni was subsequently arrested, and poisoned himself in prison rather than risk talking under torture. The PLACE D'AUSTERLITZ is dominated by the gigantic **monument of Napoleon** by Seurre (1938). The original, which now stands in the grand courtyard of the Invalides in Paris, from 1833 to 1863 surmounted the column in the Place Vendôme, Paris.

It is Napoleon in his most familiar stance, dressed in frock coat and bicorne hat. He is looking down the Cours Grandval and over the town of Ajaccio. Alone of his many statues in the town, it has majesty and grandeur. At the base of the monument is a cave where it is said that the young Napoleon, before being sent away to school when he was nine, may have played.

A.   Expeditions inland from Ajaccio

MONTE SALARIO AND THE SALARIO FOUNTAIN, 5km from the Place Austerlitz. Leaving Ajaccio, a road just before the Place leads off to the right (marked) and at just under 5km reaches the *Salario fountain*. Actually a spring with a faucet, it was said in the past to have been an area populated by salamanders, thence *funta Salamandra*. There is a good view over the surrounding countryside which is even better from the summit of *Monte Salario* (311m) reached easily by a stony track. From here one can see the valley of Saint Antonine, the former prison of Castelluccio and the pinnacles of Punta di Liza (790m) to the north-west. A track called the Chemin de la Serra leads down directly into the town.

LES MILELLI: leaving Ajaccio to the north, either by the Boulevard Sampiero or by the Cours Napoléon (the latter is busier), take the D 61 and follow the clear 'Monuments Historiques Les Milelli' signs north-west for under 5km to the former Bonaparte property (today it belongs to the town of Ajaccio and is open to the public). This plain, solid, small-windowed and architec-turally unremarkable house conveys a stronger sense of Napoleon's deep Corsican roots than does the Maison Bonaparte in Ajaccio.

It was to les Milelli that Napoleon's mother on 25 May 1793, accompanied by her half-brother Abbé Fesch, brought her two daughters from her house in the Rue Malerba which was then threatened, and later commandeered by, the Paolists and their British supporters. The party left les Milelli during the night of 1 June, skirting Ajaccio to reach the Tour de Capitello (south of the present airport) where Bonaparte and 50 men, who had been put ashore by the French navy, were planning an attack on the town. This plan became impossible and Napoleon, his family and soldiers boarded their vessel on 1 June, reached Calvi on 3 June and Toulon on 13 June.

B. Les Iles Sanguinaires

Les Iles Sanguinaires can be reached either by road or by boat (3-hour round trip, leaving twice a day at 09.00 and 15.00 from the Quai Napoléon), a voyage of 18.5km to *La Grande Sanguinaire* (or Mezzo Mare) from Ajaccio through the north of the Golfe d'Ajaccio. The boat stays there one hour before making the return trip, giving time to walk on this, the largest islet of the tour (1200m long by 300m wide, highest point 80m). A lighthouse with a flashing beam visible for 56km is where Alphonse Daudet lived during part of 1863. From both the shore and from the lighthouse there are very good views of the gulf and of Ajaccio.

Although the granite of these islets glows fiery red at sundown (one of the essential sights of Corsica) the name is less likely to be connected with this than with the Golfe de Sagone which the isles separate from the Golfe d'Ajaccio; on old maps they are named as *Sagonares insulae*.

To reach the islands by road take the Boulevard Lantivy east along the coast from the Place de Gaulle, passing (2km) the *Chapelle des Grecs* founded in 1632, where the Greek refugees came in 1731 before settling at Cargèse. A 'Couronnement de la Vierge entre des saints et les donateurs' recalls the foundation of the chapel by Artilia Pozzo di Borgo, widow of the comman-dant of the Corsican Papal troops, in 1619. View over the gulf from behind the chapel. Just beyond the chapel is the extensive cemetery where family vaults and tombstones are spread thickly over the steep hillside.

The road is *en corniche*, cut into the granite and hugging the shore. The road leads past sandy beaches, Scudo (on the road) and Vignola (off road to north), before reaching the *Pointe de la Parata* (Punta di a Parata) crowned by a tower built by the Genoese (1608) in defence against the Moorish raiders. (Car park at the foot of the promontory.) A footpath leads to the end of the point (about 35 minutes there and back) from which there is a superb view of the islets. (Restaurant and bar by the car park.) If possible, and if the sky is clear, the Sanguinaires should be seen in the light of the setting sun.

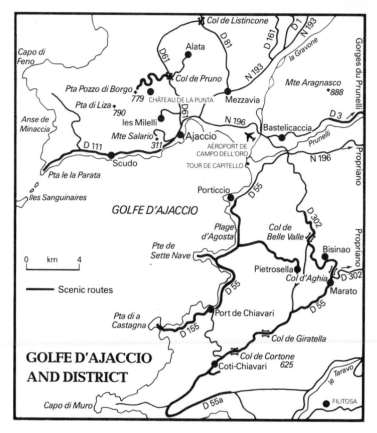

GOLFE D'AJACCIO AND DISTRICT

C. Castello di a Punta and Alata

Leave Ajaccio by the Boulevard Sampiero and take the D 61 to Alata passing through (7km) the Col de Pruno (Faccia di Campo 216m) on the high ridge of the peninsula running between the Golfe d' Ajaccio to the south and the Golfe de Lava to the north-west. Take the road to the left at the col (good views of the gulf). 13km from Ajaccio are the burned ruins of the **Castello di a Punta** or Château de Pozzo-di-Borgo. Standing on a terrace at 600m, it was built by the Pozzo di Borgo family (1886–94) of materials brought from the Tuileries which had been burned in 1871. There was a faithful reproduction of a Tuileries pavilion. The iron railings come from Saint Cloud. The north façade, overlooking the Golfe de Sagone, used to be at the Place du Carrousel; the south façade, overlooking the Golfe d'Ajaccio once fronted the Jardin des Tuileries. An inscription explains: 'Jérôme, du Pozzo di Borgo, and Charles, his son, had this building constructed with stones from the Tuileries Palace (burned in 1871), to preserve for the Corsican people a precious souvenir of the French mother country'. Like the Tuileries the Castle in turn was burned down (1980) but the contents were saved. Still worth visiting for the outstanding views.

Cars are not allowed on the track that continues to the Punta (even more outstanding views). Allow an hour there and back by the clearly marked footpath. The tower (restored) that one passes is all that remains of the Pozzo di Borgo village, razed by Barbary pirates in 1594. From the *Punta* (780m) on which stands a telecommunications (Corsica-mainland) relay station, you can see: north-east the peaks (usually snow-covered) of Monte Renoso and Monte d'Oro; north the Golfe de Lava and the Golfe de Sagone; south the Golfe d'Ajaccio; south-west the Punta di a Parata and the Sanguinaires.

If, instead of turning left from the D 61 at the Col de Pruno, you carry along the D 61, 10km from Ajaccio is the village of *Alata* (450m, 2077 inhab.). Built like a balcony on the side of the Serra mountain, it commands extensive views over the Golfe d'Ajaccio. This is the centre of the countryside dominated for centuries by the Pozzo di Borgo family, one of whose castles, the *Château de Mattone*, now in ruins, stands to the left of the D 61 just before the Col de Pruno. At Alata was born in 1764 the most famous of the Pozzo di Borgo family, Comte Charles-André (originally Carlo Andrea).

He was elected Député for Corsica in 1791. In 1793 he campaigned with Paoli for Corsican independence from France. In 1794 he supported Paoli and the Anglo-Corsican kingdom and was outlawed together with Charles Bonaparte and left for England when the French reoccupied Corsica in 1796. In 1803 Charles-André became private adviser to Tsar Alexander I and worked to strengthen the coalition between Russia, Austria and Great Britain against his own arch-enemy Bonaparte, who put pressure on Russia to get rid of him, whereupon he returned to England. The Tsar invited him back in 1812 during the Russian campaign. He represented the Tsar in Paris for 20 years from 1814 and in 1839 was appointed Russian ambassador in London. He died in Paris in 1842.

2   From Ajaccio to Propriano and Sartène

A. The Inland Route, Ajaccio to Propriano

ROAD (N 196) 74.5km.—21.5km *Cauro* (—*Bastelica* 20km to east) —51.5km *Petreto-Bicchisano*—61.5km *Sollacaro* and *Filitosa* (to west of road)—65.5km *Olmeto*.

Leave Ajaccio by the Boulevard Sampiero to reach the N 196 which skirts the eastern side of the Ajaccio Campo del Oro Airport, crossing two rivers, the Gravona and the Prunelli. At 12.5km from Ajaccio, at the Prunelli bridge, the coast road D 55 forks right. Follow the N 196 to Cauro, 21.5km from Ajaccio, passing less than 2km from a tiny hamlet called *Barracone*, scene of the assassination of Sampiero Corso on 17 January 1567 (for history of Sampiero see Bastelica). To Bastelica (20km) take the D 27.

DETOUR TO BASTELICA. To visit Bastelica is to get to know the heart of the island, although only 40km from Ajaccio. The road climbs steadily for about 10km to the Bocca di Marcuccio (661m) and then descends (1km) through the Bastelica pine forest to the Pont di Zipitoli over the Ese, the main tributary of the Prunelli. A road (it becomes the D 27a) to the right mounts the Ese valley on the left bank of the river, taking a 5km-longer but dramatic route to Bastelica.

On the D 27 5km beyond the bridge at the Bocca di Menta (756m) a road (left) skirts the northern shore of the Tolla reservoir, built 1956–64, and winds by way of *Ocana* (350m, 296 inhab.) through the Gorges de Prunelli to rejoin the N 196 to Ajaccio just north of Cauro. North-west of this lie the central Corsican forest and mountain barrier, which include the Monte Renoso and Monte Giovanni peaks and ranges.

Bastelica (808m, 436 inhab.) is set in a saucer surrounded by chestnut trees and virtually encircled by mountains (walks to Monte Renoso; 2352m

Statue of Sampiero Corso, Bastelica

and Monte Niello; 2250m). Its hamlets are scattered within its sheltered position, containing many old and elegant houses with fine doorways and windows. There is a late 19C statue in bronze of Sampiero Corso opposite the church of Bastelica's hamlet of Santo. The church is 19C but of no particular interest.

Bastelica is cherished by Corsicans as the birthplace of the national hero Sampiero Corso. On 23 May 1498 in Dominicacci, one of the six hamlets that form the commune, was born 'the most Corsican of Corsicans' who struggled ceaselessly to rid the island of Genoese occupation. In 1555 he sought the aid of France, in whose army he had served, only to be betrayed in 1559 by France handing Corsica back to Genoa. Sampiero then travelled through the courts of Europe, asking for help but in vain. In 1564 he landed in the Gulf of Valinco with an invasion force of 20 Corsicans and 25 Frenchmen. Resistants rallied to him and he fought on for three years until he was murdered in an ambush set by Genoese and their Corsican collaborators, 17 January 1567. Among these Corsicans were members of the Ornano family bent on avenging the death of their kinswoman Vannina, strangled four years earlier by her husband, Sampiero, who suspected her of being in league with the Genoese. Tall, bearded, strong and handsome, of mountain shepherd stock, Sampiero and his life were cast in a Shakespearean mould, for he could, like Othello, have said he was 'An honourable murderer, if you will; For nought did I in hate, but all in honour'.

After the detour to Bastelica, return to the N 196 at *Cauro* (Carru, 37m, 849 inhab.), dominated by two hills on which are ruins of the respective châteaux of the della Rocca and Bianca families.

Boswell, in Corsica to meet 'a people actually fighting for liberty', and having left Corsica's leader Paoli (whose advice to James was to go home and get married) on 27 October 1765 at Sollacaro, just north of Olmeto, fell sick of the tertian ague (or malaria), but was cheered up on the ride to Cauro by the company of 'a great swarthy priest who had never been out of Corsica' who had, with two other Corsicans, taken a castle garrisoned by 15 Genoese. 'I have often heard them say [reported Boswell] 'Our women would be enough against the Genoese.' I was returning to Corte but…at Cauro I had a fine view of Ajaccio and its environs…I was lodged at Cauro in the house of Signor Peraldi…before supper Signor Peraldi and a young abbé of Ajaccio entertained me with some airs on the violin.' His host also put on a show for Boswell of Corsican dances which appeared to have 'the idea of an admirable war dance'. On his way to Cauro Boswell had stayed at Ornano 'where I saw the ruins of the seat where the great Sampiero had his residence: They were a pretty droll society of monks…when I told them I was an Englishman 'Ay, Ay,' said one of them, 'as was well observed by a reverend bishop, when talking of your pretended reformation, *Angli olim angeli nunc diaboli*' [Once the English were angels, now they are devils]. I looked upon this as an honest effusion of spiritual zeal. The fathers took good care of me in temporals.'

In Cauro turn left and south down the N 196 through mountain foothill country. 30km from Cauro is *Petreto-Bicchisano* (Pitretu-Bicchisgià, 550m, 585 inhab.). Really two villages face to face, the former, Petreto, the higher and on the D 420, and Bicchisano the lower village on the N 196, with a view over the Taravo valley. These villages stand where ancient pathways came to a crossroads. There is the megalithic complex of *Settiva* in the mountains close by, with the Furchiccioli peak (1335m) at the centre. The possible routes are so complicated that those wishing to get there should ask in the village. Persistence will elicit more-or-less precise directions, so try your luck in local cafés and shops.

10km south of Petreto-Bicchisano on the N 196 is the Col de Celaccia (594m) from which the D 307 to the right leads (2km) to *Sollacaro* (Suddacarò, 450m, 324 inhab.), a fine old Corsican village and former seat of the d'Istria family of whom Vincentello d'Istria was a 15C Viceroy of the King of Aragon.

Dumas' brief stay there in 1841 inspired his novel 'The Corsican Brothers' which, however, has little to do with Corsica. Boswell arrived here on 21 October 1765 after a fortnight of rough travelling from Centuri. 'My journey over the mountains was very entertaining. I past some immense ridges and vast woods.' On arrival 'I was shewn into Paoli's room. I found him alone, and was struck with his appearance. He is tall, strong, and well made; of a fair complexion, a sensible, free and open countenance, and a manly, and noble carriage. He was then in his fortieth year. He was drest in green and gold...I had stood in the presence of many a prince, but I never had such a trial as in the presence of Paoli... For ten minutes we walked backwards and forwards through the room, hardly saying a word, while he looked at me, with a stedfast, keen and penetrating eye, as if he searched my very soul...I then ventured to address him with this compliment to the Corsicans: "Sir, I am upon my travels, and have lately visited Rome. I am come from seeing the ruins of one brave and free people: I now see the rise of another."' Boswell spent a week in Paoli's company. A plaque, recently set on a wall almost opposite the Post Office states that *'James Boswell, écrivain britannique et ami de la Corse, rencontra dans ce village du 22 au 29 octobre 1765 Pasquale Paoli 'Babbu di a Patria.'*

Just beyond the northern edge of Sollacaro the D 57 goes left and in under 8km reaches the **Station Préhistorique de Filitosa**, Corsica's major prehistoric site, which remained practically undiscovered and ignored for nearly 5000 years.

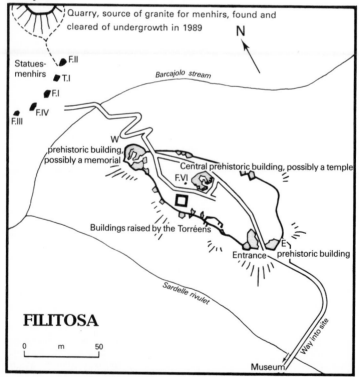

Quarry, source of granite for menhirs, found and cleared of undergrowth in 1989

N

Statues-menhirs
F.II
T.I
Barcajolo stream
F.I
F.III F.IV

W
prehistoric building, possibly a memorial
Central prehistoric building, possibly a temple
F.VI

Buildings raised by the Torréens
E
Entrance prehistoric building

Sardelle rivulet

FILITOSA

0   m   50

Way into site

Museum

Statue-menhir at Filitosa

Towards the end of summer the grass is worn but visit Filitosa in early spring when the banks of the streams and the meadow are bright with flowers, the olive trees are green and cows camera-consciously pose beside the statues, and you can comprehend why successive peoples chose this rocky height set in a verdant saucer.

In 1948 Dorothy Carrington, who was staying with the Cesari family on whose land Filitosa stands, was taken by her host Charles-Antoine Cesari, 'to look at the statues' which he had begun finding in 1946. 'I had been prepared for disappointment,' she wrote in 'Granite Island', 'right up to the instant when I reached the spot...but the block of granite lying before us on the ground, six feet long or more, was without doubt carved by the human hand in the human form...The head was clearly shaped: a large round head with protruding ears, sinister close-set eyes and a faint indication of mouth and nose. Neck and shoulders were carved from the block;

but the body was simply a flattened shaft of stone, with a ridge, just discernible, crossing it diagonally: not an arm, it seemed, but a sword. It was still monstrously impressive, this hero-image lying on its back in the maquis worn by uncounted centuries of wind and rain. The head recalled nothing I had seen so much as one of Picasso's more brutal drawings'.

With M. Cesari's permission and active participation excavation began in earnest in 1954 and the name of the late Roger Grosjean is inseparable from the record of discovery and initial interpretation of Filitosa (see bibliography).

Conservation of the site and discoveries and their availability to visitors has been organised most efficiently by the sons of Charles-Antoine Cesari. Jean-Dominique is Directeur du Centre de Préhistoire de Filitosa and his brother Joseph is Ingénieur à la Direction des Antiquités Préhistoriques de Corse, Ajaccio. Both write on archaeological subjects (see bibliography).

From the visitors' car park at the entrance to the hamlet it is a short walk to the museum and entrance to the site and the bar and restaurant where books and postcards are on sale.

In the MUSEUM are three restored statues. Left, as one enters, is the upper part of a figure known as Scalsa-Murta, 1400–1350 BC. He carries a sword held vertically, his back is protected by armour and he is helmeted. Two holes in the helmet may have held horns, Viking style. Facing the door is Filitosa XII where hands and arms are indicated in the sculpture, and a head catalogued as Tappa II.

A tree-bordered track leads downhill from the museum, crossing the Sardelle stream. About 80m on the right stands Filitosa V, the largest of Corsican statue-menhirs. He bears a sword, held vertically, and is also armed with a dagger. After crossing the Sardelle, the track makes a 90 degree turn to the left to enter the OPPIDUM OF FILITOSA, 130m long by an average of 40m wide, set on a boat-shaped spur of rock between the Sardelle and the Barcajolo rivers which join 100m to the west. There is a surrounding wall of massive blocks of stone, supposedly raised by the 'Torréens' (so named by Grosjean because they built tower-like fortresses, usually on the tops of hills). The Torréens re-used statues sculpted by the megalithic people they defeated after invading and ranging through the southern part of Corsica. The *East Monument* is a tumulus and the *Central Monument* was a Torréen building used for religious purposes. Here again statues from an earlier age were incorporated into the walls but have since been retrieved (for example Filitosa IX, with its clearly defined features, to the right of the entrance). The *West Monument*, at the point of the rocky spur, was, according to Grosjean, both for religious use and for defence. The central part is divided into two, and it has been calculated that the last time it was used was about 1200 BC.

A steep path to the right of the West Monument leads down to a pasture where the Barcajolo is crossed. On the other bank five statue-menhirs have been set up in front of an ancient olive tree. Three of them, armed, date from the megalithic era.

A path behind 'the five' leads up a hillock where maquis-clearing in 1989 uncovered a granite quarry, one of the oldest in Corsica. The occupants of Filitosa utilised the fault-lines dating from the liquid rock's cooling stage to obtain blocks from which to fashion their statue-menhirs. A fragment of one still lies there.

To reach Propriano there is a choice of two routes. One is to return to Sollacaro and the Col de Cellacia, turn right and proceed south on the

Tomb at Olmeto, typical of Edward Lear's interpretation of Corsican scenic grandeur

N 196. From here on there is a view out to the Golfe de Valinco and to (4km) **Olmeto** (Ulmetu, 360m, 1019 inhab.), a large village terraced on the southern slopes of the Punta di Buturettu (870m) and surrounded by olive groves from which it has made its living. It is a typical old Corsican village, with ancient stone houses and mellow-tiled roofs. Situated some 6km from the long sandy Plage de Baraci, Olmeto is now launched into tourism. On a peak to the east, facing the village, stand the ruins of *Castello della Rocca*, 14C stronghold of Arrigo della Rocca, great grandson of Giudice (see p 13).

A dedicated patriot, Arrigo della Rocca enlisted the King of Aragon on his side and returned to Corsica in 1372 and hounded out the Genoese from everywhere but their citadels of Calvi and Bonifacio. As Count of Corsica he ruled the island wisely and well for four years before dying in 1401 at Vizzavona of a 'stomach ailment'. There was a lot of it about at the time and he, like so many, was probably poisoned.

Colomba Carabelli, the original of Prosper Mérimée's heroine Colomba in the novel of that name, died in Olmeto aged 96 in 1861.

A turning to the left, just over the Baraci stream and on the outskirts of Propriano, used to lead to the Baraci baths where there was treatment for rheumatism and skin afflictions. The Baths still figure on 1990 maps and are described in the latest editions of the principal French guides but in mid-1991 the hotel and treatment centre were closed and abandoned.

The alternative route to Propriano from Filitosa (18km), is by the D 57, south along the lower valley of the Taravo to where it meets the D 157. Continue straight along this road which hugs the coast and the sandy beaches of the Golfe di Valinco most of the way, joining the N 196 4km outside Propriano.

B. The Coastal Route: Ajaccio to Propriano and Sartène

ROAD (D 55 and 55 A, D 757, D 157, N 196) 124km.—40km *Coti-Chiavari*—79km *Propriano*.

Leave Ajaccio by the N 196 and immediately after crossing the Piscatello bridge over the Prunelli, just past the *Campo del Oro airport*, turn right onto the D 55. 3km beyond the bridge and 1km by a track to the shore and the mouth of the Prunelli is the *Tour di Capitello*.

The tower is in good condition although seriously cracked by Bonaparte's attempt to blow it up. The Tour di Capitello played two parts in the history of the Bonapartes. First was in April 1793 when Bonaparte with 50 men and a cannon installed himself there with the intention of attacking Ajaccio while the French fleet bombarded the Paolists and their British allies. A storm held the French ships offshore and Bonaparte and his men were besieged in the tower for several days until they managed to get out and rejoin the fleet. In June 1793 Bonaparte met his mother, two sisters and uncle, Abbé Fesch, at the tower and took them off to Toulon.

This stretch of the coastline has been much developed recently for tourism at Porticcio, and the D 55 continues along the Plage d'Agosta hugging the shore closely as far as the Plage de Verghia and the tiny port of *Chiavari*. From here the D 155 goes out in the direction of the *Punta di a Castagna* from which there is a fine view of the Golfe d'Ajaccio. To reach the point there is a 30-minute round-trip on foot from the hamlet of *Portigliolo*. At the Plage de Verghia the D 55 goes due south and away from the sea to the village of *Coti-Chiavari* (Coti Chjavari, 614m, 399 inhab.) which is 40km from Ajaccio and 40km from Propriano. It is a terraced village with a nearby television relay station and a military camp set on a height. Both are out of bounds but the service road may be used to reach a twin peak (581m) from which there are views over the Gulfs of Ajaccio and Valinco. To avoid crossing the rocky spine of the peninsula that ends in the Capu di Muru the D 55 goes to the hamlet of Acqua Doria before turning west and crossing the foothills on its way to the Taravo valley and Propriano. A few hundred metres to the south of Acqua Doria a turning to the right is marked *Capu di Muru* 5km. It leads also to isolated and fine beaches, but the track is unmetalled, very rough, and muddy after rain. On the way to the Taravo valley and the D 757 (later becoming the D 157 where it crosses the Taravo) there is a turning to the right to *Serra di Ferro* (A Sarra di Farru, 100m, 327 inhab.) which has nearby a beach of fine white sand.

Immediately before the D 157 makes a right angle to cross the Taravo, a minor road, D 757, goes straight (2.6km) to *Porto Pollo*, a small port on the east of a tiny peninsula. Protected from the west wind, it was formerly a haven for sailing ships loading charcoal and for fishing boats. Now it is a delightful and modest seaside village with a few hotels, restaurants and a camping site.

From the bridge over the Taravo it is 14km to Propriano which looks north from the southern shore of the Golfe de Valinco.

About half-way along the D 157 from Porto Pollo to Propriano is the recently excavated and carefully restored Castellu de Cuntorba, a Bronze Age complex with dwelling, milling, storage, cooking areas and central monument within the circular fortifications. There is no signpost to it but look out on the left of the road for the Paradis discothèque, follow the road left for nearly 1.5km to a rutted track rising sharply to the left for 200m to an open space. Park there, open and close behind you a gate into private grazing land. At 50m the castellu stands on a hillock surrounded by oaks and olive-trees with the blue of the Golfe de Valinco beyond. Because the walls and living spaces have been so meticulously reconstructed (note the archaeologists' numbering on the blocks of granite) one enters here, perhaps more than in any other Torréen site in Corsica, the atmosphere of how people lived in a carefully chosen place more than 1200 years BC.

Propriano (Prupià, 3217 inhab.) is the port serving Sartène (13km) and the Sartenais district which produces wine, honey and fruit, and pastures cows, goats and sheep for their milk and cheese. Propriano is also roughly mid-way between Ajaccio (74km) and Bonifacio (67km) and 76km from Porto Vecchio. SNCM car ferries ply to and from Marseille and there is a large *port de plaisance.*

There has been a port here since at least the 2C BC. Greeks, Romans and Carthaginians left traces of their visits as did Turkish and Barbary raiders. It was occupied by the Pisans in the 10C and by the Genoese in the 13C. Here Sampiero Corso landed in 1564 to free Corsica. By the end of the 18C, mostly due to the barbarian raids, there was little left of the town. Only four houses were reported there in 1794. Its long history of settlement is due to the rock called Scoglio Longo which shelters the harbour from the west and north-west winds. The harbour jetties were built on Scoglio at the beginning of this century. Turbulent history has left very little of architectural interest, chiefly one long street running down to the port. Rapid growth in tourism has brought prosperity to Propriano.

There are elegant hotels on both sides of the N 196 in the north of the town, on and around the port imaginative development in a formerly commercial district is evident in the transformation of a wine warehouse into an hotel where the owner, Paul Coti, used his painter's eye to achieve a Scandinavian-style blue and white spacious comfort. It has a name—The Loft—to stay in the Anglo-American traveller's mind. This area has good non-touristy fish restaurants, *not* always to be found in ports.

Spin'a Cavallu, 13C bridge over the Rizzanese (its single arch gives it the 'horse's back' name)

The route to Sartène lies along the valley of the Rizzanese (50km long, rising at the foot of the Incudine). Take the N 196 out of Propriano as for Campomoro but cross the Rizzanese 6km from Propriano by the Pont de Rena Bianca. There are two menhirs, marked on the map and signposted to the right of the road called *u Frate e a Suora* (monk and nun), illicit lovers turned to stone as they fled from Sartène and divine wrath.

At 1km beyond the menhirs the D 69 to the left follows the Rizzanese valley north-east. At 4.5km from the turning is Spin'a Cavallu (horse's back), a finely proportioned single arch bridge of 13C Pisan construction, marked on maps as Genoese.

At a junction 3km beyond the bridge the D 69 turns north and in 25km reaches *Aullène* (Auddè, 850m, 149 inhab.) a village among chestnut groves on the western edge of the Parc Naturel through which the D 69 wends it way (Rte 16) to Vivario and the N 193.

At 2km beyond the D 69 turning the D 148 right follows the Fiumicicoli stream, crossed by a narrow bridge to (1.5km) the hot (40° C) Caldane spring (long local reputation for treatment of rheumatism and skin). Small open-air pool on private land, bar and restaurant where Corsican specialities may be ordered.

The D 119 forks left from the D 69 at the above-mentioned junction and joins the D 19 at Arbellara (350m, 120 inhab.) overlooking vineyards and orchards and dominated by a tall, square crenellated tower. North for 4km on the D 19 to **Fozzano** (Fozzanu, 350m, 152 inhab.). Two Genoese towers, 16C and 17C, narrow stepped streets between tall houses, the village is built solidly on a spur of rock. Two 17C houses are those of the Durazzo and Carabelli families whose long vendetta, in which Colomba Carabelli played a significant part in 1833, inspired Mérimée's novel 'Colomba' (see Bibliography). The tombs of Colomba and her son, killed in the vendetta, are in the nearby whitewashed chapel. There is a painted wood 17C statue of the Virgin, said to have been found in the Golfe de Valinco and to possess miracle-working powers, in the church which also has some notable tombs and a tall bell-tower.

The southern extremity of the Golfe de Valinco is at the *Punta di Campo-moro* (camp of the Moors). Take the N 196 from Propriano towards Sartène, cross the Rena Bianca bridge over the Rizzanese, turn right onto the D 121 that follows the river and skirts the southern edge of the Propriano-Tavaria airport and a racetrack. At 8.5km from Propriano is a good bathing beach at Portigliolo. 3km further Belvédère-Campomoro (BelvederiCampumoru, 230m, 128 inhab.) is a village on a terrace with a view over the gulf. The road goes down to the sea, and a track to the left leads to the 2.5m high menhir of Capu-di-Luogu and three megalithic coffers nearby.

Campomoro, at 16km from Propriano, isolated out on the point is never crowded with tourists. It has a beach of fine sand. A half-hour's walk or gentle climb up through the maquis brings you to the Genoese tower on the Punta di Campomoro (built to prevent the Moors setting up camp again?). For those who enjoy walking this is an ideal area. There are no roads for 10km as the crow or seagull flies between the Punta di Campomoro and *Tizzano*, set in a deep and narrow cove, on the west coast to the south (19km from Sartène). Tizzano has a small port overlooked by the ruins of an old fort.

3km to the north-east on the D 48, the road to Sartène, is the megalithic complex of **Palaggiu** (Pagliaju) which Roger Grosjean calls, in his '*La Corse avant l'histoire*', 'the most important in the Mediterranean countries, comprising 258 monoliths of which three are stele statues, set out in seven alignments'. Serious excavation began in the mid 1960s and continues. It was also in the 1960s that important discoveries were made on the plateau of Cauria. A road to the right off the D 48 just past the Alignments of Palaggiu, going towards Sartène, leads in 5km to the site. The direction is clearly marked and so is the site itself. The **Dolmen of Fontanaccia** in Corsican, Stazzona di u Diavuli—the devil's forge) is the finest and best-preserved dolmen in Corsica, complete with funeral chamber and roof, measuring 2.60m by 1.60m with a height of 1.80m. There is a signpost to the *Alignment of Rinaiu* and a walk of 400m to the collection of 45 menhirs. At the *Alignment of Stantari* (signposted) 25 menhirs some with swords in relief. Spend some time in the excellent *Musée de Préhistoire Corse* at Sartène (see Rte 3) before visiting these and other sites in the area.

To visit Tizzano and Palaggiu without returning to the outskirts of Propriano go back to Belvédère by the D 12 and take the only right turn out of the village, signposted to *Grossa* (325m, 44 inhab.). Just off the road in a cul de sac, it is a small village of venerable granite houses. In 1388 Giovanni della Grossa was born there. During an eventful working life as a lawyer he was pro-Genoa in sentiment but when he retired to his native village he wrote the most valuable surviving chronicle of life in medieval Corsica.

All the roads in these bare mountains wind around the D 21 and the D 321, which takes a detour to the village of Bilia, meet up with the N 196 at Bocca Albitrina, 2.5km south of Sartène.

Dolmen de Fontacaccia

3   From Sartène to Bonifacio through le Sartenais

ROAD (N 196) 54km—24km *col di Roccapina*—29km *Monacia d'Aullene* (north of the road)—34km *Pianottoli-Caldarello*—49km *Col d'Arbia*.

Sartène (Sarté, 330m, 3525 inhab.) is sous-préfecture of Corse-du-Sud.

The most famous description is by Prosper Mérimée: '*la plus corse des villes corses*', as famous as Edinburgh being 'the Athens of the North' and Sartène could very well be called '*la plus écossaise des villes corses*'. The tall, solid, granite houses, austere to the point of grimness, the narrow streets and steps of the Old Town are reminiscent of Edinburgh or Stirling.

Coming into Sartène from the south by the N 196 you cross the Pont de la Scalella and from the bridge there is the impression of a town built into and forming part of the great cliff that faces you. The fortified appearance is justified: the Barbary pirates landed on the coast and made their way inland to lay siege to Sartène. In 1583 they took the town and carried off 400 citizens into slavery in Algiers. These raids continued until the 18C. Another reason for the semi-fortified status of the houses was that Sartène kept alive the old traditions of honour and the vendetta for longer than any other Corsican town. Not only was there violent rivalry between families but also between different parts of the town well into the 19C. Now, Sartène is one of the cleanest and best run towns in Corsica.

The strong attachment of the Sartenais to tradition is most strongly expressed in the Eve of Good Friday Procession du Catenacciu (literally the 'Chained one' from *catena*,

GOLFE DE VALINCO PROPRIANO AND SARTÈNE

a chain). The identity of the man who leads the procession, dressed in a red robe and hood through which only his eyes are glimpsed, is a closely guarded secret known only to the priest. This principal role of the Penitent Rouge is much sought after and has to be 'booked' many years ahead. Often it was a bandit or murderer or someone guilty of a crime which he wished to expiate by walking barefoot for three hours through the tortuous and candle-lit streets of the old town, bearing a wooden cross (31.5kg) and dragging a metal chain (14kg) shackled to his right ankle. The Grand Penitent is followed and aided, when he stumbles or falls (often due to the pressure of the crowds curious to discover his identity) by the Penitent Blanc, also anonymous, representing Simon de Cyrène who aided our Lord. He in turn is followed by hooded Penitents Noirs.

The procession starts from the Eglise Sainte Marie, close to the Hôtel de Ville and the Place de la Libération, at 21.30 and returns after midnight to the Place de la Libération with the effigy of the dead Christ from the church lying on a shroud and borne by the Penitents Noirs. An old Corsican chant, *'Perdono mio Dio'*, is repeated endlessly and sung by the crowd until the last moment when the silent throng is addressed and blessed by the priest. The effect of the whole ceremony is strongly medieval, chilling rather than moving, with the constant chanting, the sound of the chain dragged over the stones and the almost palpable excitement bordering on hysteria of the packed crowd lining the route where the windows of houses are lit with candles. Not to be missed if one is there or nearby at Eastertide. Get to the route early and remember that as well as the ecstatic religious side there is a considerable degree of commercial exploitation. During the rest of the year the cross and chain used in the procession may be seen hanging from the north wall inside the church of Sainte Marie. (There is also a Catenacciu procession the same evening in Propriano. It is less crowded, less exploited, less dramatic but very moving.)

The centre of Sartène is the Place de la Libération with a market and cafés. An archway under the Hôtel de Ville, formerly the Palace of the Genoese Governors, leads into the Old Town and the Middle Ages. At 100m (south-west and downhill) from the Hôtel de Ville to the right of an alley is an *échauguette*—a 16C Genoese watch-tower and one of the few relics of the wall that originally surrounded the town. The old town is very well signposted, as is the more modern part of Sartène. One of the great advantages of its situation on the side of a hill is that it is possible to walk everywhere. Follow the signposts to the hospital, and from there to the Musée de Préhistoire Corse which is a few minutes' walk from the Place de la Libération, or by steps leading down from the Boulevard Jacques Nicolai.

The Musée de Préhistoire Corse (15 June–15 Sept, 10.00–12.00 and 14.00–18.00 daily except Sun; 16 Sept–14 June, 10.00–12.00 and 14.00–16.00 daily except Sat, Sun, public holidays). The way to it, set high above the town, is by way of the hospital and is clearly marked from the Place de la Libération. The museum is in the former prison (1843) a granite building, pleasantly plain in a somewhat Borders manorial style. Founded in 1970 as a centre for bringing together objects found during archaeological excavation it was designated a Corse-du-Sud departmental museum on 1 January 1977.

First Floor, Entrance Hall: a synoptic chart of the major periods of Corsican prehistory which are illustrated by the exhibition of characteristic objects presented in chronological order through the six display rooms.

Room 1: Early Neolithic (6000–4000 BC) pottery with incised decoration by shells or pointed instruments, some coloured by ochre, tools of local flint or obsidian.

Room 2: Late Neolithic (3500–3000 BC) tools, arrowheads, shaped and some polished, axes, bowls, ornaments, grinding and crushing implements, glazed pottery. From burial places (3000–1500 BC) vases, cups, ornaments, small daggers, gold and silver jewellery.

Rooms 3 and 4: Bronze Age (2600–2000 BC) flint arrowheads, polished axes. Melting-pots, pottery with perforated and chevron decoration.

Room 5: charred human bones found in places under eroded rocks, pearls, rings cut from serpentine.

Room 6: Bronze Age (1800–800 BC) objects found in domed monuments, Torre settlements and dwellings close to them; pottery, coarse and rarely decorated, fragments of bronze weapons, melting-pots and moulds, imported Italian pottery. Iron Age (700 BC–AD 100) pottery with 'combed' decoration or incised patterns, iron tools and arms, bronze ornaments, a reconstructed cremation tomb. Armed, incised statue-menhirs.

A visit to this museum is essential for an appreciation of the archaeological discoveries throughout the island.

(In mid-1991 the Conservateur, Paul Nebbia, spoke of plans for an extension and reorganisation of the Museum with the object of improving and enlarging both permanent collections and occasional exhibitions and to bring together all research documents relative to the Museum's work.)

To reach (54km) Bonifacio leave Sartène by the southbound N 196. On the edge of the town on the right is the *San Damiano monastery* (318m) from which there is a view of Sartène, the estuary of the Rizzanese and the Gulf of Valinco. The Penitent Rouge spends the day and night here in constant prayer before the Good Friday Catenacciu procession. The 19C monastery, occupied by a community of Belgian monks who are responsible for the repair and maintenance of the building, is not of great architectural interest.

The journey south is through the pleasant cultivated country of the Sartenais, mostly vineyards where often the local wine, honest, unadulterated and not rough, is on sale by the bottle or case.

LE SARTENAIS could almost be in northern Europe: there are farmhouses and scattered cottages but practically no villages along this road which crosses (20km) the River Ortolo (rises on the Puntadella Vacca Morta, 18km long). 4km *Col de Roccapina* (150m), with a view of the pink granite rocks of Roccapina and a Genoese tower. The most famous of the rocks is supposed to resemble a lion couchant and to the right of it, the head of an elephant. (Restaurant and bar l'Oasis du Lion and parking across the road from which Lion and Elephant can be photographed.) The next tower along this coast is the *Tour d'Olmeto* perched out on a point.

5km. A road to the left leads (2km) to the village of *Monacia d'Aullène* (A Munacia d'Auddè, 120m, 412 inhab.), well-known for its excellent wines. Monacia is also a good starting point for the climb to *l'Uomo di Cagna* (1217m). This 'Man of Cagna' consists of a great spherical block of about 10m in diameter balanced on top of a slender base, giving the impression of a human form from many points in the southern plains (it marks the south end of the central mountain ranges of Corsica). The ascent of the 'man' itself is for experienced rock climbers only and the first scaling to the top of the head dates only from 14 June 1970. The climb to the foot of l'Uomu takes about 2½hrs and the reward is a view of Bonifacio and northern Sardinia.

5km **Pianottoli-Caldarello** (Pianottuli Caldareddu, 80m, 653 inhab.). Pianottoli, is on the N 196 and Caldarello, 1km to the south, with houses scattered about in a great tumble and jumble of rocks. Until the 17C caves and grottoes among the rocks were inhabited and they still give shelter to farm animals. Now there is extensive cultivation of vines to produce the Figari wines which can be sampled in the *caves de dégustation* at Figari (125m, 914 inhab.).

After 2km the D 22 leads left to *Figari-Sud Corse Airport* (5.5km), served by Air France and France Inter. Opened in 1975, its traffic has increased greatly year by year.

1km beyond the turning to the airport the road crosses the *Pont de Figari.* Here the narrow Baie de Figari is watched over by the 13C Genoese tower. 2km beyond the Figari bridge the D 859 turns left to Sotta and Porto Vecchio. From here to Bonifacio the road passes through an unpopulated country of maquis, interspersed with cork-oaks and boulders, followed by marshes and meres. 10km *Col d'Arbia* (138m) is guarded by the granite peak of la Trinité (219m) and bristling with wireless aerials.

Just beyond the col a road leads right to the *Trinité monastery*, a former hermitage, built on a terrace in the shade of ilex and olive trees. There is a view to Bonifacio. Pilgrimage on Trinity Sunday and Nativity of the Virgin Mary on 8 September. Small church containing ex votos.

Bonifacio (Bonifaziu, 2683 inhab.) is totally unlike any other town in Corsica, of which it is the most southerly—and indeed the most southern town of all France.

To the north is an extensive region of scrub (*garrigue*) growing on the inhospitable granite which in the past effectively shut off Bonifacio, set apart on a mighty plinth of limestone and chalk, from the rest of the 'granite island'. The nearest town is the Sardinian port of Santa-Teresa di Gallura, 12km across the Straits of Bonifacio, while the nearest Corsican town, Porto Vecchio, is 27km away. There is a special Bonifacien dialect derived from ancient Ligurian and often not understood by Corsicans from other districts.

The town is built on a long high promontory whose cliffs fall sheer to the sea. Between the promontory and the mainland to the north is a fjord 1600m long and 100–150m wide. This is Bonifacio's traditional port. There is a new *port de plaisance* at the east end.

It is believed that the first description of Bonifacio was made by Homer in The Odyssey (Book X). Odysseus tells of arriving at the fortress of Lamos held by the Laestrygons and coming into a good harbour protected all around by an unbroken wall of rock with two jutting headlands guarding the narrow entrance. The Greeks went ashore and near the settlement met a girl drawing water from the spring of Artacia that supplied the town. Her father the king, being of the cannibal persuasion, began murdering the Greeks and started to eat one. The Greeks fled to their boats but the Laestrygons dropped boulders from the cliffs, holing the boats, while others speared the swimmers 'like fish' in preparation for a feast. The topography described certainly sounds uncommonly like Bonifacio.

Originally called Giola, Bonifacio owes its later name to Boniface, Marquis of Tuscany, who took the town in 828.

In 1187 the Geonese seized Bonifacio, built the citadel, banished the inhabitants and replaced them with Ligurian families. It became virtually an autonomous republic while still acknowledging Genoa. Besieged by the Aragonese in 1420, the French and their Turkish allies set siege to the town in 1554. In early 1793 Bonaparte entered peacefully as a young artillery officer and spent several months there.

From the main port car ferries leave for Sardinia and boats make exursions to the grottoes and along the shore below the cliffs.

The only main road into Bonifacio is the N 196 and where it finishes at the east end of the Marina there are two car parks. The QUAI JEROME COMPARETTI along the south of the harbour is the centre of commercial life with shops, cafés, restaurants, taxi rank, embarkation point for boat trips to the grottoes and the Lavezzi Islands, bus agency, and the excellent *aquarium* in a cave in the rock: comprehensive presentation of fish and crustaceans

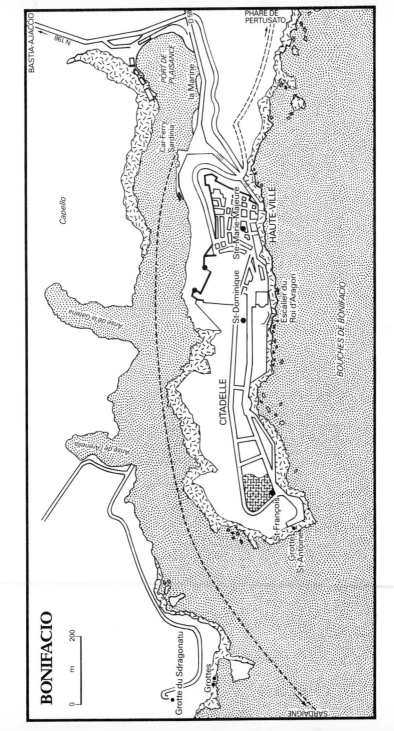

Bonifacio

from the surrounding waters. Off the Quai Banda del Ferro is the fishing port, further west beyond that and off the Quai Sotta Portigliola is the Customs shed and the embarkation point for the car ferries to Sardinia, a busy and thriving part of the town's tourist industry.

To drive up to the old town on leaving the Marina car park do not turn right along the Quai Comparetti but go straight into the Avenue Charles de Gaulle which winds its way up to the top of the rock where a left turn leads into the Rue Fred Scamaroni. In Ajaccio there is a monument to this Corsican Resistance envoy of de Gaulle (see Rte 1, Ajaccio). Follow the Rue Scamaroni into the Place Fondaco-Montepagano. (There is a car park next to the Foreign Legion monument.) On the way up from the port and immediately before coming into the Avenue de Gaulle on the right is the *war memorial*, a grey granite Roman column discovered on the islet of Bainzo (San Bainsu). At the far end of the Avenue de Gaulle, by the turn into the Rue Fred Scamaroni, one enters the Citadel by the Porte Neuve (1854) or Porte de France as it is usually known.

To reach La Ville Haute (the Citadel and the Old Town) on foot follow the Quai Comparetti to the Place St Erasme then climb the steps of the Montée Rastello. The small church (*St Erasme*) on the right was that of the fishermen, barred from the town by the Genoese. Striking in its simplicity, it has a model wooden sailing boat hung from the timbered roof constructed like an upturned boat. The Montée Rastello passes underneath the Avenue de Gaulle and is succeeded by another flight of steps, the Montée Saint Roch, which leads to the *Col Saint Roch* (32m) where there is a natural belvedere, looking over the harbour on one side and out to sea on the other, beyond the great white blocks of limestone that have fallen from the cliff. One of the largest is called, inevitably, the 'grain de sable'. The sheer white cliffs and the peninsular isolation of Bonifacio recall the Dorset Purbeck coast and Portland.

To the left of the Col Saint Roch a path marked at the beginning by a black wooden cross leads to the *Pertusato semaphore and lighthouse* (ask at the Office de Tourisme, 12 Rue Longue, with the Mairie in the centre of the Old Town). This is a walk of about 45 minutes along the ridge. The lighthouse stands 90m above sea level and its light can be seen for 27km. There is a fine view of the Bonifacio peninsula, the granite mass of the Trinité to the west and the northern shore of Sardinia. The lighthouse may also be reached (5km) by car, taking the D 58 out of Bonifacio and then the first to the right.

The *Chapelle St Roch* (closed to the public) was built on the spot where died the last victim of the plague of 1528 during which Bonifacio lost two-thirds of its population. The Montée St Roch enters the *Bastion de l'Etendard* by the Porte de Gênes, until the 19C the only gate to the old town. The 1598 drawbridge mechanism and massive gates can still be seen. Pass through the gateway and turn right into the Place d'Armes which contains the plinths of four late 15C grain silos which, with others on the Place Manichella, provisioned the Bonifaciens during sieges.

Opposite the Porte de Gênes take the Rue du Corps de Garde which runs alongside the north wall of L'EGLISE SAINTE-MARIE, formerly the cathedral church, begun by the Pisans at the end of the 12C and refashioned with Gothic additions by the Genoese during later centuries. The vast *loggia* in front of the church, where the notables of the town used to meet and where proclamations were made, is built over a great water cistern (now dry and transformed into a conference hall). The *podesta*, the ruling magistrate, dispensed justice here twice a week and his palace (fragments of a 13C colonnade) was opposite the church. The square four-storey campanile (14C–15C) is possibly Aragonese in inspiration.

The interior is dark. On entering, directly on the left is a 3C Roman sarcophagus, now a receptacle for holy water. Above it is a 1465 Genoese tabernacle, beautifully sculpted and representing the torso of Christ, arms crossed at the wrists, the delicate long-fingered hands showing the nail wounds, supported by eight mourning cherubs. The largest is at the base, his chubby form and curly head seemingly supporting with difficulty the weight of the complete tabernacle. A carved octagonal casket in ivory and ebony is said to have contained relics of St Boniface. It is northern Italian, end of 14C. It may be necessary to ask for permission to see this casket and a so-called relic of the True Cross which are kept in a locked cupboard in the sacristy. Formerly in times of storm the relic, said to have been given to Bonifacio by 'a princess' who escaped shipwreck in the Straits of Bonifacio, used to be carried onto the terrace of the Place Manichella, 65m above the roaring waves. The clergy blessed the waves in the hope of bringing calm, in the presence of the citizens.

A *jardin des vestiges* has been made around the ruins of the medieval town walls. This public garden may be visited, and apart from the ruins now brought to light there are views of Cap Pertusato, the Straits of Bonifacio, the old houses of the town seemingly perched on the edge of the vertiginous cliffs, and the coast of Sardinia. When visiting the jardin des vestiges and the ramparts it is helpful to take a pamphlet, containing a plan published by the Bonifacio Office du Tourisme entitled *'Visite des Remparts: du siege de 1553 aux jardins des vestiges'*. To quote the opening sentence on the history of Bonifacio 'Everything hinges on the siege of 1553...'. Bonifacio (like Calvi always faithful to Genoa), was besieged from the sea by the French and Turks, commanded by the corsair Dragut and aided from the landward side by Sampiero Corso's troops in revolt against Genoa.

Apart from the path along the ridge of the plateau towards the lighthouse of Pertusato there is a cliff walk, *Promenade pédestre des Falaises*, which starts from the southern end of the melodious Rue du chante de Mai, on the other side of the Rue Doria. Go through the Rue Doria in the other direction and turn left into the Rue des Pagnas from the Place Montepagano. At the end is *l'Escalier du roi d'Aragon*, constructed in the summer of 1420 when the Spanish fleet besieged Bonifacio.

There is a legend that this stairway of 187 steps cut into the cliff face from the shore to the level of the Haute Ville was made in a single night. A self-deprecatory Corsican joke playing on their unjustified reputation for indolence declares 'It certainly was not Corsican workmen who built it'. In fact, these steps had served during earlier centuries as a route for Bonifaciens to draw water from the St Barthélémy well which is fed by a subterranean lake under the plateau (possibly the Articia fountain of the Odyssey?).

The Citadel covers the west end of the peninsula and the former presence there of the Foreign Legion's principal garrison is recalled by the *monument to the Foreign Legion*, facing the Citadel gateway which once stood in the main square of Saïda and was brought from Algeria and set up here when the Légion took occupation of the Caserne Montlaur on 23 June 1963. It is a memorial to those Légionnaires who died in the Sud-Oranais campaigns of 1897–1902.

On the south side of the Citadel the church of *St Dominique*, recently restored, was begun by the Templars in 1270 on the site of a Romanesque church of which no trace remains, given to the Dominicans in 1307 and completed in 1343. It is simple Gothic where the pillars separating the aisles from the nave are decorated with delicate small paintings (18C) of the Fifteen Mysteries of the Rosary. In the *Resurrection* Christ and two other figures are depicted in almost joyous stance on the tomb. The white marble 18C altar is encrusted with coloured stones and comes from the church of St François (see below). A Vierge du Rosaire with portraits of aldermen was given in thanks when the siege was raised in 1553. An 18C Descent from the Cross, two statues which are kept in the sacristy—a Mater Dolorosa and a Ste Marthe (Pisan workmanship 14C–15C) are carried in the Good Friday procession as is the 800kg carved wood Martyre de St Barthélémy. An exuberantly baroque detail depicts turbanned infidels excoriating the saint while a small dog is restrained from retrieving the saintly scraps.

A walk of less than 500m to the end of the promontory passes two old windmills and the church of St François, objects of recent restoration. The church, built in 1390, has a single nave, spacious and austere, a fine marble font bearing the della Rocca arms and a white marble flagstone over the tomb of Rinuccio Spinola, Bishop of Ajaccio (1437), at the entrance to the chancel. The cemetery close by encloses a wide variety of baroque tombs.

Excursions from Bonifacio

BOAT TRIPS FROM BONIFACIO to the Iles de Lavezzi, Bainsu and Cavallo, 7km south of Pertusato may be made according to the state of the weather and the chance of finding sailors at the port prepared to go for a reasonable fare. The granite isles are vestiges of the isthmus that once joined Corsica and Sardinia. They have been a nature reserve since 1982 with no trees but flora now rare or vanished from Corsica proper. Ecology does not rule unchallenged, however. Cavallo (NOT part of the nature reserve) is the property of a consortium, a fortress owned, ruled and strongly (sometimes violently) defended by multinational millionaires. This Jet Set enclave on Corsican territory has attracted the attention of the authorities and, not unnaturally and more positively, that of resentful nationalists. What does remain to be seen—from a boat—are the remains of a Roman (1C–3C AD) port at Paléva on Cavallo, an ancient granite quarry on an islet near San Bainsu where there are columns still lying for Roman ships to collect. The fine grey granite was much prized by Rome.

On 15 February 1855 the frigate *Sémillante,* bound for the Crimea, struck one of the Lavezzi rocks with the loss of all 773 soldiers and sailors aboard. The bodies recovered were buried on one of the islets. Alphonse Daudet, sailing between Sardinia and Corsica with some seagoing Customs companions, spent a night beside the cemetery ten years after the wreck. He relates in one of the *'Lettres de Mon Moulin'* an eye-witness account by a leprous old shepherd of the *Sémillante* striking the rocks. In 1893 a French steamer foundered on the same reef but without loss of life.

THE SEA CAVES AND THE BONIFACIO COAST. (Trip of 45 minutes from the Marine where there is a ticket office labelled 'Grottes et Falaises'.) The caves, Le Camere, Le Bain de Venus and the Sdragonatu, are in the south-facing cliffs to the north just beyond the inlet to the harbour fjord. The Sdragonatu is lit by the sunlight coming through a great natural cleft which is, by coincidence, roughly the shape of Corsica. The light, reflected by the red rocks and the violet-greenish water, creates the effect of a stage set. As the boat rounds the point one gets the best view of Bonifacio's houses on the edge of the cliffs, the King of Aragon's staircase, the Grain of Sand and the St Barthélémy spring. Everything that has or is said to have happened comes alive: the Laestrygons hurling boulders down upon the Greek ships, the sieges in the Middle Ages, the hacking of the stairway into the cliff face.

BOATS TO SARDINIA. Daily service to Santa Teresa di Gallura, Palau and La Maddalena (frequency according to season, duration of voyage under an hour, car ferry). Information from the offices of Corsica Ferries and Tirrenia at the port.

BEACHES IN THE BONIFACIO REGION. For the *Plage de Cala longa* take the D 58, fork left at 3km to the D 258 and reach the beach in 3km. For the *Plage de la Rondinara* take the N 198 towards Porto Vecchio. Turn right at 11km to Suartone and continue for 4km until the road ends within sight of the sea. For the *Plage du Gurzago* take the D 58 for 6km to Gurzago on the shores of the Gulfu di Sant' Amanza.

4   Le Désert des Agriates and the Valley of the Ostriconi

A. Le Désert des Agriates

Corsica, blessed with a widely varied landscape, even has its own desert, not the Sheikh of Araby kind with horizon to horizon sand, but as defined by the OED, an 'uninhabited and uncultivated tract of country, a wilderness'.

The D 81 road from l'Ile Rousse to Saint-Florent (46km) enters the **Désert des Agriates** 18km from l'Ile Rousse at *Pont d'Ostriconi*, crossing the river of that name which rises on the slopes of Monte Asto (1535m) and runs 22km to the Mediterranean at the Anse de Paraiola. The road follows the south edge of the desert, uncultivated and devoid of human presence and buildings apart from the occasional shepherd's hut. One point of entry into the desert is from the Bocca di Vezzu (312m), which is roughly half-way along the D 81, the pass between the valleys of the Ostriconi and the Zente. From here one can see over the Golfe de Saint-Florent to Cap Corse. From the col a road to the left leads to the coast, about 11km of very rough going for an ordinary car although vehicles like Range Rovers or Jeeps should have no difficulty. For the walker there is a toughish 3-hour trip that brings the energetic to the shore, where there are many deserted creeks between the Punta di Malfulcu and the Punta Negra. By taking a walk now and then one gets to know and appreciate the wildness of the desert, the conservation of which, together with its shoreline, is energetically supervised by the authorities of Haute-Corse and the communes of San Pietro, San Gavino, Saint-Florent and Palasca and protected from predatory 'developers'.

Another track leaves to the left just before Casta, negotiable by rugged motors over 10km, skirting Monte Genova (421m) and following the valley of the Liscu to the Plage de Saleccia where exteriors were shot for 'The Longest Day' (1962) the film on the 1944 Allied invasion of Normandy. From Saleccia there are footpaths to the Etang de Loto to the east and further east to the Punta Mortella where there is a lighthouse and a ruined Genoese tower.

The D 81 comes out of the Desert just beyond Casta and passes between two sectors of an Army firing range before turning north-east towards the sea and Saint-Florent (18km from Casta).

B.   The Valley of the Ostriconi

In 1990 an alternative to the N 197 route from central Corsica to the west coast was opened. Some comments are needed on it in the preparation of this new edition of Blue Guide Corsica: 1) the new D 8 (taking over the number and, in places, sections of the original D 8) is a wide, straight road of 36km between Lozari and Ponte Leccia which leaves the D 81 4km from the coast and joins the N 197 8km north of Ponte Leccia; 2) it is printed on only the latest maps e.g. IGN 73 with the note '*ouverture prévue mi-1990*' and Michelin 90 where the south end is shown as under construction; 3) it bypasses the Ostriconi valley villages so you must look out for the side-roads leading to them. Descriptions of villages, from north to south, are given below.

South of the desert, the Ostriconi valley is an area which again is different from anything else in Corsica. It used to be an agricultural region with beef herds and olive groves and the valley farmers were the last in Corsica to use draught oxen. The Lama region takes its name from one of its villages, 18km long and 6–8km wide, neither of the Balagne nor of the Nebbio but a corridor district between the two. A turning to the left just beyond the Bocca di Tostari leads to Urtaca (360m, 155 inhab.) with well-restored old houses, many with carved doors, a village set in a bowl of reddish mountains. Not too hard, fine weather, walk along an ancient mule track over the Tenda range by the Bocca di San Pancrazio (969m) to *San Pietro di Tenda* 10km away in the Nebbio.

The old road goes direct in 3km to *Lama* (480m, 98 inhab.), *chef-lieu* of the region, moulded of tall houses and narrow streets and perched on a spur of rock, rightly awarded a national prize for the success of its move from declining farming to sensitive and tasteful adaptation to tourism, presenting itself attractively for what it is—a flower-filled, unchanged Corsican hill-top village. There is an easy 6km walk along a track to the eastern side of Monte Astu on the lower slopes of which Lama is built.

Still without returning to the D 8 main road it is 4km to Pietralba (450m, 244 inhab.) in a high dry, commanding position in which traces of Roman occupation have been found and some Roman masonry has been re-- employed in the walls of the parish church of Ste Marie. A former great sheep-raising centre, as recently as 1970 there were thirty flocks in the commune. There is a panorama to the Balagne coast, and a stone-paved track that was for centuries part of the link between the Balagne and the Eastern Plain provides a good 5½ hr walk (about 6.5km) by the Bocca di Tenda (1219m) to *Pieve* (450m, 76 inhab.) in the Nebbio.

10km to the south is Ponte Leccia and the N 193 east to Bastia and south to Corte and Ajaccio. At 2km north of Ponte Leccia the N 197 winds its way up the valley of the Lagani for 11km where, as an alternative to staying on it to Belgodère and Lozari, take the D 12 right to Novella (400m, 55 inhab.) an ancient mountain village with fine houses and porches. There are vestiges of the ruined 11C Château de San Colombano; also a view to the Agriates from the Bocca di San Colombano. This lonely and picturesque region may be seen from the train which runs in and out of tunnels near Novella. The D 12 joins the D 8 close to the junction with the D 81.

5   La Balagne

A self-contained region of some 861 sq km and nearly 17,000 inhabitants, the **Balagne** (A Balagna) is a fertile area of north-west Corsica, running from Calvi on the coast, north along the coastline (50km) to the estuary of the Ostriconi. The plains and rolling hills of the Balagne are flanked by the Mediterranean to the north and west, and the forests of Bonifatu and Tartagine to the south. Further south lies the central Corsican mountain range in which, visible from most of the Balagne, are the peaks (from north to south) of Monte Grosso (1938m), Monte Padro (2393m) and Monte Cinto (the highest mountain in the island at 2710m). The rivers of the Balagne are, starting from the Ostriconi in the north, the Balagne and the Agriates, separating the Lozari and the Régina which reach the sea at Lozari, the Fiume Secco, the Bartasca and the Ficarella, which all reach the sea near Calvi. To the south of the Balagne, the Filosorma is irrigated by the Marsolino and the Fango which flow into a common estuary in the Golfe de Galéria.

The fertility of the Balagne which earned it the title of the Garden of Corsica also brought invaders seeking its riches of oil, fruit, cereals, flocks and herds. Phoenicians, Greeks, Etruscans, Romans and Moors all came to plunder or settle. Nowadays there is a flourishing tourist industry along the coast and, through an active irrigation programme dating from 1977, a revival of olive oil and wine production, both in the coastal area and in the inland hillside villages.

The Balagne is the best known holiday region of Corsica to British visitors. The Garden of Corsica is also known as Holy Balagne for its many fine churches, mainly built during Pisan domination in the 11C–13C. Their construction owed much to the feudal overlords, sent at Papal instigation to drive out the Moors and fortify and occupy the area. The Genoese built fortresses at Calvi and Algajola, and l'Ile Rousse was Paoli's fortified port to rival Calvi.

A.   Along the coast: from Lozari to l'Ile Rousse and Calvi

ROAD (N 197) 29km.—7km *l'Ile Rousse*—17km *Algajola*.

To the north of the Ostriconi River is the western part of the Désert des Agriates. The D 81 from Saint-Florent reaches the Mediterranean 2km beyond the Pont d'Ostriconi and hugs the coast for 9km as far as *Lozari* where there is a *village de vacances*.

Much more than a holiday centre, it is organised to show those who stay there what the Balagne, past and present, has to offer and is closely concerned with promoting local history and employment. It is very much part of the Balagne and visitors may learn much about Corsican traditions and history in general and about this part of the island in particular.

7km along the coast road, the N 197, brings you to **l'Ile Rousse** (Isula Rossa, 2288 inhab.). This 'Red Isle' merits its name. Islets of orange-red granite offshore (now joined to the mainland) glow a deep red in the evening sunlight reflected from the sea.

L'Ile Rousse owes its existence to Paoli who decided that there should be a western port that was Corsican and opposed to the Genoese-held ports of Calvi and Algajola, respectively 24km and 9km along the coast to the south-west. L'Ile Rousse had been a Roman settlement called Rubico Rocega, but had declined after the Romans left. Paoli, in founding l'Ile Rousse, said that he was building 'a gallows to hang Calvi', intending to put the port out of business. There was discussion at the time (1758) of calling the new port Paolina and in 1769 of calling it Vaux after the Comte de Vaux, commandant in chief of the French forces in Corsica. Its old name remained, however, and l'Ile Rousse it still is, a port exporting olive oil and dairy produce destined for Roquefort, and fruit and wine of the Balagne. Of increasing importance to the local economy is its status as an expanding tourist centre, a favourite with British holiday-makers because of its high sunshine rate and bathing beaches of fine sand.

The centre of l'Ile Rousse is the spacious, plane-shaded PLACE PAOLI. Above a fountain in the centre is a white marble statue of Paoli who surveys with a stony eye the pétanque players in the square. On the west side is the large baroque church of the Immaculate Conception, restored 1930–35 after damage by fire in 1914. There is nothing of particular interest in the church except its welcome simplicity. On the northern side of the square is a covered market beyond which you enter the OLD TOWN, and narrow paved streets leading down to the sea. At the end of the Rue Notre-Dame is the Place Tino Rossi, touching and fitting because he brought nearly as much fame to Corsica as Paoli and Napoleon. Is there a Vera Lynn Square in London or a Bing Crosby Garden in the USA? On the landward side of the square, beside the Hôtel de Ville, is a partly ruined and much-restored tower carrying an inscription about the founding of the town by Paoli. To the north of the Place Paoli is the Hôtel Napoléon Bonaparte. Built 1929–30, complete with casino, it was Corsica's first luxury hotel. Between 1953 and

1955 it housed Prince Moulay, since 1961 King Hassan II of Morocco, then in exile.

The town has many cafés and restaurants, and the railway station from which the *tramway de la Balagne*, part of the island railway system, goes to Algajola and Calvi and, in the other direction, to Belgodère and Ponte Leccia and the line down to Ajaccio and up to Bastia.

The island of *Petra* or *Isula Rossa* is now joined to the town by a causeway. At its extremity is the lighthouse and from the open space around it there is a fine view over l'Ile Rousse to the Balagne hills behind, the village of Monticello, and to seaward the neighbouring small islands.

East along the promenade—*la petite croisette*—a turning 50m inland at the end, the Musée Océanographique, founded and directed by Pierre Pernod whose long devotion to the subject of marine life includes participation in Cousteau-directed expeditions. Octopus, conger eel, skate, small shark and innumerable other creatures are studied from egg to maturity in tanks holding 100,000 litres of sea water. Pernod gives lively talks, removing specimens from the water to illustrate points. German and English translations, films, instruction in underwater exploration (10.30–13.00 and 14.30–19.00 daily).

Algajola (Algaiola, 211 inhab.), 9km from l'Ile Rousse. Here the lieutenant governor of Calvi lived. There are Genoese fortifications built after the Turkish sack of the town in 1663 of which the citadel has been restored. Pleasant very small town, Casa Corsa selling genuine Corsican produce in the Place du Château, 1.5km beach of fine sand. Between N 197 direction l'Ile Rousse and the sea, 250m up a track from beside a garage on left, 3km beyond Algajola, is an abandoned quarry of porphyritic granite (marked 'monolithe' on IGN map 4149 OT TOP 25 Calvi, Cirque de Bonifatu). A column 17.50m long, weighing 301,620kg, cut by Italian

The Algajola 'Paperweight'

*San Pietro e San Paolo, Lumio. One of two granite busts of lions
set into the south façade*

workmen in 1828 and intended for a monument to Napoleon in Ajaccio,
was too heavy to move and still lies there, known locally as 'the paperweight', attended by vociferous frogs. Granite from this quarry was used
for the base of the Vendôme column in Paris and columns of a Medici palace
in Florence.

The Marine de Sant' Ambrogio is a carefully laid-out Club Méditerranée
installation with tree-lined roads, villas to let, a commercial centre, tennis,
riding, sailing, *port de plaisance*.

Lumio (200m, 895 inhab.) at 10km north-east of Calvi rises on terraces
overlooking the narrow coastal plain and the Golfe de Calvi. It has a large
baroque church, narrow, stepped streets, and is an admirable example of
how to preserve and restore attractively an old village. 1km towards Calvi
a turning to the left marked 'cimetière' leads to the rosy granite Romanesque church of San Pietro e San Paolo, late 11C, restored 18C. Two
lions' heads, brought from some earlier building where they may have,
Tuscan-fashion, flanked a porch set into the façade. Interior decorated in
Pisan style with geometric figures. A vault, sealed with a stone slab in the
floor, holds the bones of plague victims who were left there to perish of
asphyxiation.

The variety in the monumental masonry of the tombs which crowd the
cemetery up to and all around the church is astounding as an example of
the costly effort made to ensure the durable mark of families on the territory
of their commune.

A turning seawards between Lumio and San Pietro leads, in just over 2km
and crossing the railway, to the ruined Genoese tower of Caldano. Nearby,

a triangular stele, in which two holes represent eyes, was discovered in 1959 by Dorothy Carrington.

CALVI (4815 inhab., sous-préfecture of Haute-Corse), so often fought over, besieged, destroyed, endlessly rebuilt yet still solidly there.

During the second half of the 13C it was disputed by warring factions of local landowners until the citizens appealed to the Genoese for protection. The town was rebuilt and fortified in 1268 by Giovaniello de Loreto and the Calvesi were accorded special rights and privileges by the Republic of Genoa to which it remained *'semper fidelis'*, through the centuries. The town's history is that of a fortress port prepared to repel all comers, whether raiders from the North African coast, the Royal Navy, or the forces of Corsican nationalists like Paoli who founded l'Ile Rousse as a rival port to Calvi.

When in July 1793 Paoli appealed to England for support against the French the Royal Navy besieged Calvi. From 16 June to 5 August the town resisted 6000 British and Paolist supporters. Repelled by French ships, including *l'Orient* commanded by the gallant Luce de Casabianca, the British shelled the town from the heights of La Serra. It was during these land and sea attacks that Captain Nelson was wounded by rock splinters and lost the sight of his right eye. The Royal Navy eventually took the town after having damaged it severely by bombardment. Two years later the British pulled out and in 1796 Calvi and Corsica became permanently French (see Historical Introduction).

The town is built on a traditional Corsican and established medieval plan, the chosen site being difficult to reach from seaward, where it is protected by cliffs, and so placed that the possibility of attack from landward is also reduced. Calvi has all of this. The port, entered from the Golfe de Calvi, is sheltered from the west wind by the promontory on which the Citadel stands. There is deep water in the anchorage for the ships that export the produce of the Balagne: grapes, olives, cereals, figs and other fruits; and also for fishing boats, steam, motor and sailing vessels.

Calvi is roughly divided into two parts: the Citadel (as at Bastia, Bonifacio, etc.), built on the rocky promontory and virtually impregnable until the invention of the aeroplane, containing the Haute-Ville with its maze of ancient narrow streets; and the Port or Marine district, the Basse-Ville, with a broad quay, ships lying at anchor, cafés and restaurants along the quayside and, towering protectively above it all, the Citadel's honey-coloured ramparts.

The Citadel and the Old Walled Town. Although it is possible to reach the Citadel and the Old Town by car the effect is greater if one explores on foot. Cross the Place Christophe Colomb, pausing to read the commemoration of the latest struggle for liberty: '1943 First landing on French soil [by French troops] at Ajaccio 13–14 September where the volunteers of the 1st Shock Battalion met and joined up with the forces of resistance. In this citadel of Calvi the 1st Battalion forged its spirit and its arms...300 of its members died for their country'. Calvi is proud of its history and reputation as a training centre for tough units of the French Army including the Foreign Legion.

The only entrance to the Citadel was formerly guarded by a drawbridge, portcullis and armoured gates. Over the gateway are the arms of Calvi and the words that celebrate the town's long loyalty to Genoa, *'Civitas Calvi semper fidelis'*, accorded by the Republic of Genoa in 1562 after the town had heroically withstood the sieges of 1553 and 1555 by French and Turkish forces and Sampiero's Corsicans, rebels or partisans according to point of view.

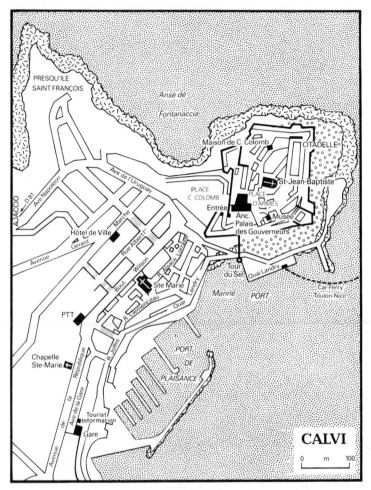

CALVI

0 m 100

A tour of the **Ramparts** encircling this fortified granite promontory rising nearly 80m sheer from the sea gives spectacular views over the Golfe de Calvi to the south-east and over to the inland villages and orchards of the Balagne with the mountains rising beyond. To the west there is a view over the Marine and the Lower Town and beyond to the Saint François Peninsula and the Golfe and Point of Revellata on which stands a lighthouse.

After completing the tour of the ramparts you come back to the Place des Armes which is dominated by the former *Palace of the Genoese Governors*, begun in the 13C and enlarged in 1554 (between the two sieges by the Franco-Turkish-Sampiero forces), by the Bank of St George. The old palace, of massive construction, restored in the 1980s, is now the Sampiero Barracks (not open to the public).

On the far side of the Place des Armes the cathedral church of **St-Jean-Baptiste** stands on the highest point of the rock on which the old city is set.

A
P. DE PAOLI
LIBERATORE
LA PATRIA RICONOSCENTE

"CORE IN FRONTE È
STRADA DRITTA, O GIUVENTÙ"

CENTINARIU DI U
RITORNU DI E
CENNERE 1889-1989

IN MEMORIA DI
PASQUALE DE PAOLI
U BABBU DI A PATRIA

Memorial to the founder of l'Ile Rousse in the Place Paoli

Built in the 13C, it suffered in the 1553 siege and was severely damaged by fire in the explosion of the Palace powder magazine in 1567. Rebuilt in 1570 and raised to cathedral status in 1576, it is in the form of a Greek cross and surmounted by a cupola.

Inside, under the dome, are what appear to be theatre boxes protected by grilles. Here sat the wives of local dignitaries when they attended mass; the grilles were to protect them from the curious or lustful eyes of the common people. To the left of the entrance are marble baptismal fonts dated 1568. The carved and painted *pulpit* was given by the people of Calvi in 1757. The central panel portrays John the Baptist and is flanked by the symbols of the four evangelists.

The *high altar* is 18C polychrome marble and surmounted by a 17C Christ in wood. The triptych (1498) in the apse is by the Ligurian artist Barbagelata and is a copy of his master Mazone's painting for the church of Santa Maria di Castello in Genoa. Below the triptych is a portrayal of St Nicholas and three children, the work of 'primitive' local artists.

To the right of the choir, above the altar, is the ebony *Christ of the Miracles* which was displayed above the ramparts in 1555 to the encircling Turks who at the sight of it fell back, raising the siege. Above the altar to the left of the choir is the wooden *Virgin of the Rosary* (16C) from Seville. Andalucian custom is followed, by dressing the figure in a sequence of robes for different holy days: for example in mourning black on Good Friday.

One of Calvi's most notable families, the Baglioni, buried below the cupola. In 1400 a member of this family overheard two men plotting to deliver the town to the Aragonese forces. Shouting 'Libertà! Libertà!' he cut them down with his sword and in gratitude the Calvesi added 'Libertà' to his surname. He and his descendants are so-called to this day.

The 15C *Oratoire St-Antoine* has over the main door a carved late portrayal of the saint with his piglet, flanked by St Francis of Assisi, St John the Baptist and members of the Franciscan order. The oratory is now the religious art museum of the Balagne, 15–18C. It houses damaged 16C frescoes and panels of a 15C altarpiece repainted in 1677. There is a fine collection of ecclesiastical vestments (17C–18C), an ivory Christ attributed to the Florentine sculptor Sansovino (died 1570), and a permanent exhibition in other rooms of the history and archaeology of Calvi, with Roman, Pisan, Genoese, and French exhibits, many recovered from the seabed.

Look at the *wall plaque* commemorating Columbus' birth in the Rue Colombo (formerly the street of the weavers, Rue des Tisserands, Carrugio del Filo). This states categorically that: *'Ici est né en 1441 Christophe Colomb, immortalisé par la decouverte du Nouvelle Monde, alors que Calvi était sous la domination génoise; mort à Valladolid le 20 mai 1500.'*

René Massoni, an eminent Calvais, president of the Association Christopher Columbus, has worked for 30 years in research on Columbus. Many books have been written asserting that Columbus was born here and 1992, 500 years after his landing in the New World, is an important date for Calvi. The claim rests on the fact that he was Genoese (as was Calvi at that time). Another famous figure connected with Calvi is the real-life Don Juan, Miguel de Leca y Colonna y Manara y Vincentello. He was born in Seville in 1627 of a father from Calvi and a mother from the Balagne village of Montemaggiore.

From the Place Christophe Colomb follow the Rue Albert 1er to where, on the right, approached by stepped terraces through well-tended gardens, is the *Hôtel de Ville* (open 08.30–12.00 and 14.00–16.00, except Saturday, Sunday and public holidays). The Council Chamber contains paintings given by Cardinal Fesch (whose main collection belongs to Ajaccio), three of which are said to be by Rubens. Others are of 17C Italian provenance.

The Basse Ville containing the Marine, the Port de Plaisance and the quays, is overlooked by the church of *Ste Marie Majeure*. It was begun in 1765 on the site of earlier churches destroyed during the Barbarian incursions in the 5C and later in the 16C, the cupola belonging to the second quarter of the 19C. Follow the Boulevard Wilson 230m south to just beyond where it becomes the Avenue de la République. On the right stands the *Chapelle Sainte-Marie*, rebuilt in the 14C incorporating vestiges of the 4C basilica. At the north-eastern corner of the Marine on the Quai Landry is the *Tour de Sel*, storehouse for salt, originally a strongly fortified lookout tower.

To visit the *Chapelle de Notre-Dame di a Serra*, 6km south-west of Calvi, take the D 81 from the Avenue Napoléon, clearly marked as the road to Ajaccio. A turn to the left at 4km leads in 2km to the chapel, standing 216m high on the summit of a hill. A 19C building on the site of a 15C sanctuary destroyed during the 1794 siege of Calvi, the chapel is of no architectural interest but contains a painting on parchment above the altar of the Immaculate Conception with a Franciscan monk *'en donateur'*. On 8 September (Feast of the Nativity of the Virgin) or the following Sunday there is a procession to the chapel from Calvi. A footpath to the left leads back to Calvi in 40–50 minutes. The visit is recommended above all for the view from the chapel north-east across the Gulf and town of Calvi, east across the Calenzana valley to the Monte Grosso, and north-west to the Revellata peninsula and out to sea.

Punta di a Revellata. Still on the D 83 to Ajaccio from Calvi, take at 4km the turning to the right (almost opposite the turn to the Chapelle de la Madona di a Serra) to the point (2.5km) where there is a lighthouse and an oceanographic centre founded by Liège University. There is a view over the Golfe di a Revellata and to the Citadel of Calvi. It may be impossible to drive all the way to the point but there is a footpath. Another footpath also leads back to Calvi (two hours).

BOAT EXCURSIONS FROM CALVI to La Grotte des Veaux Marins (3 hours there and back), to sea-caves once inhabited by Mediterranean seals. Fine views of the cliffs of the Revellata Point. Day trips to the landlocked fishing port of Girolata, Nature Reserve of Scandola, Porto, Ile Rousse, Algajola, Sant' Ambrogio. Details are available from the Office du Tourisme on the Port de Plaisance, outstanding for its staff's friendly efficiency.

After the Foreign Legion left Algeria in 1962 it was stationed in Corsica at Bastia, Corte, Bonifacio and Calvi. Since 1985 the only Legionnaires remaining on the island are the 2000 crack commando troops of the 2nd Foreign Legion Parachute Regiment at Camp Raffalli to the east of Calvi on the right of the N 197. Immediately before it is the D 151 turning to Calenzana and the turning to the right before that is the D 251 to the airport of Calvi–Ste Catherine, recently much extended to cope with increasing domestic and international traffic.

Following the D 251 to its end, 22km from Calvi, at the Maison Forestière and mountain inn of Bonifatu. There is a choice of walks of varying duration in this beautiful area of towering red granite pinnacles, Laricio pines, ilex and tumbling water. Full information on paths, walking time, altitude, vegetation etc. is given on a notice board in the car park. (Map IGN 4149 OT TOP 25 Calvi, cirque de Bonifatu; Parc Naturel Régional de la Corse; 1:25000. 1cm=250m.) (See also Rte 16, Asco.)

If the Foreign Legion is today in evidence there is a record of past Royal Navy presence to the other side of Calvi, west on the D 81 towards Ajaccio for 2km, past the Gendarmerie on the left, left turning at the first garage, park at 500m, on foot towards the house closest to the sea. There, on a seaward-facing rock on top of which the house and its garden sit, is a plaque stating that here on 12 July 1794 Nelson was wounded in his right eye (see p 69). The plaque is just visible from the main road, difficult to find and nearly impossible to photograph but it is still there, scarred as a target for Italian bullets during the Second World War.

RELIGIOUS FESTIVALS IN CALVI AND DISTRICT: on *Maundy Thursday* the Canistrelli procession in the town. The name *Canistrelli* comes from the biscuit made with eggs baked in Corsica at Easter and called in other parts of the island *caccavelli*. On *Good Friday* there is the Granitola (the snail) procession at 21.00–23.00—barefoot, hooded penitents carry a life-size statue of the dead Christ followed by a statue of the Virgin of the Rosary (p 72) in mourning. For the *Assumption of the Virgin*, 15–18 August, there are three days of games, fireworks, processions, etc. The *Pilgrimage of our Lady of the Serra* takes place on 8 September (or the following Sunday).

B.   Belgodère to Corbara: some inland villages of the Balagne

ROAD (D 71) 29km.—10km *Speloncato* (to left of road)—16.5km *Muro*—24km *Aregno*—*26.5km Pigna.*

Instead of taking the N 199 from Lozari to l'Ile Rousse, take the N 197 going directly south from Lozari for 8km to *Belgodère* (Belgudè, 310m, 331 inhab.). This is a 'balcony' village with its natural protection enhanced by an old fort on a jutting rock, now in ruins, overlooking the olive groves and orchards of the fertile Prato valley. The village owes its name, meaning '*beau plaisir*' or pleasant place, to its situation. The best view over the valley is from the ruins of the old fort, reached by a narrow lane and steps. The church of *St Thomas de Belgodère*, founded in 1269 by André Malaspina, marquis de Massa, contains a painting (late 16C) on wood of the Virgin and Child flanked by two apostles and members of the fraternity who donated the painting.

Leave Belgodère by the D 71 in the direction of Calvi. At 4.5km on the other side of the hamlet of Costa the road rounds the *Convent of Tuani*, now a private house.—10km beyond Belgodère, south of the D 71 on the minor D 63, a left turn is marked to *Speloncato* (Spiluncatu, 550m, 194 inhab.), built on an outcrop of Monte Tolo (1332m). The rocks on either side of the village have numerous grottoes, the most famous being the *Pietra Tafonata* (Pierced Stone), 8m long and 6–7m wide. On 8 April and 8 September at around 18.00 the setting sun goes temporarily out of view and reappears for a few instants, shining through the hole in the rock. Speloncato is characterised by narrow streets of tall granite houses. From the village there are superb views over the Balagne to the sea.

Return to the D 71 by the D 663 and on reaching it turn left, passing two villages, *Nessa* (Nescia, 350m, 91 inhab.) and *Feliceto* (Felicetu, 300m 145 inhab.) on detour roads among great chestnut trees and olive groves. The trees may be up to eight centuries old but many groves have been destroyed by fire.

6.5km beyond Speloncato is **Muro** (Muru, 320m, 276 inhab.), a village consisting principally of a main street of houses on one side only, the other being the open side of a 'balcony' poised above a precipitous drop down to gardens, orchards and olive groves. On the street the church of the **Annunciation*, very large for the village, is one of Corsica's baroque

Aregno, La Trinità

masterpieces. The interior is a riot of polychromatic marble covering the altar, altar rail, pulpit and organ loft. Note the inscription inside: 'On 4 March 1798, Ash Wednesday, part of the roof of the church fell in during the service and killed 59 parishioners.' Local oral tradition has it that at the moment this took place the priest in Calenzana interrupted his sermon to ask his congregation to pray for the parishioners of Muro and their church.

Near the end of the village street is a tall square house, once a centre for the cultivation of silkworms imported from Syria and fed on mulberry leaves from trees in the Regina valley below. The building was originally two storeys higher but these were removed as being unsafe (heeding ecclesiastical warning perhaps?)

In many places along the D 71 there are fine views across the Balagne countryside and also from the villages lying along the road, Avapessa, Catteri and, 2km west along the D 71 leading to the N 197 coast road, *Lavatoggio* (Lavatoghju, 200m, 138 inhab.) with a vista over Algajola Bay and to the surrounding villages.

At 500m along the D 151 from Catteri take the D 413 to *Sant' Antonino* (Sant Antuninu, 500m, 60 inhab.), on a ridge between two valleys. Founded in 9C it is perhaps the oldest village in Corsica. Narrow cobbled streets, tall granite houses, its church and a chapel are set below on a greensward which serves as a car park.

Return to the D 151 and turn right for 1km to *Aregno* (Aregnu, 219m, 544 inhab.), among orange and lemon groves. Just before the village look out for a cemetery and church in a loop of the road. **La Trinità San Giovanni Battista** is a 12C masterpiece of Pisan Romanesque architecture.

EXTERIOR. Striking polychromatic walls of granite ranging through dark green, shades of yellow, orange and ochre. Bold sculptures in high relief on the western front: left of the door a woman in a long dress, hands on hips, wearing a small cap; to the right a naked, bald man (Moses?) holding what might be the tablets of the law on his knees. Under the apex of the pediment is a seated male figure with the ankle of his left leg resting on the knee of his right in 'removing thorn from foot' posture. The door was originally surmounted by a low rounded arch without a tympanum, replaced in late 19C restoration by a monolithic lintel. The *teghie* (flat stones) covering of the nave has been replaced by round tiles but has been retained on the roof of the semi-circular apse.

INTERIOR. An admirably bare single nave. Two frescoes on the north wall. The first represents *Quatre Docteurs de l'Eglise latine* (Augustine, Gregory, Jerome and Ambrose) dated 17 May 1458, probably the work of a local artist because Jerome, for example, is given in the Corsican form of Gilormi. The second fresco is dated 1449 and depicts St Michael slaying the dragon, his expression that of a matador confident of tail and ears.

2.5km north of Aregno is *Pigna* (230m, 92 inhab.) to the left of the D 151, its houses tightly grouped in narrow paved streets on a rounded hillock girded by orange and lemon groves and olive trees. Exceptional views over to Algajola Bay, particularly at sunset. Park in square on entering the village. The 18C church of l'Immaculée Conception has slender bell-turrets with cupolas at either end of the façade and a fine organ by Antonio Ferrari. The Salle du Conseil Municipal on the square has a theatre-like interior and a 16C painting given by Cardinal Fesch (see Musée Fesch, Ajaccio). In this lovingly-preserved Balagne village the true heart and spirit of Corsica is everywhere apparent and available to the visitor—the past still living vigorously, the present actively creative in arts and handicrafts, all adding up to an optimistic and constructive view of the island's artistic and

Pigna, the Casa Musicale

economic future. In 1964 La Corsicada started here as a co-operative association with the aim of reviving old village crafts with an apprentice system to ensure that ancient skills, some nearly lost for ever, are revived and taught to future generations of craftsmen. In the village, together with shepherds and farmers, are potters, engravers, a print-maker, an organ-builder, a maker of lutes and other ancient instruments, sculptors, painters, musicians, specialists in Corsican products and cooking. The Casa Musicale, in a spacious and restored old house, is the village arts centre where several concerts are given each week, with traditional instruments such as the *cetera* (cithern in English) the medieval lute-like instrument now being made in Pigna, and with the participation of visiting folk and jazz musicians. These concerts, usually given out of doors with the setting sun and sea as backdrop, are unforgettable. In summer a bar and restaurant specialising in Corsican and Moroccan dishes is open in the Casa Musicale (the Casa

*Couvent de Corbara with, in the foreground, the Chapelle
Notre-Dame-de-Lazio*

is closed Jan and Feb). Galleries and studios where work (for sale) by local
artists is always on show, including that of the painter and sculptor Toni
Casalonga who, among his many activities and exhibitions throughout
Europe, has been arts adviser to the Corsican Assembly.

1km north of Pigna is the *Couvent de Corbara*, founded in 1456 by the
Franciscans who occupied it until 1792 when it was abandoned until in
1857 the monastery was re-founded by the Dominicans. In 1884 they
established their Studium Provinciale there, a college teaching theology
and religious philosophy to local students. Paoli stayed frequently at
Corbara. There is a footpath, or more correctly, a mule-path from the
convent (80 minutes there and back) to *Monte Sant'Angelo* (562m) with a
view over the Balagne, the Agriates Desert and the west coast of Cap Corse.

Corbara (Curbara, 170m, 583 inhab.), long known as the 'key to the
Balagne', is a large village spread out over the slopes of the gran-
diloquently-named Monte Guido (a hill rather than a mountain). Ruins of
the Castel de Guido and the Castel de Corbara. The Savelli de Guido family
ruled this district from the beginning of the 14C. They built a château
(c 1375) at Corbara, in effect a fortified castle which the Genoese pulled
down in the early 16C as being a threat to their rule, whereupon the
stubborn Savelli restored Castel de Guido which the Roman prince Guido
de Savelli had built in 816. He had been made Count of Balagne after
despatching the Saracens. The village of Corbara has almost a North
African or southern Spanish air with its narrow streets, Barbary fig cactus
and covered passageways. The 18C church of the *Annunciation* is another

baroque triumph in polychromatic marble (1750) imported from Liguria or Tuscany.

3km north of Corbara the D 151 joins the N 197 running north-east to l'Ile Rousse and south-west to Algajola and Calvi.

C. Balagne villages inland from L'Ile Rousse

From l'Ile Rousse itself there are easily-accessible villages, such as *Monticello* (200m, 944 inhab.). From l'Ile Rousse take the D 63 which winds up the hillside to this village with a large square, and a late 17C parish church (St Sébastien). The views down to the coast at l'Ile Rousse, over the cultivated fields, vineyards and orchards, are alone worth the climb to the village. Take the D 263 from Monticello, a winding road, to *Santa Reparata di Balagna* (260m, 784 inhab.), very typical of the villages of this area, with wide views across the lower-lying Balagne lands.

D. Balagne villages inland from Calvi

Calenzana is easily accessible from the main N 197 Calvi–l'Ile Rousse coastal road. At 4.5km from Calvi, going east towards l'Ile Rousse, take the D 151 to the right which in 13km reaches **Calenzana** (Calinzana, 250m, 1535 inhab.). This is a very large village (it would be accounted a town in Devon or New Hampshire) with a surreptitious urban air about it. I first went there in 1975 with an ebullient Calvais who pointed out to me that: 'the large villas with the very high walls belong to 'businessmen' from Marseille, the small villas with lower walls belong to their lawyers. And if you are looking for the priest he is the youngster in jeans sitting over there at the café'.

Set among olive and almond trees, against the slopes of Monte Grosso, Calenzana is the starting point of the GR 20, the long-distance mountain walk that ends up at Conca, near Porto Vecchio, in the south-east of Corsica. There is a Mountain Information Centre at the Mairie. The church of *St Blaise* (end 17C, finished in 1715) is of astonishing proportions with much polychromatic marble inside. The black-and-white tiled floor sloping (one can check it against the edges of memorials along the walls) towards the west door 'Lets the water out when there's a flood from the mountain', the Monte Grosso, a local informed me. The polychrome marble altar is 1767. There is some cunning *trompe l'oeil* of 1880 and medallions around the ceiling of the 18C nave depicting St Blaise.

The clock tower bears an inscription to one of the most famous Corsican legends allied to hard history. It has to be retold straight-faced, legend, history, myth and all. In 1729 the Corsicans rose against the Genoese rulers. The Genoese hired German soldiers to help them put down the Corsican nationalists. Early in 1732 Genoese troops, supported by 500–800 German mercenaries, did battle in Calenzana. One version says that the citizens of Calenzana attacked the invaders with scythes, sickles, hayforks and spades, but a more romantic version is that the villagers hid in their top storeys until the mercenaries were in the village and then hurled down beehives. The Germans, stung

CAMPO SANTO
DEI
TEDESCHI
—
ICI TOMBERENT
ET FURENT ENTERRES
CINQ CENTS ALLEMANDS
TUES AU SERVICE DE GENES
BATAILLE
DE CALENZANA
14 JANVIER 1732
—

to distraction, rushed to the fountains where they were butchered by the Calenzenais. The number of Germans killed varies in the telling from 100–800, but those who fell were buried on the spot in a mass grave called the Cimetière des Allemands.

1km from Calenzana is the church of *Ste Restitute*, Corsican martyr beheaded in 303 on the orders of the Emperor Diocletian. Two processions take place, the first on Easter Monday, the second the first Sunday after 21 May. The sarcophagus of the saint, in Carrara marble, from the late 4C, was until 1951 concealed under a cover in a 15C tomb decorated with frescoes, described by Moracchini-Mazel as 'naive and touching paintings belonging to the art of miniatures as though the painter had tried to reproduce a manuscript which he held in his hands.'

24km from Calvi along the D 451 lies *Montemaggiore* (Commune de Montegrosso, 400m, 333 inhab.), a 'terrace' village set at the end of a rocky spur above the basins of the Secco and the Ficarella, overlooking the Golfe de Calvi. There is a large baroque church but more interesting is the Romanesque church of *St Rainier* (San Raniero) about 1km above the village, set in the middle of olive groves. Built during the second half of the 12C in black and white granite, it has good marble sculptures both inside and outside the church.

6 From Calvi to Porto and Ajaccio

ROAD (D 81) 164km.—23km *Argentella*—58km *Bocca a Croce*—67.5km *Partinello*—81km *Porto*—93km *Piana*—112.5km *Cargèse*.

Leaving Calvi by the D 81, which cuts across the foot of the Revellata peninsula and passes close to the chapel of Notre Dame de la Serra (see Rte 5), this winding road keeps for the most part within sight of the sea (a few easy tracks down to the shore).

16.5km from Calvi the road turns south and inland from the *Capo a u Cavallo* to which there is a track (2km) to the semaphore (295m). There is a magnificent view from this point: to the east the Cinto range and further ranges of high mountains in the Corsican interior tower above the pine forests and maquis, to the north Cap Corse and to the south the serrated western coastline of the island.

22.6km from Calvi *Argentella*, which owes its name to the silver-bearing lead sulphide or galena formerly mined there, the ore being shipped from the nearby tiny port of Crovani. Mine buildings are now abandoned ruins. 5km further south is the Bocca Bassa (120m), a col taking the road over the *Punta di Ciutonne*, with a view over the gulf of Galéria and the village of the same name tucked into the north-north-east-facing slopes of the Capu Tondu (840m).

To reach *Galéria* (305 inhab.) turn right off the D 81 after the bridge over the Fango, on to the D 351. Sandy beach north of the mouth of the Fango. In summer the boat from Calvi stops mid-morning at Galéria on its way to Girolata and Porto and late afternoon on the return journey. Details from the Tourist Information office in Calvi.

From the Galéria turning the D 81 winds it way through the Fango Forest to the Bocca a Palmarella (374m). The D 351 turns left at le Fango, to follow the Fango valley into the Parc Naturel Régional (see Rte 16).

To the west of the D 81 lies *Girolata*, magnificently isolated except for footpaths and the summertime cruise boats mentioned above. It is a small fishing port at the farthest inland point of the Golfe de Girolata, set on a promontory with wooded and maquis-covered hills inland and a Genoese watch-tower, one of many along the coast. Girolata makes its living from lobster fishing and tourism.
    To reach Girolata on foot follow a section of the Mare e Monti long distance path leading right off the D 81 at 1km south of Bocca a Palmarella (see *Walks in Corsica* and *Corse entre Mer et Montagne* in bibliography).

1km south of the Bocca a Croce a turning to the right, the D 424, leads to the hamlet of *Osani*, above which is a prehistoric circle about which little is known. From Osani a track descends (4.5km) to a lonely pebble beach at *Gratelle*. The going is not easy, either down or on the return journey. The beach at *Caspio*, 3km from Partinello on the D 324, is easier to get to.

Genoese tower guarding the estuary of the Porto

10km south of the Bocca a Croce along the D 81 is *Partinello* (Partinellu, 207m, 113 inhab.). A further 13.5km brings you to **Porto** (500 inhab.), forming part of the commune of Ota and built in the form of an amphitheatre at the foot of Capo d'Ota (1220m). (At 5.5km from the village of Porto the D 124 winds up into the hills to *Ota* which is built in layers on the hillside, with a number of small but very good restaurants.) Porto itself is set at the point where the Gulf of that name penetrates furthest inland. Possessing one of the most beautiful situations not only in Corsica but in the whole of the Mediterranean, Porto has suffered the consequences. The little bay has been transformed into a marina and Porto is expanding into its new buildings, shops, hotels and commerce. The basic attractions of the place, the Genoese tower, the eucalyptus groves and the almost Chinese-style wooden bridge over the estuary of the Porto, remain, but Porto itself has developed almost beyond recognition in the past 20 years.

Take the D 81 south out of Porto. After it crosses the River Porto, the road turns right to follow the Vaita valley almost to the sea and then turns south-west along the coast within sight or reach of Corsica's most astonishing coastal strip, LES CALANQUES (Les Calanche, E Calanche; same pronunciation however spelt). Red spires, steeples, seemingly sculptured heads and shapes, all of granite ranging in colour through reds and pinks, often rise sheer from the sea for 300–400m. The best centre from which to observe these (and do not try rock climbing on them) is from *Piana* (A Piana, 500 inhab.) at 93km from Calvi, 71km from Ajaccio (many good hotels). It hangs above the Gulf of Porto, with a large white church of *Sainte-Marie* (18C) and a fine campanile. Les Calanques and Piana form perhaps the best-known sights of Corsica and, by no means typical of the whole island, are well worth seeing, particularly at sunrise and sunset.

Little less than 20km south of Piana is **Cargèse** (Carghjese, 915 inhab.).

Cargèse was founded in 1676 by Greek refugees from Turkish rule who asked the Genoese rulers of Corsica for the right to settle on the west coast of the island. The Genoese (often, and for the most part rightly, criticised for their harsh rule in Corsica) allowed 730 Greeks who had arrived in Genoa in March 1676 to leave in May of that year to set up their new homes. The Genoese typically took little account of the native Corsicans' attitude to this apparently generous gesture and in 1731 the Corsicans, finding themselves excluded from the traditional pastures to which the shepherds of the Niolo and Vico brought their flocks, burned the Greek villages and the inhabitants took refuge in Ajaccio. Once Corsica became French (1769) the Greek village and church were rebuilt at Cargèse and 110 Greek families returned there with a grant of 22 hectares per family. Over the years the Greek and Corsican families of Cargèse worked out a way of living together and tolerated each others' Roman Catholic and Greek Orthodox Churches. Between 300 and 400 Greeks, observing the Orthodox ritual, still live in Cargèse. To confuse this ecumenical example a little further, families of Greek settlers went to Algeria in the 19C and established the village of Sidi Merouan. After the Algerian war some of their descendants returned and took their place again in Cargèse's Greek community.

The *Greek Orthodox church* was built in the second half of the 19C, decorated with the icons donated by the Greeks in the late 17C. The icon of a winged St John the Baptist (16C), splendidly coloured in blue, green and grey, is signed by 'a monk of Saint Athos'. The early 19C *Roman Catholic church*, facing the Orthodox building, has an extravagant *trompe l'oeil* interior, and must be one of the last churches to have been adorned in this flamboyantly baroque style. The two churches, facing each other in location as well as in faith, and reached through peaceful gardens full of poppies, fig-trees and nasturtiums, are at the heart of Cargèse. Down the hill there is a rather neglected fishing port which revives in the summer. Cargèse is built on the south side of a granite promontory from which the D 81 goes due east inland and then sharply south, following the coast closely (with fine views over the Mediterranean shore) and rounding the capes of the Gulf of Sagone until reaching the site of historic *Sagone*.

The Romans founded a town here which became the seat of a bishopric in the 6C. In the Middle Ages the diocese of Sagone was enormous, but in the 12C it was put under that of Pisa. By the 16C Sagone had become unfit to live in (possibly malaria was the cause): the town was in ruins, the cathedral had to be demolished and in 1572 Pope Gregory XIII directed that the bishopric be transferred to Vico. In 1625 Urban VIII, having decided that Sagone was more-or-less abandoned, transferred the bishopric from its temporary seat at Vico to Calvi. Just beyond the bridge over the Sagone a narrow road to the right leads to the ruins of the cathedral of *Sant'Appiano* (early 12C), which may stand on the site of the original basilica (4th or 5C). Two menhirs, Sagone I and Sagone II. The latter was incorporated in the cathedral wall.

13.5km from Cargèse is the port and village of *Sagone*, set on the estuary of the river of the same name. The Sagone River rises on the slopes of San Angelo (San Anghiulu, 1272m) and is some 20km long from source to estuary, creating a wide delta which is responsible for the extensive sandy beaches. The Golfe de Sagone runs from the Punta di Cargèse in the north to Capo di Feno in the south. 4km south of Sagone the D 81 crosses the marshy delta of the Liamone, which runs 46km from where it rises on the

Cimatella. The sand it carries, as in the case of the Sagone, has built up a bar to enclose a lagoon.

At the *Punta Capigliolo* (Genoese tower) the D 81 makes a right-angle turn to the east and along the coast to the tiny seaside resort of *Tiuccia* on the shore of the Gulfu di u Liscia, a gulf within a gulf, whose south point (not on the D 81 but on a minor track which hugs the shore) is *Punta di Palmentoju* where another Genoese tower faces that of Capigliolo 3km across the Gulf.

On the hillside beyond the shoreline buildings stand the ruins of the *Castello Capraia*, formerly the stronghold of a notorious Corsican family, the counts of Cinarca (Cinarchesi) who achieved great power during the struggles between Genoa and Pisa in the 13C. One of them, Sinucello de la Rocca, who earned the name of Giudice, 'Judge', because of his impartial administration of justice, succeeded for a while in ruling the whole of Corsica. When fighting broke out again one of his many bastard sons betrayed him to the Genoese, in whose mainland dungeons he died in 1306, blind and nearly 100 years old.

The area of the CINARCA, which lies to the east of the D 81, is that of the basin of the Liscia River (today it is the canton of Sari d'Orcino). Surrounded by mountains, it is well-watered and very fertile, 'a garden amidst the maquis' as it is often described. It has citrus groves, olives, peaches, maize, vineyards, sweet chestnuts and pastures. The D 601, turning left off the D 81 less than 3km south of Tiuccia, leads by a narrow and winding road to (7.5km) *Casaglione* (Casaglio, 292 inhab.). The church of San Frediano contains a painting dated 1505 of the Crucifixion, with St Francis, and a 16C portrait of the Virgin.

Leaving Casaglione, 3.5km to the west on the D 25 is the Bocca di San Antonio (358m). Alternatively turn right along the D 1 to (3.5km) *Sari d'Orcino* (Sari d'Urcinu, 300m, 236 inhab.), two hamlets spread in a semi-circle above the Liscia valley, cultivating olives and citrus fruits. Extensive views over the valley and over the Golfe de Sagone. This short tour gives a good idea of this small and verdant area but although the signposting is usually adequate a large-scale map of the district is advisable. It is very pleasant walking country.

Return to the D 81 at Calcatoggio and continue south 11km to meet the main N 194 road, thence 5km to Ajaccio.

A.   Vico and local excursions

Before leaving the region of the Sagone Gulf, instead of following the D 81 south down the coast, take the D 70 to the left out of Sagone and in 20km cross the Col de San Antoine (496m). The road forks almost immediately and for Vico take the right. The other road also leads to Vico but in a circular and more complicated route.

21km from Sagone, **Vico** (Vicu, 400m, 921 inhab.) is a small town set on well-wooded hillsides overlooking the fertile valley of the Upper Liamone with its olive groves and sweet chestnut woods. To the east is the mountain of *la Sposata* (Punta di a Spusata). It owes its name 'The Bride' to the legend that a beautiful local girl, having married a rich husband, left her old widowed mother penniless. The mother cursed her daughter for her flinty heart and the daughter turned to stone. The outline of the mountain could be thought to resemble a woman on horseback.

Less than 2km south of Vico is the *monastery of St François*, founded by Gianpolo di Leca in 1481. The Franciscans left in 1793 and in 1836 the Oblats of Marie Immaculée settled there. The convent church is 17C and has a polychrome marble altar (1698) and massive carved chestnut wood sacristy furnishings. This church has a crucified Christ in wood, said to be the oldest in Corsica. It predates the establishment of the monastery in 1481 and is believed to have been brought from Italy by the founding monks.

Some 4km to the south of Vico, on a massive rock, stood the castle of the Leca family. In the Middle Ages this was one of the most important and powerful families in west Corsica. The castle was a fortress during the long struggle against Genoa, and after 1453 against the forces of the Bank (or Office) of St George, a Genoese business organisation with its own private army. Murder, treachery and clan warfare continued and, in 1459, 22 members of the Leca family were captured and had their throats cut by order of the Genoese Governor, Antonio Spinola. Three hundred years later the curé of Guagno, Dominique Leca, known as Circinellu, spent his life fighting for Corsican independence. In 1769, when Paoli retired to England, Father Dominique continued the fight for freedom, this time against the new rulers, the French. He led his partisans in guerrilla warfare for three more years and died of exposure and exhaustion in a mountain cave, gun in one hand and crucifix in the other. His memory is kept alive in story and song in the Fium'Orbo and by the 1937 memorial in Guagno.

Vico is a good centre for exploring the district. Take the D 23 east from Vico for 12km to reach *Guagno les Bains* which has two hot springs, exploited by the French in the 18C. After a long period of dilapidation the spa centre has been rebuilt (open May–October). The top spring (37°C) of 'l'Occhio' on the D 323 (turning to the left off the D 23) was long used in treatment of the eyes as its name suggests, and the lower spring called Venturini (52°C) is used in the treatment of rheumatism, skin afflictions, arthritis and sciatica.

Guagno (Guagnu, 800m, 145 inhab.), 8.5km beyond Les Bains, overlooks the valleys of the Fiume Grosso and the Albelli. Set in thick woods of sweet chestnuts, oaks and Corsican pines and larches, it is a good starting point for mountain expeditions. Guagno is 3km inside the western border of the Parc Naturel Régional (see Rte 16) and walkers may join up with the GR 20 mountain path.

B. Vico to Evisa

The D 70 north from Vico reaches the D 84 in 23km. You can then take the D 84 north-east, crossing the Parc Naturel Régional diagonally to meet the N 193 north of Corte, or, alternatively, go left to Evisa and take the D 84 to the coast at Porto. The D 70 leaves Vico to the north to become a climbing, winding mountain road. 2km beyond the Chapelle St Roch (755m) on the left there is a right turn for *Renno* 6km (Rennu, 900m, 84 inhab.), a group of hamlets among chestnuts, walnut orchards, and ilex. It is claimed that, together with those of Bastelica, the *pommes reinettes*, or pippin dessert apples, are the best in Corsica. Sheep, pigs and chickens are raised here and St Roch Fair is held 16–18 August, with a pilgrimage to the Chapelle St Roch.

Return to the D 70 and continue north to the Col de Sevi (1100m). There is a good and fairly easy walk from the Col, leading up to *l'Incinosa* or Chieragella (1510m) where there is a panoramic view over to the Gulf of

Porto, about 2 hours there and back. The D 70 continues high and winding, at just under 1000m, until it begins the descent to the valley of the Tavulella and the village of *Cristinacce* (East Cristinacce, 835m, 49 inhab.), its houses built on the steep chestnut-covered slopes of Capo di Melo (1564m). The D 70 climbs for 3.5km through thick chestnut woods (this is the southern border of the Forêt d'Aïtone) to the Bocca a Zora (897m). Fork left here on the D 24 or continue on the D 70 for less than 2km to the first turning left, a hairpin bend signposted (2km) to Evisa.

C.   Evisa and local excursions

Evisa (835m, 914 inhab.), one of the most beautiful Corsican villages, stands on a rocky spur that separates the upper valley of the Porto River from the ravine of the Aïtone stream. It is the gateway to the Aïtone Forest and a good centre for expeditions by car or on foot. Excursions from Evisa include the 12km by car to the *Col de Vergio* (Verghju 1477m) through the forest of towering straight Corsican pines, firs, beech and ilex. The col is the highest point (1464m) for a motor road in Corsica and is the gateway east to the Niolo and the connection between the valleys of the Porto and the Golo. The Station de Ski at Vergio is open, according to state of the snow, from December to April (five ski lifts, restaurant, hotel, bar, equipment hire; open in summer for mountain expeditions). The GR 20 long-distance path passes within a few 100m of the hotel and actually crosses the D 84 close by.

The other expeditions from Evisa can only be undertaken on foot. On the D 84, 4.5km north of Evisa and 1km beyond the Maison Forestière de Catagnone, is the village de vacances called *Le Paesolu d'Aïtone*. Immediately beyond the Paesolu is a turning to the left, the *Route Forestière 9a*, which will lead off to a 6–7 hour walk by way of the Bocca a u Saltu (1350m, refuge hut), the Col de Cuccavera (1475m) above the pines of the Lindinosa Forest and the Bocca di Guagnerola (1837m) to the River Golo and the GR 20 down to the D 84 near the Col and Ski Station at Vergio. It is essential to carry the IGN map of 'Corse Nord de Calvi à Vizzavona, No. 20 Itinéraires Pédestres; Scale 1:50,000'.

Other walks from Evisa include the 2-hour round journey to Le Belvédère. From Evisa, 3km along the D 84 in the direction of Vergio, a track leads off left and winds among the pines to a rocky spur, the *Belvédère* (975m), poised above the Aïtone torrent. Impressive view of great jumbled red rocks beyond which the sea is glimpsed. Taking the same road towards the Col de Vergio, turn left into the first *route forestière* for the Aïtone waterfall and the sparse ruins of the watermill, about 2½ hours there and back.

Leaving Evisa by the D 84 in the direction of Porto, after 1km there is a sharp bend at the church of *St Cipriano*. From this point there is a view of the Porto valley, the village of Ota and out to the Golfe of Porto. In fact along the 20km to Porto there are many self-evident stopping places from which to admire the view down the valley and, to the right, the *Cirque de la Spelunca*, where the Aïtone joins the Porto River, a massive red pyramid with finials and crockets. The village of *Ota* (c 1km to the north on the D 24) can be seen set in a hollow on the further bank of the Porto with behind it, as a rosy-red backdrop, the Capu d'Ota. At 21km from Evisa the D 84 reaches Porto.

Also starting from Evisa, *Les Gorges de la Spelunca* is one of the easiest and most impressive walks in Corsica. Involving no serious climbing or scrambling, it has to be made on foot, there being no nearer roads than the D 84 on the south bank of the Porto, or the D 124 which turns right off the D 84 (14.5km from Evisa) to cross to the north bank of the Porto at the renovated Genoese Pianella bridge, from which it is 3.5km to Ota. The D 124 continues along the north bank to Porto and the sea (5.5km).

Allow about 3 hours to walk from Evisa to Ota by the Spelunca and about 3¾ hours for the return walk. Leave Evisa by the D 84 in the direction of Porto for 1km to St Cyprien's Chapel. At the end of the cemetery wall, take the path to the right (waymarked in red). It zigzags down maquis-covered rocky slopes to the Tavulella River which it crosses in a well-shaded spot by the Genoese Pont de Zaglia, just above the Tavulella's confluence with the Aïtone (at roughly 1½ hours from Evisa). The path follows the precipitous south bank of the red granite ravine, high above the torrent. After 1 hour's further walk the path reaches the D 124 road at the Deux Ponts d'Ota where the Aïtone and the Onca meet to become the River Porto. There is a bridge over each river. Carry on downstream for 3km to *Ota* (335m, 460 inhab.), built in an amphitheatre below the Capu d'Ota (1220m). The commune of Ota, to which Porto belongs, is in a very fertile area producing chestnuts, olives, vines and vegetables. Many of the houses retain outside stairways, a local feature. There are good restaurants in this village and it is worth coming 5.5km up from Porto, when it becomes too crowded and hot in summer, to dine in the fresh evening air at Ota.

THE EAST COAST

7   Bastia

Bastia (37,845 inhab.) is the Préfecture of Haute-Corse.

2000 years ago the site of the present town was a Roman colony; after the Romans left there was a fishing village called Porto Cardo on what is now the Vieux Port. In 1380 the occupying Genoese built a fortress or '*bastiglia*' (hence Bastia) overlooking Cardo harbour, which they enlarged, to guard against attack both from the unruly Corsicans inland and enemies planning invasion across the Tuscan Straits. The citadel was built 1480–1521 and the town became a garrison and the seat of the Genoese governors of Corsica who moved from the less easily defended Biguglia to the south. Bastia remained chief town of the island until the French Revolution when, in 1791, the Convention divided Corsica into two départements, with Ajaccio the capital of one and Bastia of the other. This division lasted for 20 years until 1811 when the island came under one administration again with the capital moved to Napoleon's birthplace, Ajaccio. There has always been rivalry between the two towns, each vaunting its past glories, and the cliché description has been forged that Ajaccio is the cultural centre of Corsica and Bastia the industrial capital where 'feet are on the ground and hands at work'. Now that each administers a département, a principal aspect of competition has gone but there are obvious differences between the two towns: Ajaccio in atmosphere and architecture is very 'French' while Bastia is much more 'Italian'.

  Although the town is now prosperous and solid it has suffered siege and depredation over the centuries, the most recent being the damage inflicted during September–October 1943. De Gaulle awarded the town the Croix de Guerre avec palme for 'the courage and spirit of its citizens' resistance', in the same spirit as Malta was awarded the George Cross.

Bastia consists of two parts, the Terra Vecchia and the Terra Nova. Pay no attention to these terms, there is nothing new about the Terra Nova which was the original quartier built, fortified and walled by the Genoese in 1480–1521.

  The 20km drive to Bastia from the Bastia–Poretta airport is not a very attractive introduction to the town. The airport is (sensibly) in the flat eastern plain near the sea but also close to the N 193 which runs north between the Biguglia Lagoon on the right and the mountains on the left. Smallholdings give way to suburban industrial estates: small factories, showrooms of agricultural machinery and packing plants where everything is handled from grapes and tomatoes to wine and refrigerators. Until the end of 1983, when the tunnel under the Vieux Port was opened to take traffic into the heart of Bastia, the town was entered by a comparatively narrow street thick with traffic, winding down a hill with side streets leading steeply down to the port on the right beyond the massive walls of the Citadel, and on the left tall Italianate tenements, gay with drying laundry splashing colours against the speckled old walls.

  Now the new expressway from the coast road goes under the Citadel and the Vieux Port and continues along the edge of the Bassin St Nicolas, with the Place St Nicolas on the left, to the Nouveau Port and ferries to Marseille, Toulon, Nice, Genoa, Leghorn, La Spezia, San Remo, Piombino and Sardinia. Bastia, Corsica's largest port, is best seen in its series of rising terraces, from the sea. At almost any time of the day or night there seems to be a large ship, usually a car ferry, either just entering or leaving harbour.

Bastia, Vieux Port and St Jean-Baptiste

BASTIA FROM NORTH TO SOUTH. In the north of the town, close to the Nouveau Port and the ferry boat arrival and departure point, much of practical use to the visitor is grouped. The D 80 goes north from here through the suburb of Toga and up the east coast of Cap Corse; the *Post Office* is a block away on the Boulevard du General Graziani; the buses for Cap Corse leave from the Rue du Nouveau Port, those for Bonifacio, Porto Vecchio, Piedicroce and Solenzara leave from the Avenue Maréchal Sebastiani, close to the Post Office. The avenue itself leads to the Rond-Point Leclerc and the *railway station* from which there are trains to Ponte Leccia, Ile Rousse, Calvi, Ajaccio, Corte, Venaco, Vizzavona, Bocognano and intermediate stations. There is a *Tourist Information Office* on the northern side of the Place Saint Nicolas, opposite the Centre Administratif and just over the road from the embarkation point on the Nouveau Port. The main *Syndicat d'Initiative* is on the Boulevard Paoli, between the Rue Abatucci and the Rue Miot.

The PLACE SAINT NICOLAS, impressive and spacious (300m long), is open on the seaward side, being built on a terrace overlooking the port. The other side is lined with cafés and shops and the Place itself is shaded by palm and plane trees beneath which at most times, but particularly in the evening, several games of *boules* are usually in progress. There is a constant parade of strollers past the bandstand and the statue of Napoleon in a toga, by the 19C Florentine sculptor Bartolini. There is a car park under the square and another between the east side and the expressway that runs along the sea front.

Parallel to the Place Saint Nicolas and running several blocks to the south of it towards the Old Town are three streets forming the main and smartest shopping district. From east to west, or from the Place Saint Nicolas inland, they are the Boulevard du Général de Gaulle (becomes the Rue Napoléon south of the Place); the Boulevard Paoli which continues under the same

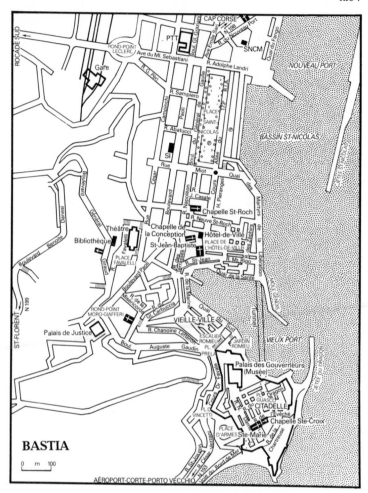

BASTIA

0   m   100

name to the Palais de Justice; the Rue César Campinchi which joins the
Boulevard Paoli, at its south end just below the theatre in the Place Favalelli.
Across the next street to the west, the Boulevard du Général Giraud, is the
impressive **Municipal Library** of over 80,000 books, many rare, including
a 'Decameron' of 1529, as well as an extensive collection of Corsican
interest. This part of Bastia and further west becomes progressively steeper.
Shorter routes for pedestrians involve many flights of steps.

On the Rue Napoléon, between the south side of the Place Saint Nicolas
and the Place de l'Hôtel de Ville is the **Chapelle St Roch**, built in 1604 by
the Confrérie de St Roch. The interior is richly decorated and carefully
preserved, with finely carved pews, and a gilded 1740 organ.

150m to the south where the Rue Napoléon becomes the Rue des
Terrasses is the **Chapelle de la Conception**, built in 1611 by the Confrérie
de la Conception. Interior walls hung with crimson Genoese velvet and

Pebble mosaic below steps to La Chapelle de la Conception, Bastia

damask silk, crystal chandeliers suspended from the painted ceiling. Carved panelling and over the altar a copy of Murillo's *Immaculate Conception*. The sacristy is a small museum of religious art and the statue of the Holy Virgin is carried in procession on 8 December to the Church of St Jean-Baptiste. The interior of the chapel is so regal that it was used by the Corsican Estates when in session during the French monarchy and by Sir Gilbert Elliot for the first meeting of the Anglo-Corsican Parliament in February 1795. In front of the chapel is a pavement with a pebble mosaic of a face with an enigmatic expression and beams radiating from the head. A sundial once stood there.

On the seaward-side of the chapel is the Place de l'Hôtel de Ville, in the centre of a collection of narrow streets leading to the port. There is a lively market in the square every morning. At the south side of the square is the back of the church of *St Jean-Baptiste*, built mid 17C, enlarged and much decorated inside in the 18C. It contains some Italian pictures from Cardinal Fesch's collection; the pulpit, altar and baptismal fonts are in Corsican polychromatic marble. The twin towers and imposing façade dating from 1666 dominate the Vieux Port.

The best view of the Vieux Port, the tall well-weathered houses of the Terra Vecchia and of the church of St Jean-Baptiste, is from the Jetée du Dragon which projects from below the Citadel towards the Môle Genois.

Around the Vieux Port and in the labyrinthine narrow streets, many with steps, are restaurants and bistros to suit all tastes and pockets. There are cafés and bars, and places where traditional Corsican songs and guitar music are performed. It is much less touristy than most seaports and if you ask for or hunt out restaurants where the Bastiais eat you will find good and reasonably priced food.

To reach the TERRA NOVA follow the street round the inland side of the Vieux Port by way of the Rue de la Marine and the Quai du Sud to the *Jardin Romieu*, reached from the quai by an elegant double staircase. The

Steps to the Jardin Romieu, Bastia

garden is a shady terrace under the ramparts and within the Terra Nova, the new town set up in 1480, with buildings around the Keep turned into the Governor's Palace, and a campanile added in 1530. Through the centuries it has retained the distinctive style which the Genoese set upon their towns, in no way marred by restoration in the reign of Louis XVI.

To reach the **Citadel** turn left at the top of the steps from the Jardin Romieu into the Cours du Docteur-Favale and the entrance is a few steps along on the left. Bastia takes its name from the 'bastiglia' or 'bastille', the great round tower, in very good condition, at the right-hand corner of the Palais des Gouverneurs. It is the oldest surviving part of the original fortifications raised in 1378 by the Genoese governor Leonello Lomellino after he had been burned out of his fortress at Biguglia by the supporters of Corsican 'resistance'.

The galleries in the inside court were vandalised when the Governor's Palace was made redundant by Napoleon's choice of Ajaccio as capital and the palace was turned into barracks. A third of the buildings were time-bombed by the Germans before they retreated in September 1943. The War Ministry passed the building over to the Secretary of State for Arts and Letters who restored it to become the **Ethnographic Museum of Corsica** 1952. (Open: 16 Sept–Palm Sun 09.00–17.00, Sat, Sun, public holidays 10.00–17.00. Palm Sun–30 April 09.00–18.00, Sat, Sun 10.00–18.00. 1 May–15 Sept 09.00–19.00, Sat, Sun 10.00–19.00. Closed 1 Jan, All Saints Day, 25 Dec) The displays indicate how geology and geography gave this island its unique character, and how its zoology, botany, archaeology and history have been conditioned as a consequence. The personality of Corsica

Head of Louis XVI, bas-relief from the Bastille in Paris, now in the courtyard of the Citadel Museum, Bastia

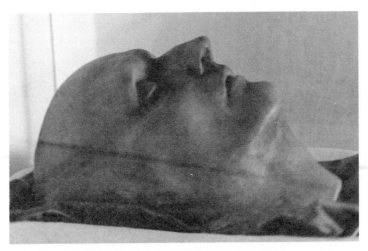

Death mask of Napoleon, in the Citadel Museum, Bastia

develops here through prehistory to the Greek and Roman presence, Pisan, Genoese, Aragonese and French occupation, Corsican patriots such as Sampiero Corso and Paoli. There are displays on every aspect of Corsican ways including the life of peasants and mountain people, implements used, the interior of a Niolo shepherd's hut complete with human figures, and the tools used in the cultivation and processing of the sweet chestnut. The Genoese dungeons and 2nd floor for art exhibitions opened in 1991.

Next to the museum is a memorial to the 173 and 373 Infantry Regiments and a roll of their battle honours through almost two centuries. At the far end of the courtyard is the **Centre du Documentation d'Archéologie Sous-marine**, in what was the powder magazine. Anchors, amphorae for oil, olives and wine, and other relics of the cargoes of boats trading in Roman times between Italy and Spain which had to pass through the Straits of Bonifacio and often foundered off the Lavezzi Isles.

On a terrace in the grounds of the Citadel is the conning tower of the submarine *Casabianca*. Having escaped from Toulon on 27 November 1942, the *Casabianca* reached Algiers and for the rest of the war, under the command of Captain l'Herminier, plied secretly between Algeria and Occupied Corsica, playing an important part in the liberation of the island. The submarine was named for the 12-year-old Jacques, son of Luce de Casabianca who commanded the *Orient* and was killed at Aboukir on 10 August 1798. His son, refusing to leave the ship, was killed when it exploded. The poor lad is on permanent duty in Mrs Hemans' lines 'The boy stood on the burning deck'.

Follow the Rue Notre Dame from the Citadel to, on the left, the church of **Sainte-Marie** (1495–1604, restored in 1938). It was elevated to cathedral status in 1570 and retained this distinction until the bishopric of Corsica was transferred to Ajaccio in 1801. The interior is richly baroque with much gold and marble. On the right is an Assumption of the Virgin in chased silver which is carried in procession on 15 August across the Terra Nova and the Terra Vecchia. Above the altar is a painting on wood of the Assumption, dated 1512 and formerly in the Canonica at Mariana (see Rte 8). The two polychromatic statues carved in wood are 17C and represent the Immaculate Conception and Notre Dame du Rosaire. The organs were built in 1845 by the Serassi brothers of Bergamo.

The **Chapelle Sainte Croix**, in the Rue de l'Evêché, is next door to Sainte-Marie. Built in 1543 the added Louis XV gold stucco and cherubs gambolling in the blue ceiling give it something of a ballroom atmosphere. A figure of Christ, carved in oak blackened by long immersion in water is said to have been found floating in the sea by fishermen in 1428. This black *Christ des Miracles* is carried in procession on 3 May and the first catch of the season is offered up to Our Lord by the fishermen of Bastia. The striking appearance and dramatic lighting of the Black Christ should not deflect attention from another beautiful 13C Christ in wood to the right of the entrance.

The Terra Nova covers a relatively small area and is a very self-contained neighbourhood, differing from the rest of Bastia. It is easy to walk along its narrow short streets. Half-way along the Rue du Dragon is the Place Guasco: small, peaceful and tree-shaded, with the atmosphere of a medieval village square. Unless it is very windy or raining it is worth walking some of the way out on to the Jetée du Dragon for the view of Bastia and beyond: to the north Cap Corse, and to the south the Biguglia Lagoon and the great Eastern Plain which is overlooked by Bastia and emphasises why and how the fortress city came to be placed where it is.

8 Bastia to Solenzara: the Eastern Plain

ROAD (N 193 and N 198) 102km.—30km Mariana (to left of road)—70km
Aléria—85km Ghisonaccia.

The history of the Eastern Plain of Corsica, lying between the Tyrrhenian
Sea and the central mountain spine of the island, on average 12–16km
wide, has been dictated by its geography. Low-lying, it was easy to invade,
and in 565–540 BC Phocaean Greeks from Asia Minor settled and built the
town of Alalia. In 259 BC Alalia was conquered by the Romans together
with the rest of the island. Alalia became Aléria, a military colony with a
naval base on the Étang de Diane with an estimated population of around
20,000 while it was the capital of Rome's Corsican province (259–162 BC).
As the power of Rome declined so did Aléria and the Plain. The land was
no longer drained and cultivated and water from the mountains turned the
fields into marshes where mosquitoes and malaria flourished. This, and
invasion by the Vandals in the 5C, drove the inhabitants away from the
Plain and into the hills, only descending to pasture their beasts in winter.

The Plain remained more-or-less abandoned for some 1500 years and
until the present century the average expectation of life among Plain
dwellers was 22 years. Baedeker obviously thought things went from bad
to worse, referring in 1895 to 'the somewhat bleak and desolate east
coast...the malarious plain of Aléria' then deleting 'somewhat' from the
1907 edition of his *Guide*. Periodic incursions and settlement by Pisans,
Genoese, Aragonese, French, Italians and Germans brought scant improvement to the area.

It was occupation by the liberating US Army that dispelled the murderous
blight that had lain there for a millennium and a half. American forces were
stationed in Corsica from 1943–46. Their main enemy was the anopheles
mosquito and their weapon was DDT. Once the mosquito had been elimi-
nated the area began to be cultivated again and in 1957 impetus was given
towards reclamation by the creation of SOMIVAC (Société pour la mise en
valeur de la Corse). Thirty years later the cultivated area of the Plain
amounts to 80 per cent of agricultural Corsica, producing citrus and other
fruits, vines, cereals, vegetables, sheep, goats and cattle. Reservoirs in the
central Corsican mountains ensure irrigation. In the late 1950s and 1960s
many of the French colonists (or *pieds noirs*, the name given by North
Africans to those who wore shoes) acquired land in the Plain. They had
experience of similar conditions, climate, and crops in North Africa and
many of their Arab workers came with them. They set a high standard of
farming but this massive incursion of non-Corsican settlers did not, in the
early years, take place without strong and sometimes violent opposition by
Corsican farmers.

Apart from the overwhelming agricultural importance of the present-day Plain there
has been a rapid development of tourism along the magnificent and for the most part
sandy coastline broken by a half-dozen lagoons. Baedeker reported in 1895 that the
railway from Bastia to Ghisonaccia was 'to be prolonged'. The line was extended to
Solenzara in 1930 and thence to Porto Vecchio in 1935. It would eventually have
reached Bonifacio had it not been for the Second World War which began four years
later. The Germans, in retreat in 1943, destroyed bridges, tunnels, locomotives, signals,
freight vans, passenger cars and stations. Rebuilding was never undertaken so that
now the farthest south one can go is to Casamozza on the Golo where the line turns
inland to the centre and west coast of Corsica.

Leave Bastia by the N 193, heading south and at 3km look out for the town *cemetery*. On the corner is a stone commemorating the landing on 23 August 1553 of Sampiero Corso (at that time a colonel in the French army), when the French aided by a Turkish fleet invaded and conquered the whole isle with the exception of Calvi and Bastia which held out for Genoa. 2km further on, to the right of the road, is the ruined castle of *Furiani*, on a hill above the new factories. The Genoese besieged the castle in 1729. It was defended and held by Luigi Giafferi, another Corsican hero. 8km *Casatora* from which the D 82 leads to the Défilé de Lancone and Oletta in the Nebbio (see Rte 13).

On the eastern slopes of the inland mountains, reached from Casatora by a minor road (2.5km), lies **Biguglia** (270m, 4073 inhab.), capital of Corsica after the destruction of Mariana in the 8C, first under the Pisans and then under the first of the many Genoese occupations. At that time it was the diocesan seat. When Biguglia was taken by the Corsican rebels, led by yet another Corsican hero, Arrigo della Rocca, in 1372, the Genoese moved north and built a fortress, a '*bastiglia*' which was the beginning of Bastia. From Biguglia the Étang de Biguglia, a lagoon open to the sea by a narrow mouth to the north, takes its name. Renowned for its eels. The seaward bar has a *village de vacances* called *Pineto*.

The railway follows close to the N 193, crossing it a couple of times. 16km, *Borgo* (U Borgu, 320m, 3773 inhab.), 3km to the right from the main road.

Set on a rocky spur overlooking the Plain, Borgo has tall old houses with elegant carved doors and porches. Those who fled the unhealthy plain moved to higher villages such as these. In 1768 Pasquale Paoli defeated the French here after the ignoble treaty between France and Genoa brought the Corsicans out in arms once more.

1.5km south of Borgo to the left is the road to the *Bastia-Poretta Airport* (20km from Bastia, buses from Place de la Gare, Bastia). At the airport there is a memorial stone to the writer Antoine de Saint Exupéry who, as a Free French pilot, left here 31 July 1944 on a reconnaissance flight over the Mediterranean from which he never returned.

At the same turning there is another road, the D 107, forking to the left, further south, and reaching in 5.5km the archaeological site of the Roman city of **Mariana** and the churches of La Canonica and San Parteo.

The Roman general Gaius Marius (157–86 BC) founded two military colonies in Corsica in 93 BC, one at Alalia (Aléria) and the other at Mariana. It would seem that the soldiers sent to the latter were penal battalions raised in Italy who aroused the violent opposition of the Corsicans. Mariana was several times destroyed and rebuilt until in the 5–6C, under the onslaught of the combined forces of mosquitoes and Vandals, the city fell into ruins. The Christian Church was strongly established here from the 4C onwards. The church of **Santa Maria Assunta**, the former Cathedral of Mariana which is known as *La Canonica*, stands 50m to the north of the site of a 4C paleochristian cathedral, remains of which have been brought to light by recent excavations under the foundations of the 12C episcopal palace. The square *baptistry* is flanked by two small apses. In the centre is a piscine, later used as a baptismal pool and now roofed over for protection. The floor is decorated in mosaic (4C) depicting fish, ducks, dolphins and stags, with the Four Rivers of Paradise represented by male heads whose bearded faces are portrayed in the classical style of water gods such as Neptune.

La Canonica, the church of Santa Maria Assunta, the former cathedral of the diocese of the Bishop of Mariana, was consecrated in 1119 by the Archbishop of Pisa. The architectural form was inspired by the Roman

La Canonica, Roman paving

basilica: the nave is flanked by two aisles and is 35m long, both wider and higher than the aisles and ending in an oven-shaped apse (*cul de four*). Impressively simple in design, great effect was achieved by the use of *calschiste*, marble quarried at Sisco and Brando in Cap Corse whose colours range through a honey-tinted grey to light greenish-orange and blue. The stone slabs were cut to a remarkable perfection and a feature of this church is that the square 'putlog' holes in the stone, to support the scaffolding, were left unfilled and thus form a pattern in this admirably undecorated interior. The west front reflects the relative heights of the nave and side aisles: two flattened pilasters on either side mark the width of the nave, balanced by two broader pilasters at the corners.

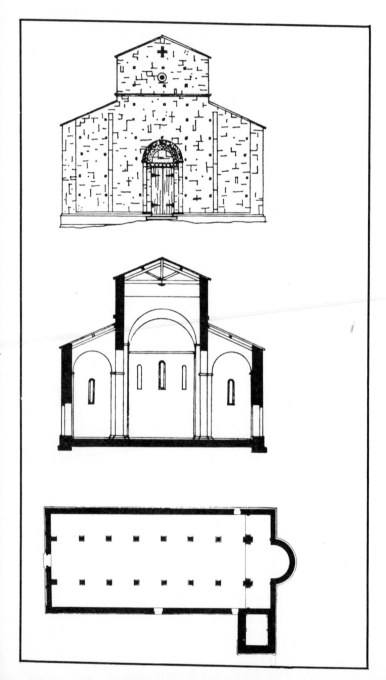

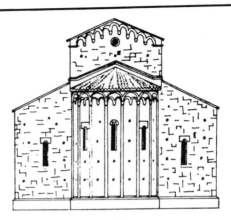

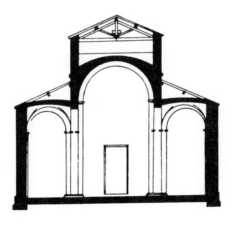

SANTA MARIA

The frescoes inside the west door are unexpectedly ample in this austere church. The archivolt is decorated with animals: a lion, griffins, a wolf, a stag pursued by hounds and a triumphant Lamb of God. The south façade is bare but its rhythmical proportions are perfect as is the east façade. The Canonica is perhaps the prototype of Corsican Pisan churches and with the former cathedral of the Nebbio it is one of the architectural jewels of the island.

The church of **San Parteo de Mariana** stands about 300m to the south-west of the Canonica. Pisan, and of excellent proportions, it was built in the 11–12C (construction possibly interrupted by a Muslim invasion). Excavation of the fields surrounding the church has revealed a cemetery, first pagan, later paleochristian and medieval. The present church was built in continuation of an earlier building dedicated to the memory, and possibly housing the relics of, San Parteo, one of Corsica's martyrs (excavation has uncovered some foundations). The outstandingly elegant apse is decorated with granite columns and arcadings; some of this material may have come from the ruins of Mariana.

Madame Moracchini-Mazel writes in 'Corse Romane' '...it is astounding that a few years ago [in the 1960s], on the direct orders of a company of Paris architects, such a 'curious' restoration should have been undertaken. The pediment was reset much too high; the side walls were heightened in grey cement, without trouble being taken to respect the proportions, which the Pisan builders sought as ardently in their apses as did the Greek architects in the façades of their temples...red tiles were used while the original framework was covered by slabs of mauve *teghie* (stone). The best thing for the visitor to do is to try to imagine the outline of the ramparts of the pediments, the level of the side walls and the colour of the roof...'.

The south door lintel has a sculpted decoration of two lions facing each other with comic snarls, a stylised tree between them, their tails looped gracefully: an Oriental design copied by European craftsmen from imported woven cloth. The west door lintel has a string course decorated with sculpted geometrical patterns.

Return to the N 193 by the D 107 but at a T-junction 1.5km beyond San Parteo turn left into the D 10 and left again when it reaches the railway which runs parallel to the road for 2km to *Casamozza*, one of the most important junctions in Corsica. Here, on the River Golo, the N 193 makes a 90° turn to the west to follow the course of the river through dramatic ravines to Ponte Leccia and thence to Corte and Ajaccio. To the south of the road lie the regions of the Casinca and the Castagniccia (see Rtes 11 and 12).

In the direction of Solenzara–Ponte Vecchio–Bonifacio the road continues south as the N 198. Turnings to the right lead to the Casinca villages and those to the left, such as the D 106, lead, 6.5km beyond Casamozza, to the beach and *village de vacances* of *Anghione*. 4km further at *Folelli* the D 506 leads to a fine beach and good hotel at *San Pellegrino*. At Folelli the Fium'Altu, a river rising in the Castagniccia, is crossed and the road runs ever closer to the sea until reaching (8.5km) *Moriani Plage*. Some of the famous in the past arrived or left here. Pasquale Paoli, aged 15, entered his first exile (from the then naval base called Padulella) with his father Hyacinthe and Luigi Giafferi in 1739 and in 1815 Napoleon landed, having escaped from Elba and before setting sail for the French mainland. 4km to the south is a new *port de plaisance*, serving Campoloro, well sheltered by the mountains further inland. Campoloro itself is rapidly developing, like so many places on the east coast, into a holiday town. In 2.5km you reach

Prunete–Cervione. 6km by the D 71 to the right leads to Cervione and a small road to the left (about 500m) goes down to one of this coast's finest beaches.

For 25km from Prunete the road passes through rich farmlands with orchards, vineyards and cornfields, undramatic but beautiful, wide and calm; but not so wide that the mountains some 12–15km inland are not always in view as a backdrop to this intense cultivation. There are practically no villages until Caterraggio and Aléria. To the left, clearly marked and 1–2km from the road are occasional *villages de vacances.* After crossing the River Bravone at the hamlet of (another) Casamozza (Marine de Bravone to the right, 2.5km), there is a military firing range lying between the N 198 and the sea.

Immediately to the south of the Champ de Tir is the extensive ÉTANG DE DIANE (600 hectares), a lagoon which served two purposes for the Romans: as a naval base for Aléria and as a bed to cultivate oysters which they both consumed and exported to Rome. While Napoleon was on Elba a boat was sent twice weekly to collect Diane oysters for him and secretly bring back news from France, no doubt kept as close as an oyster. An island in the étang consists solely of oyster shells and there is a road from the N 198 to a store where oysters and fish may be bought.

Caterraggio, 70km from Bastia, on the north bank of the Tavignano (rises at the Lac de Nino, 1743m) is the spreading modern counterpart to Aléria. From here it is 3km to the left by the N200 to a wide sandy beach at *Padulone.* On the N 198 cross the Tavignano and continue 1km then right onto the D 343, a road clearly marked with the ancient monument sign (white on dark blue) and arrowed to Aléria.

Aléria (10m, 2022 inhab. in the commune, including Caterraggio), founded by the Phoceaen Greeks in 540 BC on the plateau about 50m above sea level on the right bank of the Tavignano.

The settlement dominated the estuary where there had been a trading post since 565 BC. The Phoceaens made it their capital when they were chased out of their own Asia Minor city of Phoceaea by the Persians. They won the sea battle of Alalia against an invading force of Etruscans and Carthaginians in 535 BC but subsequently transferred their capital to Massalia (Marseille), retaining Alalia as a mercantile link with their new colonies in southern Italy as well as with Greece, Carthage, Gaul, Sicily and Spain. In 259 BC Alalia was taken by the Romans from the Carthaginians, who had been in control since 280 BC. The Romans conquered the whole of Corsica and made the city, with a population of 20,000, capital of their Corsican province. In AD 81 Sulla established a military base, subsequently Augustus constructed a naval base in the Étang de Diane and a mercantile port was built in the loop of the Tavignano. The city flourished until it was sacked by the Vandals in the 5C and sank into obscurity but was partially revived on a much smaller scale in the 13C by the Genoese and was a diocesan seat for 2 centuries. It was still an important place in 1736 when Theodor von Neuhof landed here before travelling to Alesani where he was crowned King of Corsica. Prosper Mérimée noted that there were traces of the Roman city remaining in 1840. Some test excavations were made in 1920 but it is only since 1955 that a systematic archaeological search has been made by Laurence and Jean Jehasse, directeur des Antiquités historiques de la Corse.

The car park for visitors is on the left, just before the village with its one wide street leading to the square where the church of *St Marcel* faces the *Fort de Matra,* built by the Genoese in 1572 and since 1969 the Musée Jérôme Carcopino (1881–1970, archaeologist and historian of ancient Rome).

Aléria

The Musée Jérôme Carcopino (price of entry includes visit to the site. Open 16 May–30 Sept 8.00–12.00, 14.00–19.00; 1 Oct–15 May 8.00–12.00, 14.00–17.00). The museum consists of 12 display rooms grouped around the central courtyard of the former fort. It should be visited before going to the site but a second tour of the museum rounds off the experience.

ROOM 1. Life in Aléria as a city of the Roman Empire: oil lamps, coins, rings, amphorae, pots and earthenware water pipes. Iron and bronze objects dominate the metal discoveries, very little silver and gold. ROOM 2. The evolution of ceramics during the period of the Roman Empire, the advances in methods of glazing etc. A fine marble head with ram's horns of Jupiter Ammon (2C), reconstruction of a Roman tomb. ROOM 3. Pre-Roman Aléria (4–3C BC). Red-figure ware in which the baked orange clay showing through the painted black glaze creates the pattern or figures, a method that preceded the red-glazed pottery which dominated in the Roman period. Examples of Etruscan and other imported ceramic objects attest to Aléria's importance as a large trading port. ROOM 4. The showpiece here, and the most renowned exhibit in the museum, is *Attic vase with erotic figures* ascribed to a master artist of Panaitios, 480 BC. Other objects recovered from tombs are displayed, such as a curved Greek sword (5C BC). ROOM 5. This room contains an assembly of objects attesting to Aléria's rôle in the economic and military development of Corsica in the ancient Mediterranean world and demonstrating its importance as a link between the Greek possessions in Spain and Provence and Greece and the Near East. A display of Greek influence in Corsica in the 6th, 5th and 4C BC. Note the *crater*, a wide-mouthed vessel for wine and water (c 425 BC) decorated with a design of a seated Dionysos with two satyrs and a nymph,

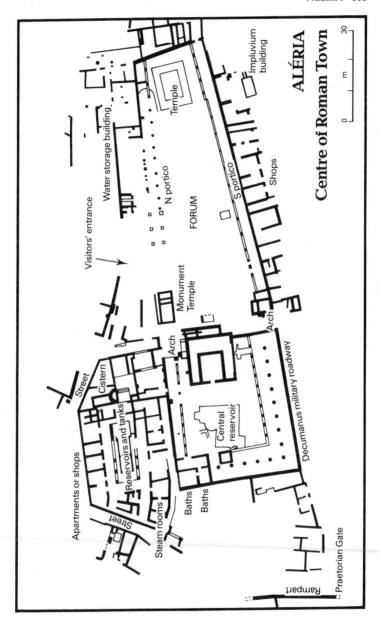

ALÉRIA
Centre of Roman Town

Impluvium building

Temple

Water storage building

Visitors' entrance

N portico

FORUM

S portico

Shops

Monument
Temple

Arch

Arch

Street

Cistern

Central
reservoir

Reservoirs and tanks

Decumanus military roadway

Apartments or shops

Street

Steam rooms

Baths

Baths

Rampart

Praetorian Gate

0 m 30

by a painter of Dinos (c 425 BC). ROOM 6. Reconstruction of a burial chamber (c 450 BC) containing over 100 objects found in tombs including Etruscan bronzes and Attic pottery. ROOM 7. Objects from the oldest tomb found at Aléria. Two Attic rhytons, drinking vessels, in the forms of the heads of a dog and a mule, of exceptional grace and exquisite workmanship. ROOMS 8–9. Assorted objects discovered in the tombs. ROOM 10. Attic ceramics and iron weapons from a tomb. ROOM 11. Finely decorated craters and cups including Hercules and the lion, Theseus (450 BC) and Dionysos keeping an eye on the grape harvesting. ROOM 12. Reconstruction (1991) of a 4–3C BC tomb.

The Roman city of Aléria. A pathway leads from the square up a gentle rise to the plateau and the excavations, south-west of the village. This archaeological site is unique not only in Corsica but in the whole of France by virtue of discoveries there dating back to the 6C BC. The present excavations began in 1958 and there is undoubtedly much more to be found.

Explanatory boards display clear plans and descriptions of the site.

Entry is directly into the FORUM, 90m long running east–west, which was colonnaded and lined with shops. Columns of the north and south porches have been uncovered; of brick originally stuccoed. A small *temple* at the east end of the Forum has a foundation platform of pebbles brought from the bed of the Tavignano. Against its north side is the apse of a later Christian building. Also on the north side of the temple are traces of a large dwelling place known as the *Domus 'au dolium'* because of the discovery in one of the rooms of a huge earthenware jar. At the west end of the Forum is the *Praetorium* from which the Romans ruled the city and the whole of their Corsican colony. Entrance is by an archway from the period of Sulla Felix (138–78 BC) of which a column is still standing. There is a courtyard with water tanks and porches on three sides. To the north of the Praetorium were the *baths*, the *balneum* with cisterns and pools and the *caldarium* heated by a system of underground pipes, the hypocaust, above which lies a decorative mosaic floor. Additions and alterations to the complex date from 1C BC–early 5C AD. To the west of the *balneum* lies what is thought to have been an area for the storage and preservation of fish including, no doubt, the Diane oyster.

Facing the museum is the 1462 church of *St Marcel*, in whose walls are incorporated blocks of stone from the Roman city.

Return to the N 198, following the road south and passing on the left the *Domaine de Casabianda* (no visitors), an open prison where the inmates are employed in farming. Valuable agricultural discoveries have resulted from experimentation in crop raising and domestic animal breeding. The nearby Réserve National de Casabianda (1765 hectares) was established in 1951 to ensure the conservation of Corsica's rarer wild creatures. Eucalyptus nurseries send saplings throughout Corsica for replacement afforestation in areas ravaged by fire. To the left of the road is another lagoon, the Étang d'Urbino where oysters and mussels are cultivated.

Ghisonaccia, 15km south of Aléria and 85km south of Bastia (Ghisunaccia, 16m, 3270 inhab.), is the 'capital' of the Eastern Plain. It is lively and cheerful, with many new shops and houses; and manufactures agricultural machines. The population today is four times what it was 30 years ago. Formerly Ghisonaccia was a large village whose living depended on the flocks and herds which were the Plain's major source of income. The 'accia' ending means 'bad' in the sense of 'unhealthy': there used to be mosquitoes and malaria. The eradication of the mosquito and the transformation of the Eastern Plain into a rich agricultural region has sent Ghisonaccia upwards on a spiral of activity and prosperity.

The D 344 leaves Ghisonaccia for Ghisoni in a straight line north-west for 27km through intensely cultivated flat farmlands and smallholdings, a countryside of vineyards, orchards and cereal crops. In summer and autumn every other house seems to offer peaches, apricots, grapes and vegetables for sale at the roadside. After St Antoine the D 344 turns due west and there is a sudden and dramatic change in the landscape. The Fium'Orbo (the 'blind or turbid river', 45km long, rising at 2352m on Monte Renoso and reaching the east coast at Calgarello south-east of Ghisonaccia) forces its way through the canyon of the Défilé de l'Inzecca. 2km upriver is the Défilé des Strette where the river thunders and froths over giant boulders at the bottom of the 300m deep ravine.

Ghisoni (658m, 335 inhab.) is set deep in a valley between the heights of the Col de Sorba to the north and the Col de Verde to the south and is surrounded by the forests of Sorba and Marmano. In 1985 vast tracts of forests in this part of Corsica were devastated by fire. Ghisoni is in the Parc Naturel Régional de la Corse (see Rte 16) and by taking the D 69 north over the Col de Sorba one reaches (19km) *Vivario* on the N 193 Bastia–Ajaccio road, 30km south of Corte. Vivario is also on the railway line between Bastia and Ajaccio.

From Ghisonaccia, across the Fium'Orbo and south down the N 198 for 2km, is Migliacciaru where a turning to the right, the D 145, leads up into the Fium'Orbo by the valley of the Abatesco.

The FIUM'ORBO is a small region known for its turbulent history and the independent and recklessly brave spirit of its people. At 19km from Ghisonaccia *Prunelli di Fium'Orbo* (I Prunelle di Fium'Orbo, 580m, 2339 inhab.), built on a rocky promontory giving, in clear weather, fantastic views of the Plain, the lagoons and the sea. At the highest point of the village stands the church of *Santa Maria Assunta* and a 20-minute walk below the village reaches the ruins of the church of *St-Jean-Baptiste* (6–7C) on a spur of rock overlooking the Plain and the sea. A nave with one door and no light apart from one tiny east window. A beautifully engraved lintel with the Cross, the Hand of God and the Dove. Moving and impressive, this small *pième* survived the Barbarian invasions and its stones have outlasted both the church built in the 11C to replace it and a nearby abbey. Nothing remains of either.

On the N 198 going south the next hamlet after Migliacciaru is yet another Casamozza. After crossing the Abatesco 5km south, on the left, is the Étang de Palo, the smallest and most southerly lagoon on the east coast. Between the étang and the estuary of the River Travo is the military airfield of Zara (public not admitted). 2km beyond and a few 100m to the left is the *Marine de Solaro* which takes its name from the village of Solaro, built safely in the mountain foothills 8.5km to the west but keeping an outlet to the sea. 3.5km south on the south bank of the River Solenzara (rises 20km south-west in the Punta de Taffanatu di Palin) is the small town of the same name, 102km south of Bastia, 41km north of Porto Vecchio and 67km north of Bonifacio.

Solenzara is part of the commune of Sari-Solenzara (300m, 1178 inhab.), 8km inland by the D 68 south-west from Solenzara. A good centre for a traditional seaside holiday, Solenzara has to the north a wide sandy beach shaded by eucalyptus trees planted in the 19C to drain the marsh and to the south of the town a rocky coastline begins. The Côte des Nacres (the Mother of Pearl Coast) takes its name from the large number of shells along the shore. There is a *port de plaisance* for 350 berths. Holiday camps, caravan and camping sites, and a variety of hotels. Most of the building has been done recently and quickly, partly to house the families of the Zara Air Force base personnel and to meet the growth of tourism. The small, light and airy church on the port, has glowingly cheerful modern stained glass in pink, lime, turquoise, and a clear, almost Scandinavian interior. Solenzara is only 30km by the D 268 from the Col de Bavella and some of the most dramatic Corsican mountain scenery.

9 From Solenzara to Porto Vecchio and Bonifacio

ROAD (N 198) 68km.—41km Porto Vecchio—27km Bonifacio.

Going south from Solenzara the N 198 stays very close to the shore and there are many good places for swimming reached from the road itself or from seaside hamlets. Access is easy but as there is little shade it is as well to look out for the patches of maritime pine and scrub to seaward of the road. 10km from Solenzara, *Les Logis de Favone*, holiday village and motel and 1km further south the *Marine de Favone* at the mouth of the river of that name. A fine beach of 800m. 15km beyond Solenzara is the *anse* or cove of Tarco, at the mouth of the Tarco River. Here too is a long fine beach and 5km beyond is the Bocca di Parata (44m) a crest between the estuaries of the Rivers Conca and Cavu. Remains of Genoese tower out on the *Punta di Fautea*. From the Bocca the N 198 turns almost due west-south-west inland for 4.5km to Santa Lucia di Porto Vecchio, crossing the Cavu.

From here the D 168A goes right up the valley of the Cavu, a very worthwhile but tortuous (and not to be considered in wet weather) route through deserted mountains. The road eventually finds its way to the D 368 and up to Zonza. The D 168A going left out of Santa Lucia leads in 4km to the tiny port of *Pinarellu* and the tree-shaded beach around its bay.

11.5km beyond Santa Lucia watch out for the second turning left after crossing the River Osu. It is marked to Torre with the blue *monument historique* sign but it is easy to miss. The road leads to the hamlet of **Torre**, 8km north of Porto Vecchio, and then stops. This is the place from which the Bronze Age (c 1600 BC) Torréens (see Filitosa, Rte 2) were given their name. Go into the village and anyone will show you how to reach the site which appears to be over and above some back gardens, but is in fact easy to get to. The best-preserved and most complete of Torréen fortresses in Corsica, semi-circular and built up against a granite mass, it has retained some of its stone roofing slabs.

This is a region of Corsica particularly rich in archaeological sites and a few hundred metres further down the N 198 from Torre is the D 759 to the right which leads in 2.5km to a T-junction with the D 559. Turn left and immediately you are among scattered houses forming the hamlets of *Arragio* (Araghju). Look out or ask for the way to the site. The most I have found there is a roughly-painted sign on the side of a house saying 'Ruines'. A path crosses a stream and then the footpath, narrow and stony, winds up through the maquis. Wear tough shoes, feel energetic, and allow 30–40 minutes each way (longer if there has been rain).

The **Castellu d'Araghju** is one of the most complete and largest of Torréen fortresses. Impressive in its cyclopean proportions, the great entrance gives access to the fortress and the ruins of the religious centre. Surrounding the fort is a circular wall, on average 2m thick and 4m high, with rooms built against it and steps to a walkway from which there are extensive views over the Araghju to Porto Vecchio.

There are two alternative ways to return to the N 198 to Porto Vecchio. Either continue south along the D 559 to the junction with the D 368 Zonza–Porto Vecchio road, turn left and in 4.5km reach the N 198 and turn right into the northern suburbs of Porto Vecchio or return by the D 759 to the N 198 and turn right.

At Ste Trinité (2km), south of the turn-off to Arragio, the D 168A leads left (2km) to *Golfo di Sogno* (a big camping site and 1200m-long beach). Continue 1km further and turn right to *Cala Rossa*, with pine trees and a tourist development. 2.5km further east the road reaches *Punta San Ciprianu*. If you continue along the D 168A direct from La Trinité you reach the 2.5km-long beach of San Ciprianu; a further 7km to the north-north-east leads to Pinarellu (see alternative route from Santa Lucia di Porto Vecchio).

Porto Vecchio (Porti Vechju, 70m, 9307 inhab.) is 143km from Bastia, Solenzara 41km, Ajaccio 149km, Corte 121km and Bonifacio 27km.

The 'Old Port' of its name is apt because this safe harbour, deep in an almost fjord-like gulf at the south end of a long, flat and mostly harbourless coastline has attracted voyagers from distant antiquity until the present day. The Torréens, of course, made their presence clear; the Romans whose *Portus Syracusanus* this may have been, the Etruscans, Barbary pirates and then, inevitably, the Genoese, all made use of the port. The Bank of Saint Georges established a fortress here in 1539 to complete the chain of defences around the island and it became their second most important fortress, after Bastia, on the east coast. In 1564 Sampiero Corso, needing a port but failing to take Ajaccio from the Genoese, turned his attention to Porto Vecchio which he succeeded in taking on 30 July 1564. A true politician, cynically finding allies where it suited his purpose, Sampiero made common cause with the corsairs against Genoa. The Genoese in their turn called in their ally, Spain, whose ships defeated the corsairs and whose men, under Genoese command, took Porto Vecchio on 26 November 1564. Prosperous under the Genoese, the town fell later into a decline, largely due to malaria.

The American DDT campaign at the end of the Second World War, so important and often referred to in this Guide, enabled Porto Vecchio to regain its prosperity. Export of cork from the oak forests of the district has suffered from the competition of plastic but more than a third of Corsican wine is exported from the town and the tourist industry flourishes, exploiting the pink rocky coves, superb sandy beaches, and the *port de plaisance* next to the *port de commerce*. Figari Airport, 25km south-west, and Italian and Corsican ferries, bring close to 2 million Italian visitors yearly yet the atmosphere is that of a friendly, easy-going place that copes well with the influx although there is little style in the architecture of the extensive hotel and apartment building going on. Many good shops and boutiques. Walk in Porto Vecchio, there are no great distances or hills and parking in the centre is difficult.

The old town and the fortifications have retained their original character. Of the 15–16C *Genoese fortifications*, raised on outcrops of rosy pink porphyry, five bastions have survived as well as the Genoese Gate opening east, with a view of the Golfo de Porto Vecchio, the port and the salt marshes (with the only salt pans on the east coast of Corsica). The streets in this part of the town are narrow, often with steps, finely carved old doors and covered alleys. The parish church, plain and solidly built, with a square tower, dates from 1868.

From the centre of the town the road to the Marina and the commercial port (1km), goes down through olive groves. The quayside has nothing of

Porto Vecchio, the Genoese fortifications are being carefully restored

note architecturally, mostly modern houses, shops, cafés and restaurants. You can walk beyond to the commercial port but, apart from looking out to the gulf or back inland to the mountains beyond the town, there is little of interest. The harbour is on the estuary of the River Stabiacciu (22km long, rising on the east face of the Punta di a Vacca Morta at 1314m).

A. Excursions from Porto Vecchio: the Coast

The beaches on the Gulf to the north of the town—Golfo di Sogno, Cala Rossa, San Ciprianu and Pinarellu—are described above. To the south the Gulf and the port are protected by the peninsula of Piccovaggia, a round tour of which (29km) takes in some of the best beaches in southern Corsica. Take the N 198 out of Porto Vecchio towards Bonifacio. After 2km and crossing the Stabiacciu take the first turning to the left (it is almost opposite the turning to the right onto the D 853 to Sotta). This road follows the northern shore on the peninsula to (7.5km) Piccovaggia from which a minor road left leads to the *Punta di a Chiappa*. This is the furthest point east on the peninsula. From the foot of the lighthouse there is an incomparable view of the Gulf, to the Punta San Ciprianu on the north side of the Gulf and inland to the mountainous backdrop. Return to Piccovaggia, 3km to the south. Continuing south through cork oak woods, there is a track 500m down to the sea and the beach of *Palombaggia* (Palombaja) backed by rosy-red rocks and with sandy dunes shaded by umbrella pines. The sand is white, the bathing safe, the water clear and of every shade of blue and green.

5km offshore an archipelago of half-a-dozen uninhabited islets (15km from Porto Vecchio). Five of them constitute *La Réserve Naturelle des Iles Cerbicale* (founded 3 March 1981) covering 36 hectares. Predominantly gneiss and schiste and a little granite, the islets formed part of the Corsican coast until 10,000 years ago. All information regarding flora and fauna and visiting (very limited) can be obtained from M. le Conservateur des Réserves, Mairie de Porto Vecchio, 20137 Porto-Vecchio.

From Palombaggia keep to the coastal road to the hamlet of Bocca di l'Oru, then right for 1km to the N 198. Turn right and 6km back to Porto Vecchio. Or turn left on the N 198 and after 1.5km turn left again and 600m to Golfo di Santa Giulia. Do not be bewildered as to how to get to the sea beyond the large hotel and apartment complex with macadamed paths and streetlighting. By going on to the end one can both park and walk down to a fine and sheltered sandy beach, crowded in high season.

B. Excursions from Porto Vecchio: the Mountains

Leave Porto Vecchio by the N 198 towards Solenzara and, in the suburbs, take the first road left, the D 368, crossing in 4.5km the D 559 (Arragio 3km to the right). The thick woods of cork and evergreen oaks give way to maritime and Corsican pines as the road rises steadily through a landscape of giant granite masses, the Forêt de l'Ospedale.

19km from Porto Vecchio, *l'Ospedale* (812m), a hamlet in the commune of Porto Vecchio, that owes its name to a hospital in Roman times. Here are views over the Gulf, north along the east coast, south to Bonifacio and beyond to the coast of Sardinia (weather permitting, of course). Just beyond the village, on the left, is the artificial lake made by damming the high waters of the Osu. This is the *Barrage de l'Ospedale* whose waters supply the Porto Vecchio area. 10km beyond the village you cross the Bocca

Sunday wild boar hunters (back to camera, friend from Porto Vecchio who has just been given a joint of sanglier)

d'Ilarata (1008m). To the left are views over the valleys of the Rizzanese and Ortolo rivers.

40km from Porto Vecchio is *Zonza* (762m, 1600 inhab.). Built in terraces above the valley of the Asinao, solid old granite houses and narrow streets make this a village of 'mountain' character and its position, high above the surrounding forests of Ospedale, Zonza and Bavella, justifies its reputation as a pleasant summer resort, while the forests create employment to tend the Corsican pines. Zonza is at a mountain crossroads, one road coming up from l'Ospedale, the D 268 going north-east to the Col de Bavella (see Rte 16) and south to Levie and Sartène, and the D 420 going west to Aullène and Petreto-Bicchisano where it joins the N 196 to Ajaccio.

From Zonza head south on the D 268 9km to *Levie* (Livia, 656m, 781 inhab.), a large village spread out on the granite Pianu (plateau) de Levie that lies between the valleys of the Rizzanese and the Fiumicicoli in the Alta Rocca region. This is one of the richest archaeological areas of Corsica and discoveries at sites on the Pianu have been brought and displayed in the **Musée Départemental de Levie** (1 June–30 Sept 10.00–19.00 daily; 1 Oct–31 May 10.00–12.00 and 14.00–16.00, closed Sat, Sun and public holidays). The museum, clearly signposted in the main street, is on the ground floor of the Hôtel de Ville, an elegant old house standing in its own grounds, a gift to the community. The collections, constantly added to, come mainly from the Pianu sites (Calecula, Capula, Cucuruzzu, Curacchiaghju, Nuciarese, and Santa-Catalina). The displays are well-arranged and clearly described in an excellent brochure. Notable among the objects which date from 7th millennium BC–15C AD are the 6570 BC skeleton of a handicapped (arthritic?) woman known as the Dame de Bonifacio, the skeleton of a long-extinct rodent, *Prolagus sardus Wagner*, flint tools and weapons, the first metal objects, Bronze Age pottery, Iron Age tools and ornaments and a female skeleton from Capula bearing evidence of the practice of funeral rites, Pisan pottery and coinage struck by the Genoese.

Local tradition maintains that Félix Peretti, Pope Sixtus V 1585–90, was born of Levie parents. It is a local family name and during the preparation of the 1st edition of this Guide Jean-Baptiste de Peretti, a teacher from the village, acted as guide to the sites and invited us to his parents' house. He also introduced us to the priest who showed us the exceptionally beautiful ivory crucifix, 15C Florentine work that captured the muscular contortion induced by great pain. Pope Sixtus V is said to have given it to the Levie parish church of St Nicolas. I photographed it against the wall of the priest's house where it used to be kept but since his death it has been sent to Paris 'for restoration' (in 1991) before eventual display in the Levie Museum.

15C ivory crucifix, Levie

To reach the fortified Torréen complex of *Castellu de Cucuruzzu* take the D 268 out of Levie, in the direction of Sainte Lucie de Tallano. At 3.5km watch for a signpost to the site. Follow this road to the right and after 3.5km there is parking space and an easy 800m walk up a shaded track to the site. Those wishing to visit Curacciaghiu and other archaeological sites on the Pianu di Levie, some of which involve moderate walks and climbs, are advised to ask for information at the Levie Museum. On the way, at 2km from the main road and to the right of the track is a footpath leading to the *Caleca* site of a 1st millennium BC funeral chamber within three concentric stone circles.

The c 1400 BC **Castellu de Cucuruzzu**, like other Torréen fortified sites, makes use of a hilltop to incorporate the natural rock into the structure of the settlement. Entrance is by a roughly-formed stairway between two rocks, mounting up to and passing through a rampart within which were constructed casemates with narrow slits from which to keep watch on the countryside below. A walkway leads round to the east side and an open space or terrace on one side of which were raised the great boulders of the central monument, backed by a rock wall. Entry is by two successive openings framed by massive lintels set on equally massive vertical rocks serving as pillars. The chamber itself is ingeniously vaulted with stones without benefit of any kind of mortar. The summit of the monument can be reached from outside by a stairway of boulders and from there can be appreciated the strength of this position with extensive views in every direction. The eastern extent of the rocky spur was occupied by the fortified Torréen village.

When the fortress and village were occupied dense forest surrounded the site, providing game. A torrent just below supplied fish as well as water. The inhabitants cultivated cereals—charred grains of wheat were found during the excavations. The *castellu* was set on the hilltop so that it had sun throughout the whole day and in every season of the year.

From the parking place a track leads off and after about 300m there is a signpost, to the Castellu de Capula and the Chapelle Lorenzu (about 20 minutes walk). The site of the *Castellu de Capula* was in constant human occupation from the Bronze Age until the destruction of the medieval castle in 1259 after a long period of clan warfare. In the construction of the castle practical use was made of a dolmen (it can be seen protruding from the wall as one climbs the rock stairway to the remains of the castle). There is also a headless menhir with vestiges of a vertical sheathed sword held in front of the figure and the etching of a spine and ribs on the back still visible.

The *Chapel of San Lorenzu*, the product of pious but misguided zeal, has the ruins of an earlier chapel next to it. The original chapel was 13C Romanesque and each 10 August, the feast of St Laurence, a pilgrimage was made to it from Levie and the other villages below. In 1916, when all able-bodied men were away at the First World War, the good *curé* of Levie noticed that the roof of the chapel was in bad repair. He therefore had it demolished and some of its stones employed in the construction of a splendid new chapel which met with the disapproval of many of his warrior parishioners when they returned. It is however very plain and inoffensive and the ruins of the old, rising just above the ground, attest to continuity under the boughs of the oaks.

Sainte Lucie de Tallano (Santa Lucia di Tallano, 450m, 424 inhab.), 8.5km to the south-west on the D 268, is one of Corsica's loveliest villages, set on a wooded hillside in a landscape rich in orchards and vineyards. It had to be repopulated from the surrounding villages after the inhabitants were decimated by plague in 1348. This was della Rocca territory and Rinuccio della Rocca, a '...tempestuous Corsican warlord...a true prince of the Renaissance, a discriminating lover of the arts' (Dorothy Carrington: 'Granite Island'), endowed a Franciscan monastery at Sainte Lucie in 1492. Six years later he gave the monastery church a Crucifixion and a reredos of the Virgin and Child with Saints by the Master of Castel Sardo, a painter of probably Catalan origin, and his studio. Rinuccio also presented to the parish church of Sainte Lucie a 15C marble font in the shape of a hand and a marble bas-relief in Florentine style of an adolescent plump-faced Virgin and Child, dated MCCCC LXXXX VIIII at the top and flanked by the arms of 'Rinuccio de Rocha' at the bottom.

In a quarry (30 mins walk) due south of Sainte Lucie was worked the extremely rare rock (thought to be exclusive to Corsica until some was found in Finland) *diorite orbiculaire*. The walk to the quarry (now fenced) is not easy but you can get an idea of what the rock is like from the fragment set into the village war memorial. Marked like a panther skin, the orbs of the *diorite orbiculaire* are formed of concentric circles up to 6cm in diameter of white feldspar and black amphibole.

Return to Levie, retracing the route north up the D 268. From here an alternative way back to Porto Vecchio by a picturesque route is to leave the village by the D 59 which goes south.—8km on is *Carbini* (600m, 96 inhab.), with rows of lime trees bordering the road, and long low houses, many with elaborate and well-fashioned porches. The church of *San Giovanni Battista* was built in the first half of the 12C and is the former *piévanie*. Originally there were two churches, San Giovanni Battista and San Quilico of which only a bell tower still stands, very well restored in the late 19C by the Historical Monuments Service (taking action on a letter of Mérimée sent to the Minister about Carbini a mere 40 or so years earlier). Fine decorative arcading, particularly on the west front.

Carbini may exude peace and calm today but 600 years ago there was an outburst of heresy which was violently suppressed. The Giovannali sect was founded in Carbini c 1354, taking its name from the church. Franciscan in origin, it sought spiritual perfection, the sharing of worldly goods and family life and equality of the sexes. Its members defied the feudal and ecclesiastical laws and their teaching spread in the east of Corsica. Pope Urban V, declaring them Satanists, mounted a Papal Crusade in 1362 and sent soldiers who hunted down and massacred the heretics, not only at Carbini but far away at Alesani in the Castagniccia. There are many fascinating and baffling sides to the whole story and links with similar movements in continental Europe.

2km south from Carbini a footpath to the left of the D 59 leads to some vestiges of the Torréen *Castellu de l'Accinto* in 1km and then to the Punta di a Vacca Morta. 7km beyond Carbini the road climbs sharply into the mountains between the scrubby oaks to the Col de Bacinu.

To the right, 4km beyond the Col, there is a stony track, which gets ever rougher, climbing up into the dramatic wilderness of the Montagne de Cagna. After about 6km there is a plateau with a few stone cabins and houses called *Bitalza* and a view eastwards over to the Golfe de Porto Vecchio and south over the Bouches de Bonifacio to the Sardinian hills behind the port of Santa Teresa di Gallura. The twin summits of Capelu form a backdrop to Bitalza. Only sturdy and high-slung motors can negotiate this track without too much risk of fractured sumps but with provisions, rucksacks and stout footgear this is a good day's exploration. For dedicated walkers, well equipped and experienced in mountain travel, there are a dozen or so good itineraries in the Massif de Cagna, including the *Uomo di Cagna* (1217m), a sphere of rock 10m in diameter balanced on a narrow socle. It can be seen from most places in the southern plains and marks the south extremity of the central mountain ranges of Corsica. This Man of Cagna is most easily accessible from the village of Giannuccio at the end of the D 50 which leads north from the Sartène–Bonifacio road N 196 (see Michel Fabrikant: 'Guide des Montagnes Corses').

At the foot of the southern slopes of the Cagna Massif the D 59 goes through the Tunnel d'Usciolu and after crossing another mountain ridge reaches (10km) Sotta, just before which take the left fork, the D 259, into the village. *Sotta* (130m, 762 inhab.) recalls a mountain village in its fine granite houses yet is a village of the plain, set among fields and cattle pastures. 10km to

Porto Vecchio by the D 853 and the N 198. At 4.5km is the village of *Ceccia* above which stands the 3rd millennium BC monument of *Tappa*. It can be difficult to find: do not go into the hamlet but watch out for a track through the vineyards to the right after the turning to the right to Cardetto. The track is almost opposite a small house standing on the road. Follow this straight, flat track as far as it goes. Immediately to the right is a maquis-covered high mound, a typical Torréen site. Ascent is relatively easy to the cyclopean walls and the central chamber they surround.

Porto Vecchio to Bonifacio is 27km by the N 198. Access to the sea and the beaches are described in the passages on the coastal environs of Porto Vecchio and Bonifacio respectively. The road crosses a desert region of a low plateau covered with maquis and dotted with cork oaks. At the Bocca d'Aresia (68m) there is a view west to the Cagna Massif. 4km beyond the D 59 leads off to the right to join the D 859 road to Sotta (right) and Figari Airport (left). Closer to Bonifacio the landscape becomes less arid and desolate, with areas of cultivation and olive groves. Approaching Bonifacio from the north brings home the extent of its geographical and geological isolation and explains much of the distinctive character and speech of the Bonifaciens or Bonifazinchi.

10   Le Cap Corse: from Bastia to Saint-Florent along the coast road

ROAD (D 80) 110km.—10km *Erbalunga*—15.5km *Commune de Sisco* (to left of road)—28km *Sta Severa* (and detour to west along the D 180)—61.5km *Pino*—93.5km *Nonza*.

CAP CORSE is a peninsula, an extended index finger pointing to France from the clenched right fist, seen palmside up, of Corsica.

The Cap is broadly that part of the island to the north of the D 81 road from Bastia on the Tyrrhenian coast in the east to Saint-Florent on the Mediterranean coast in the west via the Col de Teghime (541m), a distance of 23km. This winding road is the divide between Cap Corse and the Nebbio (see Rte 13). Cap Corse itself is 40km long and 15km across at its widest point. Bastia in the south forms the divide between the Eastern Plain and, to the north, the Cap's mountainous spine which hugs the east coast, the continuation of the central mountain chain of the island. The highest point of Cap Corse is Monte Stello (1307m).

The D 80 follows the coastline around the Cap Corse peninsula so the circuit may be made either clockwise or anti-clockwise, either from Saint-Florent or from Bastia. Starting from Bastia the variety of the Cap Corse landscape opens out more dramatically.

Leave Bastia from the north-east corner of the Place St. Nicolas. This is the starting point of the D 80, the corniche road that follows the entire coastline of the Cap (translated in a French guidebook as 'a cornish road with rocky coasts'!).

3km north of Bastia, *Pietranera* is a residential suburb of Bastia with villas tucked into the hillside on the left of the road and fitted into most of the available space above the sea on the right. 5.5km, *Miomo*, a small fishing port with a mostly residential village clustered around it. There is pleasant bathing and a Genoese tower in a well-preserved state. 7.5km, *Lavasina*, one of the hamlets forming the commune of Brando. *Notre Dame des Grâces* (1677) is rough-cast in a pleasantly faded pink but flanking it is an ugly thick-set campanile surmounted by a Virgin in the worst 'plaster saint' style. Inside, above the black-and-white marble altar, from a Pistoia monastery in Tuscany, hangs a painting of the Virgin and Child (school of Perugino, 16C) known as the Madonna of Lavasina (darkened with age). It is credited with miraculous powers to protect the local fishermen. In an ex-voto collection on the interior walls of the church, stories are inscribed, usually in the vernacular, of sailors delivered from peril on the sea. A confessional box in carved wood dates from 1680. The pilgrimage on 8 September (Birth of the Holy Virgin) is attended by large crowds, with a torchlight procession on the shore the night before.

To the left of the D 80 lies the commune of BRANDO (Brandu, 300m average, 1334 inhab.) that gives its name to a number of hamlets none of which is actually called Brando. Take the D 54 to the left, just south of the bridge over the Lavasina and before entering the village to which the river gives its name. At 4km is *Pozzo*, the starting point for the ascent of Monte Stello, (1307m).

The summit of *Monte Stello* is reached by a stiffish climb, the round trip taking 5 hours. Park in the Rue Napoléon, left of the church, and ahead is the footpath through the maquis. The path passes two ruined buildings and immediately after the second one the mountain ridge comes in sight. From the summit there are views (according to weather, and the earlier in the day the ascent is made the better) north to the tip of Cap Corse, east to the Golfe de Saint-Florent, south-west to the Balagne and south and east to the mountains of Central Corsica and down along the Eastern Plain. Check by telephone (36 04 96, recorded forecast) before setting out.

3km further on lies *Castello* with the church of *Sainte-Marie des Neiges* (Santa Maria di e Nevi), c 9C–10C, a single nave and oven-vaulted apse. The north wall incorporates earlier (6C or 7C) bas-relief animals, a boat, birds and rose designs. The south wall is decorated with frescoes from 1386, 15C altarpiece of the Virgin and Child on wood.— After a further 3km the D 54 reaches Erbalunga.

Back on the D 80 coastal road, 2.5km north of Lavasina and 10km from Bastia is *Erbalunga*, a fishing hamlet in the commune of Brando. A tongue of schist projects into the sea, protecting the tiny port from the north wind. The houses appear to have been built haphazardly, one against another at a variety of angles. Like a miniature Manhattan, as much as possible has been fitted onto the available rock and many of the buildings seem to rise out of the water. A Genoese tower, the seaward side somewhat weather-worn, sits at the tip of the promontory. It is not surprising that Erbalunga has for long been a favourite with painters. It is also the native village of the forebears of Paul Valéry (1871–1945), the poet. The church of *St Erasme* is set on a terrace above the road from Bastia, from which the procession of penitents called the *Cerca* (the Search or Quest), sets out before 7 am on Good Friday. Walking a 7km route the penitents visit the churches and chapels of the Brando hamlets and return at noon to Erbalunga. In the evening the torchlit procession of cowled figures enact the *Granitola*—the Snail—winding and tightening on itself. Possibly a pre-Christian fertility ceremony, it is now, to be on the safe side, followed by other penitents who form the sign of the cross.—5.5km further on is *Marine de Sisco* which takes its name from the commune of Sisco (500m average, 616 inhab.) comprised of 17 hamlets scattered along the valley of the River Sisco.

To visit the Sisco churches take the D 32 which runs along the valley, climbing nearly 700m into the mountains. It eventually peters out into a track that reaches the hamlet of *Cortina Sutana* (3km) and the D 232 coming west from the Marine de Pietracorbara. The D 32 then turns due north to reach villages as far as Carbonnace where the D 32 runs north-west towards the coast and the D 132 loops and twists its way down to the east coast at Porticciolo on the D 80, 10.5km north of Marine de Sisco. If it is planned to visit the Sisco hamlets by car allow plenty of time because the roads are narrow and winding. Walking is preferable, to take in the beauty of the hillsides on which chestnut and ilex rise above the thick growth of myrtle, heather, bramble and arbutus.

SAN MICHELE
Sisco

Up a footpath to the left of the D 32, 1km before the road ends (see above) is the little Romanesque chapel of *San Michele* (1030m) standing on a plinth of rock from which there are outstanding views of the east coast of Cap Corse and the Tuscan islands. Pilgrimage is made here from the Sisco villages on 29 September. The parish church of *St Martin*, surrounded by oaks on its terrace overlooking the sea, houses relics transferred here from the local Convent of Ste Catherine (Santa Catalina) in the 17C. Sailors, returning from Palestine in the 13C are said to have promised the best of their cargo to the first church they reached should they be delivered from the storm. Once safe ashore they forgot their promise but were reminded by a second storm and took their treasures to St Catherine's Convent. Among them were a clod of the earth from which Adam was moulded, stones from Sinai, hairs from St John the Baptist's cloak, a portion of the Virgin's coat and one of Enoch's fingers. The most striking relic is the so-called skull of St John Chrysostom encased in a mask of hammered copper, silvered and gilded, said to have been made in the 13C in the Sisco valley, a metal-working centre in the Middle Ages.

16.5km further on is *Santa Catalina*, the former convent of Ste Catherine, now a church. 2km Beyond Sisco a statue of St Catherine stands on the left, high above the road, and a hairpin bend below it leads into the road up to Santa Catalina, the first sight of which is the massive fortified square tower beside the church. In front is a kind of rough lawn dominated by an ancient olive tree and set on the low walls surrounding the grass are large Ali Baba-style jars painted cream. There is more than a hint of the East and Islam in the jars and the shells and pottery dishes set around the semi-circular window of the west façade (modern glass depicting a crimson rising sun with a gold background and sunrays represented by radiating metal strips). To the right of the window is the date of the first restoration of the church: MCCCCXLIII (1443). Note the diamond and lozenge decoration over the two west doors. The queue of pilgrims to view the relief would have entered by one door and left by the other. Unfortunately this Romanesque church is bare and in bad repair. On entering, to the left, is a massive pillar that seems to support a roughly-made modern semi-circular gallery. There is a badly battered 17C altar with baroque barley-sugar columns. Plaster is falling off the walls. An elegant organ by Mustel, Paris (no date), is in bad condition; another organ is in decrepit state against the south wall. A circular crypt (12C?) is reached by two stairs or 'tomboli', thought by Mme G. Moracchini-Mazel, the authority on Corsican Romanesque architecture, to have been an attempt to reproduce the Holy Sepulchre at Jerusalem. It was here that the relics were kept which are now at St Martin, and when one remembers that they were brought from Palestine it perhaps explains the numerous reminders of the East encountered here. The Convent is now a home for old people and is not open to the public.

Santa Catalina, Cap Corse

20km from Bastia, and at the foot of the D 232 if returning from the Sisco detour, is *Marine de Pietracorbara* (Petracurbara). Just before a sharp bend to the right that follows the line of the bay is the *Torre dell'Aquila* (the Eagle Tower) to the left.—6km *Marine de Porticciolo* with just beyond it the D 132 that corkscrews its way inland through the Cagnano hamlets to join the D 32. 3km further is *Santa Severa* with its small port, the Marine de Luri, at the estuary of the River Luri. This fertile valley, filled with vineyards and citrus groves is followed by the D 180, the principal road (apart from the D 80 further north) to cross Cap Corse, by which it is 16km to Pino.

From Santa Severa a detour can be made along the D 180 to Pino. 6km the Luri (0–600m in the hamlets, 671 inhab.) hamlet of *Piazza*, with the church of *St Pierre* (17C). Inside the pillars are painted to resemble marble and walls decorated with blue, grey and light brown lozenges in geometric patterns. The wooden reredos has a 15C painting representing the life of St Peter. The background to the Quo Vadis scene records valuable architectural details of the castles and fortified houses of the 15C lords of Cap Corse. There is a separate campanile of 1821 set, with the Luri commune building, in a large square with trees and the war memorial.

A road leads from the Col de Santa Lucia (signpost) to the path that leads by a 30-minute steady climb to *Seneca's Tower* which stands 200m above the Col de Santa Lucia on a peak of the Ventiggiole (640m). Legend claims that Lucius Annaeus Seneca (c 4 BC–AD 65), exiled from Rome in 41–49 by the Emperor Claudius, lived here, although it is more likely that he was banished to one of the Roman colonies such as Mariana or Aléria. In the Middle Ages the tower was used as a fortress by the powerful da Mare nobles, Genoese in both origin and political fidelity. There is a car park at the foot of the climb, in the courtyard of what was for over 50 years the Maison d'Enfants which provided home and education for hundreds of children in need of the healthy surroundings and outdoor activities which included the collection, classification and often reassembly and repair of pieces of pottery, necklaces, rings etc. which they retrieved from the area and set up in a museum of which they were justly proud. Although the Maison is still mentioned in some guides that have not yet been brought up to date, it is now, sadly, closed for reasons of finance and the need for structural modernisation of the building which stands on the site of the Castel dei Motti, a watch-tower guarding the Motti château (1246) which became a Capucin monastery, dedicated to St Nicolas, in 1548. The Mairie of Luri took over the museum which 'was founded on 20 November 1971 and was created by the children of the open air school of Luri 1970–71'.

At 34.5km from Bastia by way of Santa Severa on the D 80 is the *Marine de Meria*, a hamlet and sandy beach on the Luri estuary, 4km north of which is *Macinaggio*, now a small port for fishing boats but more important in the past. Paoli, returning from England, landed here on 13 July 1790. On 10 March 1793 Napoleon Bonaparte came ashore and on 2 December 1869 the Empress Eugénie landed from 'l'Aigle' on her way back from Egypt where she had attended the opening of the Suez Canal.

By a footpath leading due north from Macinaggio, 3.5km and taking 2–2½ hours there and back, you reach the chapel of *Santa Maria di a Chiappella*, on a bleak and bare stretch of coast, overlooking the tiny island of Finocchiarola. Romanesque, twin apses from 11C, restored in 18C. A Genoese tower close by, now in ruins, was built 1549. At the northern extremity of Cap Corse is the commune of *Rogliano* (Ruglianu, 480 inhab.). In the mid 17C the commune was a stronghold of the da Mare family and had a population of 4000–5000. The Romans also had a settlement here. From the 11C the da Mare were the masters of all they surveyed, and a good deal of land they could not see, until in 1553 Jacques da Mare broke with Genoa and supported Sampiero's revolt. Genoa had the da Mare château demolished and the site is called locally 'Castelacciu' (the bad château), while the nearby château of the Negroni family, old allies of the da Mare, is merely 'castellu'.

There are ruins of a Franciscan monastery nearby (on private land) and the 16C church of *St Agnel* whose classical façade was restored and enlarged in the 18C. The 16C church of *St Cosmo and St Damien* was largely destroyed by fire in 1947. The nave was probably built in the 10C or earlier and its rectangular campanile was set at an angle to the façade.

From Macinaggio the main road, D 80, turns west to cross the Cap peninsula by the Col St Nicolas (300m). The first turning right after the Col leads, by a very minor road by way of Granaggiolo and the D 253, to the north of Cap Corse and *Barcaggio*, 16km by very narrow roads. Barcaggio's fine sandy beach, where the Acqua Tignase reaches the sea, was guarded against invaders by the Genoese Agnello Tower.

On the way to Centuri Port on the west coast of the Cap there is a turning marked to the *Moulin Mattei* (some way off the road and little to see) from which there are good views over the Tuscan sea to the islands of Capraja and Elba, north to the tip of Cap Corse and south down through the island towards the often snow-capped Monte Cinto, Corsica's highest mountain (2710m).

Centuri Port (150m average, 201 inhab.) was set up in the 18C as a fishing port specialising in lobsters and anchovies, still the mainstay of its commerce and a feature of local menus. Centuri is a centre for wet-suited

Centuri Port, Cap Corse

submarine fishermen. Fishing and eating apart, Centuri is very attractive with its multi-coloured houses grouped around the little harbour. 4km to the east and seen from the road is the château of General Cipriani (1844–1918) built in the 19C in medieval style. Going south from Centuri Port the D 35 rejoins the D 80 at Pecorile.

At 58.5km from Bastia is *Pruno*, a spectacular bay enclosed by cliffs making it almost impossible to get down to the sea. At the village of *Morsiglia* (Mursiglia, 200m average, 110 inhab.) the solid towers are a reminder that the inhabitants had repeatedly to take shelter from invaders. 3km further on, *Pino* (Pinu, 145m, 143 inhab.) is set in luxuriant vegetation. It has a pebbly beach, a baroque church, a Genoese tower and a Franciscan monastery dating from 1486. Olive trees, fig trees, chestnuts and planes flourish all around. In the chapel, frescoes and 16C triptych of the Virgin, St Francis and St Bernardino of Siena. A road to the right 8km further on leads down to the Marine de Giottani and the Genoese tower of *Castelluccio*.

6km south is Marinca, one of 10 hamlets that make up the commune of Canari (360m, 291 inhab.). At its centre is Pieve where there is a fine view from the Place du Clocher over the west coast of the Cap. The church of *Santa Maria Assunta* is late 12C Pisan Romanesque dressed with finely cut light green schist. Some mistaken 'improvements' were made in the 18C, such as the window in the façade. The cornice includes masks, human figures, animal heads, geometric patterns, here and there incorporating fragments of pre-Roman sculpture. From the main square a road goes up to the church of *St-François*, a 17C former Franciscan monastery chapel. To the left on entering, you will see a 15C St Michael slaying the dragon, possibly a local work, and in the sacristy a large figure of Christ dressed as a penitent. On the right of the nave, is a 16C triptych of the Assumption, and the 1590 memorial to Vittoria de Gentile depicting a young woman holding a baby in swaddling clothes.

4km south of Marinca to the left of the D 80 is the tall dilapidated building where was crushed and processed the amianthus (a form of asbestos) from the nearby mine at Algo, between 1932 and 1966. Its closure resulted in serious local unemployment but there has been talk of converting the buildings into craft workshops and studios. At present it is desolate and depressing and the grey dust, ugly but harmless, cascades down the cliff to the sea. Pebbles of amianthus from the mine workings have changed the coastline to the north of Nonza by building up into a grey-green beach extending from the foot of the cliffs.

Nonza (152m, 86 inhab.) is 14km further south and 93.5km from Bastia. St Julie, who was born in Nonza or Carthage, was crucified for her Christian faith on the orders of the Roman Prefect Barbarus. Her body was taken to Brescia in Italy in 734 at the time of the threat of a Saracen invasion. There is a pilgrimage on 22 May to Nonza and the fountain of St Julie is approached by 164 steps from the road to Pino. From the fountain there is a good view of the village and the Genoese tower (which can be reached from the centre of the village), and views of the Cap Corse coast down to Saint-Florent, of the Balagne and the massif of Monte Cinto. In the church of *Ste-Julie*, above a polychromatic marble altar of 1694, is a 16C painting depicting the crucifixion of the saint in 303.

After the cession of Corsica by Genoa to France by the Treaty of Versailles of 15 May 1768 those Corsicans who supported Paoli resisted the French forces. Général de Grandmaison set siege to Nonza but his 1200 soldiers were unable to take the Genoese tower which kept up a constant musket fire and bombardment from the single cannon. Grandmaison parleyed with the stubborn Corsican defence and agreed to accord full military honours and a safe passage through the French lines of survivors wishing to rejoin Paoli on surrender. The terms were accepted but only one old limping man called Jacques Casella came out as the French presented arms. By an ingenious system of cables he had kept up a continuous fire giving the impression that the tower was defended by a large force. The French were full of admiration and the promise of safe conduct to Paoli was honoured. 'The defence force of Nonza tower was just me', Casella said.

The D 80 closely follows the coast, giving extensive views of the Golfe de Saint-Florent and over to the Désert des Agriates. At the Estuary of the Fium'Albino the road turns south-east towards the commune of Patrimonio, renowned for its wine, and joins the D 81 which returns to the coast at Saint-Florent.

11 La Casinca

South of Bastia and north-east of the Castagniccia, lying between the lower valley of the Golo to the north and the lower valley of the Fium'Alto to the south, is this tiny (8330 hectares) and virtually self-contained region called the **Casinca**. To the west the Monte Sant'Angelo rises to 1218m and to the east is the coastal plain. This is the most densely populated region of Corsica and, now, the most fertile area, producing cereals, citrus fruits, vines and tobacco with, on the terraces inland to the west, groves of olive and chestnut trees.

From Bastia take the N 193 south for 20km and at Casamozza cross the Golo and follow the N 198 towards Aléria. Either take the second turning to the right, the D 10, which leads to the Casinca village of Olmo, or the third turning right, the D 237, to Loreto-di-Casinca.

36km from Bastia, in the heart of the Casinca, is *Loreto-di-Casinca* (Loretu di Casinca, 630m, 225 inhab.), a village on the chestnut-covered lower slopes of Monte Sant'Angelo. There is a car park in the Piana, the town square bordered by plane trees. Go on foot to the end of the main street flanked by houses of green schist, to where the church and a campanile stand on a terrace from which there is a view of the whole of the Casinca as well as the Biguglia lagoon, Bastia and the east coast from Erbalunga in the north to the estuary of the Fium'Alto in the south, the isles of Elba, Pianosa and Monte Cristo, and, in clear weather, the coast of Tuscany.

There is a footpath to the summit of *Monte Sant'Angelo* from Loreto-di-Casinca. Leaving the village by the D 6 in the direction of Silvareccio take the first track leading off to the right. It is 90 minutes to the summit (1218m) and 45 minutes back to Loreto. Splendid panorama from the top.

From Loreto-di-Casinca there is also a pleasant walk through the chestnut woods to Olmo. Again, take the D 6, towards Vescovato. In less than 2km a narrow road, marked, goes off to the left to *Olmo* (Olmu, 540m, 98 inhab.), an amphitheatre village on the right bank of the Golo.

Take the D 6 south in the direction of Silvareccio to the junction with the D 237 (which continues west to the Bocca di Sant'Agostino, 670m, the mountain pass connecting the Casinca with the Castigniccia). Turn right and continue south along the D 237 and after 4km turn left and follow the D 206 to *Penta di Casinca* (A Penta di Casinca, 400m, 1917 inhab.). The village consists of a single street of tall grey schist houses strung out along a rocky spur, with the heights of Monte Sant'Angelo to the west and to the east a view out to the eastern coastal plain and the Biguglia lagoon. Just outside the village is a cemetery and the road to it passes under an aqueduct. Engraved on the arch is *'Oghje a me'* (today it is my turn) and on the other side mourners returning from the funeral would read '*dumane a te*' (tomorrow it will be yours).

Fork left immediately on leaving the village, then left again, and after 1km turn right onto the D 6 to *Castellare di Casinca* (150m, 389 inhab.), another typical Casinca village built on a spur of rock looking out to sea. Follow the road 2km to the junction with the N 198, turn left in the direction of Bastia, and after 3km take the second turning on the left, the D 37, reaching in 2km *Venzolasca* (U Venzulasca, 35m, 1162 inhab.) another village of a single street of tall houses built along a ridge between two valleys. Fork right after leaving the village to the west.

2.5km along the D 237 is **Vescovato** (U Viscuvatu, 140m, 2329 inhab.), the capital of the Casinca which now gives its name to the commune. Vescovato is Corsican for 'bishopric' and from 1269 to 1570 it was the seat of the Bishops of Mariana, being healthier and more easily defended than Mariana itself which had suffered the depredations of mosquitoes and Moors. After 1570 the Bishops of Mariana took up residence in Bastia.

Cars may be left close to the main square which overlooks the coastal plain and has a fine fountain presided over by an eagle. Ask at the Mairie for the key to the former cathedral church of *San Martino*, originally a chapel, enlarged in the 15C by the Bishops of Mariana. The greatest treasure of the church is the white marble *tabernacle* sculpted by a Genoese artist in 1441. It portrays the Resurrection and the sleeping Roman soldiers lying against the tomb, elbows propped on their knees and with plump childish faces, are a triumph of the expression of martial boredom. The left hand of the soldier on the right is long-fingered and elegant. Either the sculptor wished to express something about the nature of these dormant guards or his own pleasure in forming the hand got the better of him.

Vescovato, by Edward Lear

There are several historical figures, famous both inside and outside Corsica, who were natives of, or at one time lived in, Vescovato. Among them is Anton Pietro Filippini whose house displays his arms and a 1575 inscription. His 'Historia di Corsica', an invaluable source book on the island, was published in 1594. In the house in which was born the patriot Andrea Colonna-Ceccaldi (who organised resistance to Genoa in the 18C), Joachim Murat, named King of Naples in 1808 by Napoleon, stayed in 1815 before his expedition to Calabria where he was taken prisoner and shot. Luce de Casabianca (1752–98), also born here, commanded the French flagship *l'Orient* at the Battle of Aboukir on 10 August 1798. His 12-year-old son, Jacques, was beside him and when Luce was killed Jacques, obeying his father's orders not to abandon ship, refused to leave when *l'Orient* caught fire and was blown up with the ship (see Rte 7). Mirabeau (1749–91) was stationed here for a short time while a serving soldier and a couple of centuries earlier it was in Vescovato that Henri II of France, who had been persuaded by the Corsican patriot Sampiero Corso to take the island from the Genoese, had a public declaration made that Corsica was henceforth incorporated into the Kingdom of France and could no more be abandoned than the crown itself. Two years later Henri II, with cynical treachery, handed Corsica back to Genoa.

The D 237 leads back from Vescovato in 4.5km to the N 198 and, turning left to Casamozza one can return to Bastia, 20km on the N 193.

12 La Castagniccia

The Castagniccia is a high-lying region of hills and mountains of medium height (800–1700m) in north-east Corsica, bounded to the north by the valley of the River Golo, to the south by the valley of the River Tavignano, to the west by Monte San Petrone and its outliers, and reaching the Tyrrhenian Sea between the Fium'Altu and the Alesani. The district takes its name from the *Castanea sativa*, the sweet chestnut of the *Fagaceae* family of trees. Familiar to Northerners as the nut roasted in the fire in winter and sold in city streets, or as *marrons glacés* and chestnut stuffing, it once formed when ground into flour the staple diet of mountain people. The wood of the tree was used for carpentry and cabinet making, as stakes to support vines and as firewood. Both wood and fruit were used in barter with other regions to obtain oil, soft fruit and cereals. Those chestnuts not gathered for milling sustain the large troupes of semi-wild pigs so often encountered throughout the district, usually just around a bend in the road. The importance of the chestnut has declined with the development of communications that ensure a regular supply of wheat flour. The chestnut plantations which man had developed in place of the indigenous oak woods have lost their pre-eminent importance in the local economy and the trees themselves have been both neglected and afflicted with 'the ink disease'. Although to the eye of the visitor the Castagniccia in spring and summer is one vast billowing ocean of green, and of gold and russet in autumn, a closer inspection reveals the stark skeletons of dead trees.

The people of the Castagniccia have always been hard-working: they have not relied exclusively on the chestnut crop. The traditional occupations still flourish, although on nothing like the scale that they did in the past up to the 20C. Among them are pottery, woodcarving and pipe-making, the forging of arms and agricultural implements from ore brought from the island of Elba, leatherwork and shoemaking. The villages of this once most densely-populated region of Corsica were built on elevations so that the inhabitants could defend themselves against attack. The settlements are liberally dotted about the tree-covered countryside.

The approaches to the Castagniccia are easy but the roads in the interior are still for the most part winding and narrow so that enough time must be allowed and special care taken.

Approaching the Castagniccia from Bastia take the N 193 south for 20km and turn right to follow the N 193 at Casamozza where the N 198 continues south towards Aléria. The N 193 and the railway follow the course of the River Golo, a picturesque and varied route. There are a number of narrow turnings off to the left that lead into the Castagniccia but much time can be wasted in the intricacies of minor roads and it is very easy to get lost. It is preferable to continue to (46km) Ponte Leccia. Take the first road left just before reaching the Golo and the Genoese bridge, the D 71, which runs along the southern slopes of the Serra Debbione, a twisting lonely road with scarcely a building alongside but with fine views west to the red pinnacles of Popolasca and south-west to the Rotondo range of mountains.

14.5km from Ponte Leccia is **Morosaglia** (Merusaglia, 800m, 883 inhab.), birthplace of Corsica's most illustrious patriot and statesman, Pasquale or Pascal Paoli, born on 6 April 1725. He was the youngest son of Hyacinthe Paoli (1690–1768; sounding less of a spring flower with his name in its original form of Giacinto), who had been a minister of King Théodore I, the first and last king of Corsica. Theodor von Neuhof had landed at Aléria on 12 March 1736, was crowned constitutional monarch in April and by November of the same year was on his way out of his kingdom by boat from Solenzara. The Genoese appealed to the French to help them control the still-rebellious Corsicans. This suited the French who defeated the rebels and stayed in Corsica until 1741. Many Corsican patriots left the island, including Giacinto Paoli who took his youngest son with him to Naples. Pasquale Paoli's return as an adult to Corsica as General of the Nation and his two periods of exile in England belong to another part of this book (see Historical Introduction).

The solid, modest house where Paoli was born is beyond the main village street, to the left of the road. It is now converted in part into a *museum* (open 9.00–12.00 and 15.00–18.00 every day). The ground floor is a chapel with a family vault where Paoli's remains were interred when they were brought in 1889 from St Pancras old cemetery, London, where he had been buried in 1807. (There is a bust of Paoli in Westminster Abbey but his body never lay there.) The first floor, including the room where he was born, displays proclamations, the resolutions of the Corsican Parliament of his time, and engravings of the many portraits made of him by Reynolds, Gérard, Lawrence and others.

Paoli was baptised in the church of *Santa Reparata*, a 5-minute walk up and above the main street of the village. Ask the way to it because the track winds up between the town's back gardens. This single-nave church of Romanesque origin, with many later modifications, is set, as so often in Corsica, on a spur of rock overlooking the village. The sculpted pair of interlaced and tail-consuming serpents probably precede by three to four centuries the date of 1550 incised above the west door, having been saved from an earlier building. The Stations of the Cross are by an unknown late 18C local painter, *naïf* in style like those at Carcheto. The man who stands on a ladder to hand down the body of Christ from the Cross holds one end of the shroud in his left hand but, his right hand supporting Christ's arm, he holds the other end of the shroud between his teeth so that the body shall remain wrapped in decency before the eyes of the women. The Cross is held upright by two wooden stakes, the tops burred over when they were hammered into the ground, so familiar to the painter that he included this everyday sight as a matter of course.

The school at Morosaglia, the *Pascal Paoli School*, cannot be missed because its name is painted boldly on the walls. It was the former Rostino Monastery, a meeting place in the first half of the 18C of a *consulta* dedicated to the liberation of Corsica from Genoese domination. Clemente Paoli, older brother of Pasquale and much overshadowed by his brother, was a tough and effective Corsican resistance fighter against all foreign assailants who, having retired from politics, died in the Couvent de Rostino in 1793.

At 4km from Morosaglia the Col de Prato (985m) is the highest point on the D 71 as it crosses the mountain spine of the Castagniccia. Just east and beyond the Col there is, in clear weather, an extensive panorama of the Castagniccia and over the coastal plain to the Tyrrhenian Sea. Between the Col and Piedicroce there are four left turnings to the east leading to the villages of the Fium'Altu valley and to the scattered mountain villages towards the valley of the Golo. These are better visited from Piedicroce and are described below.

At 18km beyond the Col de Prato is *Campana* (A Campana, 746m, 36 inhab.). The church of *St André* is reached on foot; ask for the key in the village. It contains an Adoration des Bergers attributed to Zurbarán (1598–1664) or to one of his pupils, Sarabia.

Campana sits on the side of *Monte San Petrone* (1767m). To climb the mountain follow the road right to Campodonico and take the path leading to the right from the hamlet (about 6 hours there and back). From the summit there is a panoramic view of the chestnut forests, the Eastern Plain up to Cap Corse in the north and, to the west, the central mountain chain. 3km from Campana are the ruins of the *Orezza monastery*.

Of Franciscan foundation, the monastery became a centre of Corsican patriotism and resistance to foreigners, principally the Genoese but later the French as well. During the years of the first major Corsican insurrection, 1730–34, the mountain rebels came down to the plains and attacked the centres of Genoese government in the Eastern Plain.

Consultes (*consulta* in Corsican) were established to decide the course that the rebellion should take. Initially the assemblies had their seat in Corte but in March 1730 an assembly held at the St François monastery at Orezza gave ecclesiastical blessing to the rising against Genoa. In 1735 the *consulte* at Orezza proclaimed Corsica independent but the following half century saw the seven month wonder of King Théodore, interventions by the French, British and Sardinians and the Generalship of Pasquale Paoli from 1755–69, when he retired to England. Paoli returned to Corsica on 17 July 1790 and at the Orezza Assembly in September of that year he was elected Commander-in-Chief of the Corsican National Guards and later Président du Conseil Général du Département de la Corse. So Orezza played a large part in Corsican history but today there are only ruins of the monastery invaded by brambles, and sometimes by cows who wander off the road. The building was destroyed by Corsica's last invaders, the Germans, who blew it up during their retreat in 1943.

1km to the south on the D 71 is *Piedicroce* (Pedicroce, literally 'at the foot of the Cross', 636m, 91 inhab.). A large village in the centre of the Castagniccia, it is built on a 150m-high terrace on the south-eastern slopes of Monte San Petrone, overlooking the natural amphitheatre of the Orezza, which gives its name to Corsica's most famous mineral water and is the place where the Fium'Altu rises. There is an extensive view from the terrace of the big church of SS Peter and Paul, 1691 with a baroque façade of 1761 and a square tower. It has the oldest *organ in Corsica, built at the beginning of the 17C and recently restored to magnificent appearance and tone. A 16C painting on wood depicts the Virgin and Child flanked by two angel musicians.

There are two roads out of Piedicroce. The D 506 runs due north until it reaches the valley of the Fium'Altu where it turns due east to follow the valley towards the coast, joining the N 198 at (23.5km) Folelli. The first turn off to the right from the D 506 as one leaves Piedicroce leads to the Orezza source. There is a neglected courtyard in front of a building which looks as if it had been designed as a small château or manor house, many of its windows now broken. In the centre of the courtyard, its ornamental fountain now gone, is the spring water bubbling out of the iron-reddened ground. There is a sad air of general dilapidation, yet one finds bottled Orezza water in every café and restaurant in the island. A cascade of broken glass glitters down into the Fium'Altu ravine like greenish snow; bottles which did not survive recycling.

The D 71 leaves Piedicroce to the east and in under 2km goes through the hamlet of Pie d'Orezza (Ped'Orezza, 637m, 39 inhab.). Way up on the mountainside, hanging over it, is Campodonico. 3.5km Carcheto-Brustico (Carchetu Brusticu, 630m, 19 inhab.) where the baroque parish church of Ste Marguerite, its façade intricately decorated, contains two striking, although sharply contrasting, works of art. The delicately sculpted alabaster statuette of the Virgin and Child, with crown and sceptre, is probably 18C Italian. The Stations of the Cross, dated 1 June 1790, are the work of some local painter who, as at Morosaglia and in other Corsican churches, depicted local costume, tools and habits. In the Crucifixion a curly-haired chubby child holds out the basket of nails and a hammer to one of the two men nailing Christ to the cross and, as the body is placed in the tomb, the painter included four women mourners or voceratrices wearing 18C Corsican clothes. Ivy-covered remains of a Carcheto house that once belonged to a notorious bandit called François-Marie Castelli, one of whose victims lay dying in the street for 18 hours on 6 May 1912 with nobody daring to go to her aid.

After a further 3km the D 71 crosses from the higher valley of the Fium'Altu to the valley of the Alesani by the Bocca di Arcarota (819m). There is a broad view of the surrounding chestnut-covered countryside and over to the sea in the east and the mountains to the west. 11km, Valle d'Alesani (E Valle d'Alisgiani, 620m, 192 inhab.), a collection of hamlets in the chestnut forests on the left bank of the Alesani River.

The history of the valley and people of the Alesani is a microcosm of the history of Corsica: of invasion and resistance. Repelled or endured were Greeks, Romans, Vandals, Ligurians, Byzantines, North African and Turkish pirates and at various times the soldiers of Aragon, Pisa, Genoa, France, Italy and Germany. At the Franciscan monastery of Alesani, a centre of resistance against the Genoese, a German was crowned King of Corsica on 15 April 1736. Theodor von Neuhof (1694–1756), an adventurer with experience of both European courts and debtors' prisons met Corsican exiles in Italy and then convinced some 'Greek and Jewish merchants in Tunis whom he had somehow inspired with confidence in its success' (Carrington: 'Granite Island') to finance his attempt. He landed on 12 March 1736 at Aléria, flamboyantly dressed, equipped with money, guns, ammunition and a persuasive tongue. Monastery bells rang, a crowd sang, a laurel wreath was placed on the head of Théodore I who swore loyalty to the constitution. By November he was out of funds and left for Italy from

Solenzara. His luck never changed and on the wall of the Blitz-ruined church of St Anne's Soho, London, is a tablet which Horace Walpole had placed there (just above one to Hazlitt): 'near this place is interred The King of Corsica who died in this parish December 11 1756 immediately after leaving the King's Bench Prison by the benefit of the act of insolvency in consequence of which he registered his Kingdom of Corsica for the use of his creditors, The grave great teacher to a level brings heroes and beggars, galley-slaves and Kings but Theodore his moral learnéd ere dead. Fate poured its lessons on his living head, bestow'd a kingdom and denied him bread'.

The *monastery of Alesani* (founded 1236) is 5km along the D 17 leading out of the village of Valle d'Alesani to the right. The church (1716) contains a Virgin and Child painted on wood, c 1450, known as *La Vierge à la Cerise* because the Virgin holds a cherry to the Infant's mouth. It is ascribed to the Sienese artist Sano di Pietro (1406–81).

At (12km) *Sant'Andrea di Cotone* (408m, 182 inhab.) the road leaves the valley of the Alesani and runs along the flank of the mountains overlooking the Eastern Plain.

A minor road, the D 517, goes south and crosses the Alesani Dam but there is no right of way for motor traffic. I have walked it without being challenged and there is a fine view over the Barrage de l'Alesani and to the sea.

4km from Sant'Andrea di Cotone the D 71 reaches **Cervione** (326m, 1334 inhab.). From the village square, which has a low wall on the east side, there is a splendid view over the Eastern Plain and the sea. Up and above the village on the slopes of Monte Castello (1109m) and all around are chestnut groves, terraces of olive trees, and vines. The former cathedral church of *Ste Marie and St Erasme* (c 1580) was built at the instigation of Alexandre Sauli, Bishop of Aléria, who made Cervione the seat of his diocese. Sauli was canonised in 1904 and wall paintings on either side of the entrance depict his progress to Cervione on a white horse and his magisterial expulsion, by the force of faith, of the Barbary pirates. Choir stalls and frescoes. The *Bishop's Palace* opposite was Neuhof's first residence as king-designate of Corsica on his way to coronation at the Alesani monastery, and is now a *museum* concentrating on local archaeology and the traditional Corsican way of life in the mountains. It displays a large collection of locks and keys, including that said to belong to the lock-up 'cantarno' built by Paoli in 1760, pans for roasting chestnuts, blacksmith's tools, knives etc. (Open 10.00–12.00 and 14.30–18.00 daily, closed Sun and public holidays.) The names of streets, squares, public buildings and wall plaques commemorating notable citizens are inscribed in Corsican.

The *statue of La Madonna* is 1½ hours' walk there and back by a rough path leading out of Cervione to the west-south-west (the best way to find the path is to ask in the village). This 16C white marble statue of the Virgin was found by sailors on the shore at Prunete after a Genoese ship bound for Cordoba with Florentine works of art was wrecked. The life-size statue stands in the *Chapelle de la Madonna di a Scupiccia* (Our Lady of the heather) to which there is a pilgrimage on 15 August when Mass is celebrated at dawn. There is a fine view over the Eastern Plain to the Tuscan islands.

To visit the *Chapelle Santa Cristina* leave Cervione to the north by the D 71 and drive to the village of *Valle di Campoloro* (500m). The key to the chapel is at the Mairie: ask there for directions to the narrow track to the chapel, about 30 minutes' walk there and back (some of the distance can be covered, with care, by car). The walls of the small twin-apsed chapel (15C) are covered with frescoes dated 1473, indifferently restored at some time. Christ in Majesty is depicted in each apse. On the north wall a dark-complexioned monk who may be the *donateur* of the frescoes or the artist who painted them. Despite retouching and damp and neglect during the centuries the frescoes are remarkable for their lively colours and the characterisation in the faces. From Valle di Campoloro it is 5.5km on the D 71 to the N 198, the main road along the east coast.

From Valle di Campoloro north the D 33 is a corniche overlooking the Eastern Plain. 4km from the Valle is *San-Nicolao* (Santu Niculaiu, 250m, 1061 inhab.), a remote village set among olive groves, chestnut woods and orchards on the east rim of the Castagniccia overlooking the Eastern Plain from its mountainside balcony. The 17C baroque church with imposing bell tower stands on the site of an older Romanesque church.

From San-Nicolao the D 34 turns east towards the N 198 and Moriani Plage (5km). The D 330 winds north 10.5km to *Talasani*, birthplace of Luigi Giafferi (1680–1745), a great fighter for Corsican freedom who beat the Genoese at the battle of Furiani in 1729.—10km further is *Folelli*, at the junction of the D 330 and the N 198, just north of the Fium'Altu.

The heart of the Castagniccia: along the D 515

The D 515 wends its tortuous and picturesque way north starting from the Col San Cristofano, 7km north of Piedicroce on the D 71. In 3km you reach *Croce* (A Croce, 800m, 78 inhab.) where there is a private *museum* devoted to the former way of life in the Castagniccia (open on Saturday and Sunday afternoons). The founder-proprietor gives a graphic explanation of how people lived. The ground floor was reserved for domestic animals and at night the ladder was pulled up to the first floor where the family lived. In the museum are sieves for removing the outer skin of the chestnuts which were then baked and sieved again until the second skin came away, after which they were taken to the miller who retained 20 per cent of the flour as payment.

Because chestnuts are particularly rich in vitamins it was possible to live for long periods through hard winters or during troubled times almost exclusively on bread made from chestnut flour to which, as it is sweetish, salt was added. Baskets were carried to hold the chestnuts and three-pronged long forks to pull them off the branches. Preparation, peeling, baking and milling took place during November or the beginning of December, according to the weather and state of the crop. Now people eat wheaten bread and the falling off in demand for chestnuts has meant the neglect of the trees: one sees as many dead chestnut trees as one saw dead elms in Britain during the Dutch Elm scourge. Chestnut cultivation and industry began to fall off in the 1920s and 1930s and was not much revived during the Second World War despite severe food shortages. Chestnuts now feed the half-wild pigs and the wood is still used, though less than in the past, to make articles of furniture from cradles to coffins. It would appear from the study of fossils that the sweet chestnut, roughly the same tree as today, was growing in Corsica some 25 million years ago.

5km from Croce, *La Porta* (A Porta, 520m, 248 inhab.) has had its share of turbulence and battles against Romans, Vandals, Arabs and Genoese. The church of *St-Jean-Baptiste* planned by a Milanese architect and built in 1648–80. The façade, painted in ocre and white, is of 1707, with later additions. The organ, built in the Italian style in 1780 by a monk at Rogliano in Cap Corse, was placed in the organ loft in 1800, restored in 1965, and concerts are now held there in summer. The church contains a poly-chromatic ceiling and pulpit, grey *trompe l'oeil* decoration (1886), a 17C

Christ painted on wood and an 18C painting of the Beheading of St John the Baptist. The *campanile* built in 1720 is considered the finest baroque bell tower in the whole of Corsica.

La Porta is the birthplace of two brothers who are among France's most famous soldiers: Horace (1772–1851) and Tiburce Sebastiani (1786–1871). Horace served with distinction during the Spanish and Russian campaigns and went on to become Deputé for Corsica and first Navy Minister and then Foreign Minister under Louis-Philippe; he was subsequently French ambassador to London 1835–40. Very handsome, he was nicknamed '*le Cupidon de l'Empire*'. This First Empire cupid, Adonis rather, more than just a pretty face, became a Marshal of France. Tiburce reached the rank of general during Napoleon's campaigns. Born before the Revolution, he lived to see the Franco-Prussian war. He too was Deputé for Corsica.

The oil press or *franghju* at La Porta has been recently restored after many years of idleness and brought back into service in the Government's attempt to stimulate a revival in olive production.

8km north of La Porta is the *Col de Sant'Antone* (687m). It was in the monastery here, now in ruins, that Pasquale Paoli was elected General of the Nation (Capu Generale) on 13 July 1755 by the Casabianca Assembly. Follow the D 51 to the left from the Col de Sant'Antone, reaching in 9km *Campile* (66m, 196 inhab.). Here was forged the long thin knife which gave its Italian name to the world. The *vendetta* (from Latin *vindicta*, vengeance) has a blade decorated with scrolls and flourishes and the Italian words '*Che la mia ferita sia mortale*' or in Corsican '*Chi a mio'terita sia murtale*' ('May my wound prove fatal'). The use of *vendetta* in the sense of a family feud, usually hereditary, has been extended to mean any kind of relentless and 'vindictive' campaign between one group and another.

It is 2km to the hamlet of *Canaghia* which used to be known until the beginning of the present century for a particular kind of pottery rendered very heat-resistant by mixing asbestos in with the clay. The potters were women who moulded their pots by hand without a wheel. From Canaghia it is 5km north-east to the hamlet of Barchetta and on the N 193 by the River Golo, 28.5km to Bastia and 17.5km to Ponte Leccia.

13 Le Nebbio and Saint-Florent

The **Nebbio** (Nebbiu) is a clearly-defined geographical area, easily reached from Bastia in the east and from Saint-Florent in the west.

It is a fertile region, partly plain, partly hills and valleys, irrigated by the River Aliso (rising at 1508m on Monte Grimaseto, 20km long) and its tributaries which run into the Golfe de Saint Florent on the northern limits of the Nebbio. It is framed to the south and east by the mountainous ridges that run from the Col de Teghime to the Col di Tenda, and to the west by the Tenda massif (the watershed of the River Aliso which runs into the Golfe de Saint Florent and the River Ostriconi which flows west to reach the sea at the south limit of the Désert des Agriates).

Leave Bastia by the D 81 due north from the Palais de Justice towards the Col de Teghime (10km) and Saint-Florent (23km).

10km *Col de Teghime* (548m) where there is a monument to those who fought and those who died in the battles for Liberation 1–2 October 1943. In clear weather fine views to the Étang de Biguglia, the Eastern Plain and

Patrimonio, St Martin overlooking the vineyards

over the Tyrrhenian Sea to the Isles of Elba and Capraja and to the west
the Nebbio, Golfe de Saint-Florent and the Désert des Agriates. To the left
the D 38 runs from the Col to the village of Oletta (8.5km).

7km along the D 81 *Patrimonio* (Patrimoniu, 100m, 546 inhab.), which
gives its name to the first wine in Corsica to be designated *appelation
controlée*. Set on a hillock, apart from the village and surrounded by
vineyards the church of St Martin (16C, restored and belltower added early
19C), its warm brown stone and fine proportions most imposing from a
distance. Interior has a painted ceiling and finely worked marble altar. In
a garden near the church the statue-menhir U Nativu (900–800 BC), of
limestone with a T engraved on the sternum and the lower ribs indicated.
It was found in 1964 during excavation for vine-planting in the nearby
commune of Barbaggio. 1km further the Bocca di San Bernardino (76km)
where the D 80 goes north and to the right up the west coast of Cap Corse
and the D 81 continues south-west to (23km) Saint-Florent.

A. Saint-Florent

Saint-Florent (San Fiurenzu, 1350 inhab.) is a popular holiday resort with
many hotels and restaurants situated both along the harbour and around
the Place des Portes, the principal square of the old town. The harbour was
dredged and a *port de plaisance* created in 1971. The citadel (not open to
the public), built in 1439, is a fine example of Genoese military architecture
and was the residence of the Governors of the Nebbio.

Saint-Florent

The Roman town was 1km inland from the present port, where the Cathedral of the Nebbio now stands. When the Genoese built their citadel on the shore of the Gulf a new town grew up around it and the site chosen by the Romans was abandoned. Until the 18C Saint-Florent was the seat of the Bishop of Nebbio and of the Genoese governor of the province. Built on the marshy estuary of the Aliso, malaria was a constant menace. The strategic importance of Saint-Florent was fought over by Corsicans, Genoese and French during the war of 1553–69 and again during the struggles for independence of 1729–69. Between the mosquito and human assailants Saint-Florent fell into decay and even the attempts to revive the port during the Second Empire did not help much because the harbour silted up, but work during the past 30 years has kept it clear.

It was from Saint-Florent on 14 October 1795 that Paoli boarded an English frigate for Livorno and thence to London, never to return. A large crowd of supporters came to see him off and Sir Gilbert Elliot ordained that Paoli, as Governor of Corsica, should receive full military honours on his departure. However, the end of Elliot's Corsican career was also imminent; only 11 months later he followed Paoli to England. On 15 June 1794 a decision had been taken at Corte to put the island under the protection of the English King George III and Sir Gilbert Elliot was named Viceroy of Corsica over Paoli. But in November 1796 Bonaparte's Army of Italy took the island in the name of the French republic and Corsica has remained French ever since.

The most exciting aspect of Saint-Florent is the Cathedral of the Nebbio, approached by an unpromising narrow road leading out of the main part of the village for 1km and then, suddenly, to the left of the road on a slight rise, is the church of **Santa Maria Assunta**, the Cathedral of the Nebbio, starkly beautiful on its sward of rough grass, with a farmyard to one side and vineyards stretching below, its honey-coloured walls expertly restored in the 1980s.

Cathedral of the Nebbio

The Cathedral of Santa Maria Assunta was built by the Pisans in the first quarter of the 12C as was La Canonica, the former cathedral of the diocese of Mariana close to Bastia (see Rte 8), which it resembles. These two cathedrals are outstanding examples of Romanesque architecture in Corsica. Built of fine-grained pale limestone, the Nebbio cathedral's west front is elegant and dignified with semi-circular blind arcades arranged in two tiers, five rising from ground level and the three top ones reaching almost to the pitch of the roof, leaving room in the small triangle at the top for a slender Greek cross. The lintel and pillars are decorated at intervals in relief resembling shells engraved with concentric lines. The decorated capitals of the graceful pilasters show, on the left, a four-legged creature in high relief and, on the right, a pair of intertwined snakes. The beast is lion-like with mane and long tail and yet, the closer one looks, it becomes apparent that the animal is more fantastic than leonine. The cathedral had at one time a campanile, demolished in the 19C.

Enter the church by the door in the south wall. (The key may be borrowed from the Syndicat d'Initiative on the first floor of the Centre Administratif on the Bastia road, open 10.00–12.00 and 15.00–18.00 on weekdays. Your passport or identity card and a small sum of money are held until the key is returned.) Inside, a nave and two aisles divided by pillars whose capitals are decorated with shells, foliage, fabulous animals and serpents, a ram, and abstract designs. In the vaulted apse is a statue of the Virgin and Child in white marble (given by Jean-Jérôme Doria in 1691), placed above the gilded wooden statue of St Flor, a Roman soldier martyred for his Christian faith in the 3C. To the right of the entrance door is a glass case in which are exhibited the mummified remains of St Flor taken from the Roman catacombs and sent to the Bishop of the Nebbio by Pope Clement XIV in 1771. In size and height the body would seem to be that of a youth of 14–18 years old, possibly of North African origin, dressed in the 18C conception of a Roman soldier's outfit: a highly unsuitable kind of battle-dress made mostly of fine chain mail. There is something most touching about this small figure, dressed as it were by the theatre wardrobe.

In the nave (left) is the tomb of General Antoine Gentili (1745–98) who, when young, had been a supporter of Paoli in the fight for Corsican independence, but deserted him and became his rival when Paoli called on England for help. Bonaparte made him General commanding a division and he took part in the liberation of Corsica from the British in 1796. One of the most notable bishops of the Nebbio was Monsignor Giustiniani, whose description of Corsica in 1531 is a valuable source-book. He was a Hebraic scholar at the Collège de France in the reign of François I.

B. Nebbio villages

A circular tour of the Nebbio can be made from Saint-Florent by taking the D 81 road across the Aliso in the direction of Calvi. For 4km this road passes along the southern edge of the Désert des Agriates (see Rte 4) until the turning to the left and south on to the D 62, a narrow and winding road through pastures giving way to olive groves. At 10km along the D 62, *San Pietro di Tenda* (Santu Petru di Tenda, 360m, 291 inhab.). The houses of this village are stretched out along the flank of the Tenda ridge above the Aliso valley. Two separate baroque churches (one is in fact a chapel), are joined in a single façade by a square peach-coloured campanile built between the two, and an archway. The church of *St Jean* (open to visitors) has the chapel of the *confrèrie St-Croix* next door to it. The interior walls of the church are painted in *trompe l'oeil* marble and there is a 17C Descent from the Cross of which an old man said that he remembered it being taken down 50–70 years ago to be 'revivified'. Despite that it is still very dark and needs expert cleaning. A stage has been built in front of the altar: 'some idea of some Pope to bring the Mass to the people', commented the same informant (presumably referring to Pope Paul VI who presided over the Vatican II reforms). The marble altar-rail has been amputated at each end to make way for this revised concept of the Holy Table and each side has been panelled in plywood. The result is an aesthetic disaster.

The road from San Pietro to (7.5km) *Pieve* (450m, 76 inhab.) is a typical mountain route. In front of the church, which has been largely cement-rendered and has a green and buff campanile built in drystone style, are two menhirs (2nd millennium BC). Wandering around this scattered village I saw in the garden of a small house what appeared to be a small menhir, placed there like a garden gnome. Close-to it looked original or like a very good fake. My curiosity was unsatisfied, nobody was at home.

2.5km from Pieve is *Rapale* (400m, 102 inhab.). The striking church has a square tower and pyramidal roof with, to the right of the main door, a plaque '*A la memoire de Lapina Robert tué par les Italiens 26 août 1943*'. From the war memorial one learns that in 1914–18 eleven villagers were killed and in 1939–45 twelve soldiers and two civilians—another example of Corsica's sacrifice in France's wars.

5km from Rapale after forking right onto the D 162, the church of **San Michele de Murato** (San Michele di Muratu) stands at a T-junction about 1km from the village of *Murato* (Muratu, 497m, 565 inhab.). Set on a grassy

San Michele de Murato

level by itself, theatrical in its splendid isolation and somewhat elevated from the surrounding countryside, San Michele is one of the outstanding churches of Corsica. It is 12C Pisan Romanesque consisting of a single nave with the proportions of the façade spoiled to some extent by the addition of a belltower in the late 19C. There are striking figures, human, quadruped, two intertwined snakes and birds, and Eve tempted by the serpent, in the blind arcading and windows.

The most arresting aspect of this church is the combination of colours in the stone of which it is built. Madame Geneviève Moracchini-Mazel says in 'Corse Romane' that '...the master masons used for this church a dark green stone from the bed of the nearby Bevinco River, a kind of serpentine marble with a close, compact grain, easy to work and offering great possibilities to sculptors'. San Michele exhibits the most imaginative poly-chromatic use of stone in walls where the predominant green-and-white blocks of serpentine are mixed with pink and yellow stone.

San Michele is less arresting inside but there are remains of a 15C fresco of the Annunciation on the arch of the apse. The whereabouts of the key to the church has varied during the years I have gone there but its safe keeping remains in spirit at least with the curé of Murato who, like so many priests in Corsica, the rest of France and the UK, ministers to many parishes. I suggest enquiring at the house nearest to the church where the key was obtainable last time I was there.

5km from Murato is the *Bocca di San Stefano* on the D 82. From this 349m-high pass there is a view left over the valley of the Aliso, the Golfe de Saint-Florent and the Désert des Agriates. Take the D 82 north towards Oletta. At under 2km the village of *Olmeta di Tuda* (300m, 247 inhab.) with many tall elm trees and a fine 17C Sacrifice of Abraham. A château was built here by Marshal Horace Sebastiani (1772–1851), elder brother of Tiburce Sebastiani (1786–1871), both of whom were born at La Porta (see Rte 12).

3km further on, *Oletta* (250m, 879 inhab.), whose houses are spread out over the hillside overlooking the valley of the Guadello which has the richest land in the Nebbio and produces fine ewes' milk cheese. The 18C church of *St André* is on the site of an older church of which a relic, a very early and primitive bas relief of the Creation, is incorporated in the façade of the present church. There is a triptych painted on wood (1534) of the Virgin giving the breast to the child Jesus flanked by Saints Reparata and André.

From Oletta the D 38 runs north to the Col de Teghime (541m), a distance of 8.5km, and meets the Bastia–Saint-Florent D 81 road. Alternatively, returning south by the D 82 to Bocca di San Stefano, continue along the D 82 as it turns left and east towards the N 193 and the Eastern Plain. This road follows the course of the Bevinco River through the gorge called the Défilé de Lancone. A twisting, truly mountain route with views over precipices to the course of the Bevinco. When the canyon through which the road passes opens out there are broad views of the lower valley and estuary of the Bevinco, the Biguglia lagoon and the sea. At 22km from Saint-Florent the D 82 joins the N 193 at *Casatora*, a hamlet of the commune of Biguglia.

Turn left and north on the N 193 to reach Bastia.

III   CENTRAL CORSICA

14 Corte

Corte (Corti, 486m, 5693 inhab.) is sous-préfecture of Haute-Corse.

Set geographically only a little to the north of the very centre of Corsica, Corte is the only major town that is not a sea port (although not on the coast itself Sartène has its port in Propriano). The town stands at the confluence of the rivers Restonica (rises Lac de Melo, 1711m, flows 15km east to join the Tavignano) and Tavignano (rises Lac de Nino, 1743m, and flows east 80km, taking in the waters of the Vecchio, Corsigliese and Tagnone and reaching the sea at Aléria).

Historically as well as geographically Corte is at the heart of Corsica and the spirit of independence. From the earliest times there was always a settlement here and by the 11C Corte was a fortress town. It was conquered by the Genoese in the 13C, later taken by the Moors, who called it Mascara, and then occupied in the name of the King of Aragon by Vincentello d'Istria after he had defeated the Genoese at Morosaglia. He had the citadel built between 1419 and 1425 but in 1434 he was caught by the Genoese and literally lost his head to them. The Bank of St George took over the town in 1459; the Corsican Sampiero took it for France in 1553; it was retaken by the Genoese and then by the Corsicans themselves who lost it again in 1564. Corte thus see-sawed back and forth until in November 1755 Pasquale Paoli, the Corsican leader, had Corte named the capital of Corsica. The new constitution of Corsica, way ahead of its time, was voted by the new government convened at Corte, where Paoli also founded a university. Paoli's requests for French recognition and protection of Corsica were rejected, and when his army was defeated by the French at Ponte Nuovo, France proclaimed the island to be French on 15 August 1769, the very day on which Napoleon Bonaparte was born. Constitution, university and an independent Corsica were no more.

Corte has never been capital of Corsica again but in 1981 it recovered its status of a university town. After lengthy discussion it was decided that the new Università di Corsica (2400 students, 1989–90) should direct its studies towards defining Corsica's role in the modern world and assisting it to play an active part. Among its main objectives are the study of the Corsican language and literature and establishing and obtaining recognition of the island's culture. Arts, science, law and economics are also read here.

The older part of the town is built on a hill that rises abruptly from the river plain and on top of the hill is a cliff-sided gigantic rock on which stands the citadel. It is a town to be explored on foot (car-parks are clearly marked and cars can also be left towards the top end of the main street, the Cours Paoli, near the Post Office).

Approaching Corte along the N 193 from Bastia you enter the town by the Cours Paoli. On the left is the wide tree-lined Place du Duc de Padoue (the duke was Napoleon's General Arrighi de Casanova; 1778–1853), which then becomes the Avenue De Gaulle, a cul de sac with trees and flowers in the middle. From the entrance to the Place one can look down the Cours Paoli, over much of newer Corte to the left and up to the old town set on the rock above the Place Paoli where the Cours ends. There is not much in the newer town of architectural interest but the Cours is a pleasant, unpretentious street of shops selling clothes, fruit, shotguns, books, spectacles, local produce, etc. The Place Paoli is of modest proportions and on market days it is packed with stalls, overlooked by the grave eyes of Paoli,

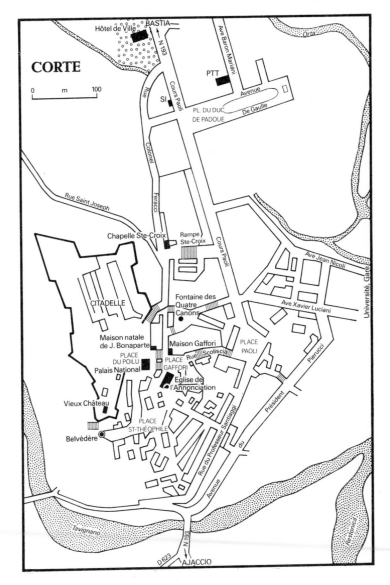

raised in bronze by public subscription in 1854, and surrounded by modest cafés and shops. In fact, there is nothing of the tourist trap about Corte.

From behind the statue of the 'Father of the Nation' the Rue Scoliscia leads sharply up over cobbles, aided now and then by flights of shallow steps, to the Place Gaffori, the Ville Haute and the Citadel. Here is a bronze statue (1901) in memory of General Gian'Pietro Gaffori (1704–53).

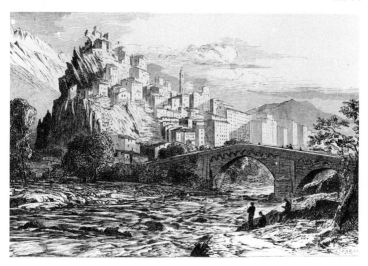

Corte, by Edward Lear

This Corte doctor of medicine was named head of state when a constitution was adopted in October 1752, to take effect when the French troops left Corsica. In 1750 the Gaffori mansion, behind the statue, was besieged by the Genoese. The general was away but his wife Faustina persuaded those who talked of surrender to hold out by brandishing a lighted torch over an open barrel of gunpowder. Gaffori arrived and the siege was lifted. This scene is depicted in bas-relief on the pedestal of the statue of Gaffori who was assassinated on 3 October 1753 in an ambush laid by members of a rival Corsican family and Gaffori's own brother, in the pay of Genoa.

The Gaffori house is still marked by the bullets fired during the struggle for independence. Facing it on the Square is the *Eglise de l'Annonciation*, built in 1450 but much altered in the 17C, including the façade. Of most interest inside are a finely carved pulpit and early 18C vestry furniture from the (no-longer extant) Franciscan monastery at Corte. A small marble statue of the Virgin is dated 1613.

The *Palais National* (Palazzu Nazionale), reached by a stairway going up through an archway from the Place Gaffori, was from 1755–69 the seat of the Corsican independent government. It has been restored and now houses, most fittingly, *le centre de recherches corses de l'université*.

The *Citadel* was built by Vincetello d'Istria, the King of Aragon's viceroy, in 1420 and the barracks added in the time of Louis XV, and 1962–83 units of the Foreign Legion were stationed there. Opposite the gateway to the citadel is No. 1 Place du Poilu, the ancestral house of the Arrighi de Casanova family, in which Napoleon's father Carlo lived in 1768 and where in the same year Napoleon's brother Joseph (1768–1844), later King of Spain (1808–13), was born.

Follow the ramp along the Citadel wall to the *Belvédère* from which one has the most dramatic impression of the fortress set on top of its rock. Below, the Tavignano and the Restonica rivers emerge from their respective gorges to join, and in the distance rise the mountain peaks of the great central ranges. Look at the oldest (15C) part of the fortress on the edge of the precipice that falls a sheer 100m to the Tavignano below: it was from here that Corsican prisoners, including members of the Gaffori family, managed to escape. One can still get down to the Tavignano, though somewhat more easily and without fear of pursuit, by a stairway and a steep path that leads to a footbridge over the river at a popular bathing spot.

A. Excursions from Corte: Gorges du Tavignano (on foot)

The Tavignano expedition is for walkers only, experienced and well-equipped, with large-scale maps, ample food and a good idea of how much and what they want to do. The route starts in the centre of town. Climb up the steps of the Rampe Sainte Croix leading off the Cours Paoli, follow the Rue Saint Joseph which begins opposite the Chapelle Sainte Croix (cars can be left on an open space at the end of this street), and it is here that the track begins, way-marked in yellow and following the left bank west. Thirty minutes' walk reaches the beginning of the gorge and in 2½ hours the footbridge to the path leading to the Lac de Nino (see Rte 15). The path to the right leads to the Bocca à l'Arinella and winds up the great left-hand wall of the gorge. Four hours from Corte is la Fontaine d'Argent whose silver water gushes out of the rock beside a gigantic Corsican pine. From here on the path goes through the Corsican pine and beech Forêt de Melo until it comes out on the stony grazing grounds of a plateau. In 6–7 hours from Corte the Bocca de l'Arinella (1592m) is reached, on the ridge dividing the valleys of the Tavignano and the Golo (see Rte 15). Views over the Niolo and the two valleys and to Rotondo and the outliers of the massif. From here the choice is between returning to Corte or carrying on along downward paths to Calacuccia (about 2 hours) or to the Calacuccia dam (about 1½ hours). For those who do not want to undertake the whole journey all sections of it are picturesque and rewarding but in my opinion the starting point of Corte is preferable to Calacuccia, and to have the sun behind you as you walk I suggest a very early morning start from Corte.

B. Excursions from Corte: Gorges de la Restonica (on foot)

The Restonica Gorge and the Melo and Capitello Lakes offer an equally pleasant but less arduous choice of walks. Leave Corte by the Ajaccio road, crossing the bridge over the Tavignano and take the D 623 to the right, where there is the Parc Régional Information Centre and the folkcraft Casa di l'Artigiani. A motor road goes up the valley for 15km but can be rough at the upper end, in early spring or after heavy rain. The river runs over tumbled rocks and the valley sides are dotted with chestnut trees that soon give way to maritime pines of a kind peculiar to Corsica. The top edges of the ravine are often jagged and spiky, with pines between the rocky turrets. Beyond the Tragone bridge the valley narrows and closes in to form a true gorge and the road clings closer to the river which can be reached at certain points where pools, ideal for bathing, have formed. The road, by this time a fairly bumpy track, dusty too when it is dry, comes to an end at the Bergeries de Grotelle (1375m) a traditional halt for shepherds taking their flocks up to higher pastures and the Lac de Melo.

For those who do not want to come as far as this there are two footpaths that can be explored in part or in their entire length. The first, to the right 500m before reaching the Tragone bridge, goes to the Tavignano valley and the footpath leading back to Corte. Allow a good 2 hours up to the Col de Cappellaccia (1600m) and an hour down the path which forks right and to the north-east to reach the Tavignano.

From the Bergeries de Grotelle there is a pleasant walk to the Melo and Capitello lakes. From the bergeries, where cars can be left, follow the visible track up to the right which levels out and crosses pastures on the banks of the Restonica. To the right is the long ridge of the Capu a Chiostru (2295m) and to the left, across the pastures of the upper Restonica, is the great massif of the Rotondo. As one draws closer to the great wall of rock that holds the *Lac de Melo* a choice of route presents itself. Either go straight ahead, climbing up through scrub on potholed paths and then clamber up the rocks direct to the top, like climbing to the edge of a giant rock saucepan, or follow the cairns to the left through the alders, cross the river and take the easier way up on the left side of the lake. When there has been rain the smooth rocks on the frontal approach are very slippery. It is three hours there and back.

To get to the Lac de Capitello take the path along the northern shore of Melo at the far end of which the path forks (that to the left goes south to the Bocca a la Soglia (2052m) and joins in 2 hours the GR 20). Follow the right fork from where in 50 minutes, after taking another fork to the south-west, you reach the *Lac de Capitello* (1930m). At 200m higher than Melo, set in a deep bowl (maximum depth 40m) carved out of the granite in the Ice Age, Capitello's waters are very cold even on the sunniest summer day and usually covered with ice for more than half the year. Above the lake tower the east cornices of Capu a i Sorbi. Going due south along the east bank of the lake leads to the GR 20. Allow a good 4 hours there and back for the Bergeries de Grotelle walk.

C.   Excursions from Corte: Monte Rotondo (on foot)

Monte Rotondo (2622m) is a mountaineering expedition presenting only medium difficulties for the experienced walker but it is a round trip of about 10 active hours and it is essential to wear stout boots, carry a change of warm clothing, waterproofs and, it goes without saying, the right maps and a compass. Optional but preferable is to reach the summit at sunrise for the spectacular view of most of Corsica and the north of Sardinia. In order to do this, the previous night, or some of it, must be spent either at the Bergeries de Timozzo or camping in the lee of rocks close to the Lac di l'Oriente (see below).

Leave Corte by the D 623 'Gorges de la Restonica' road (see above) and travel 11.8km, crossing the Pont de Tragone. About 800m beyond the bridge take the path to the left up the course of the Timozzo stream, following the mule track that winds up through trees on the left bank of the ravine in which the stream flows. In just under 2 hours the Bergeries of Timozzo are reached (1520m), a group of typical Corsican drystone huts set in a rock-strewn combe, just off the main track but clearly visible from the approach. From the bergeries the track continues up the course of the Timozzo but if the bergeries are bypassed the route continues through alders and at around 1600m rejoins the Timozzo torrent at a waterfall. At about 90 minutes beyond the bergeries you reach the Triggione spring (1920m) in an alder-covered depression which is a possible camping site. The path continues on the right bank of the stream and, where the going levels out somewhat, crosses to the left bank. In about 40 minutes from Triggione the path reaches the grassy plateau of the *Lac di l'Oriente* (Lavu di l'Oriente, 2061m). Michel Fabrikant in his comprehensive 'Guide des Montagnes Corses' (see Bibliography), in which he details seven Rotondo climbs, comments 'some maintain that this name is a deformation of 'Lac d'Argento' which is not unlikely because there is nothing 'eastern' about the lake.' Silver it certainly is, not deep and with bog on some parts of the shore. The north face of Rotondo is immediately to the south with a col to the right of the summit called the Collet du Rotondo. Camp may be made here in the shelter of the rocks around the lake (see above) in order to make an early start the following morning. If setting off in the dark carry a powerful torch to pick out the infrequent cairns marking the path. Aim almost due south for the cliffs straight ahead. A path to the right climbs to the Col de Rio Secco (75 minutes from the Lac di l'Oriente). A massive block of rock barring the way is scrambled around by the south face and from there a climb of a few dozen metres reaches the summit of *Rotondo* (2622m). Views north to Monte Cinto and around other points of the compass to the sea and Sardinia.

There are two alternatives to returning by the route just described. The first is to carry on along the track until descending due east from Rotondo, passing south of the tiny Lac de Pozzolo (2350m). The track turns north-north-east and shortly afterwards follows the course of a narrow stream. In 3½ hours the Bergeries de Spiscie (1650m, pronounced *spiché*, meaning waterfalls) are reached and in a further 75 minutes the bergeries de Rivisecco (1270m) at the confluence of two streams which form the Rivisecco stream. The track follows the stream closely to its meeting with the Restonica where, turning right and east, the Restonica is eventually crossed by the Pont de Rivisecco leading on to the D 623 to Corte (c 6½ hours from Rotondo).

The second route lies to the south of the summit of Rotondo, past the *Lac du Monte Rotondo* (2321m). (Although this name is easiest for identification, the lake appears on maps, according to date of edition, as either Lac de Bettaniella or, most recently, as Lavu Bellebone.) This is the largest of the Corsican lakes, set in a glacier-gouged basin surrounded by jagged peaks. The path passes east of the lake and in 90 minutes reaches the small Refuge de Pietra Piana (Pétra Piana, 1842m), close to the GR 20 along which it is 10–11 hours south-east to Vizzavona and 10–11 hours north-west to the Col de Vergio.

D. Excursions from Corte: San Giovanni Battista and Santa Mariona

Two notable, although ruined, churches are within walking distance of Corte. For *San Giovanni Battista* leave Corte by the N 200 to Aléria. A little under 2km beyond the railway bridge take the second turning to the right, narrow and rather rough but it can be driven over, and just beyond the railway line (800m) and on the right is a ruined church. Probably 9C and one of the oldest churches in Corsica, the fabric has been extensively pillaged up until and including this century. Slabs of the rock façade were incorporated into buildings in the neighbourhood and the altar steps and benches and the square pillars of the three naves have all vanished. The two buildings, church and baptistry, were set side by side and possibly on the site of a Roman village.

Santa Mariona church is 1km north of Corte, to the left of the N 193, just beyond the cemetery. A Pisan church, it has twin apses at the east end, one of only three such plans in Corsica. Although it now stands in ruins among the olive groves, enough remains to get an idea of its former glory.

15 Le Niolo: from Corte to Porto via Evisa

ROAD (D 84) 86km.—27km Calacuccia—49.5km Station de Vergio—63km Evisa.

The **Niolo** (Niolu) district is a basin of the upper Golo (Golu), the most important river of Corsica (84km long, reaching the east coast 20km south of Bastia).

This plateau 800–1500m high and 21km long by 10km wide, is surrounded by mountains. To the south these range up to 2400m in height (Punta Artica and Monte Tozzu), and to the north and west up to 2700m (Monte Cinto, Punta Minuta and Paglia Orba). To the east lies the jumbled granite of the Scala di Santa Regina (see below).

The most inaccessible region of all Corsica until the building of the D 84 road at the end of the last century, Le Niolo is also the most independent in spirit. Its people always opposed invaders from the lands below, Genoese and French alike: a revolt against the French in 1774 was put down with a campaign of scorched earth, torture and hangings. The inhabitants, some of whom are ruddy-complexioned, blond or sandy-haired and blue-eyed, and above average height for the island, may (as they often choose to believe) be descendants of an earlier race in Corsica, perhaps those who built the megaliths. Physical characteristics have been preserved down the centuries through isolation and intermarrying.

The Niolins relied for a living on their flocks of sheep and goats and travelled to the high pastures in the surrounding mountains for the summer, staying in stone huts close to their animals. From early September to the end of May there was the flock-migration—transhumance—to the west shore by the Fango valley or to the east shore pastures by way of the Scala di Santa Regina. The raising of sheep and goats is still the major occupation, on a smaller scale than in the past but much helped by the Roquefort cheese industry. The Niolo forests of Corsican pines are an important source of employment and income. Work, followed by tourism, came to the region with the building in 1968 of the Calacuccia dam and artificial lake on the River Golo for the irrigation of the Eastern Plain and provision of electric power and water to the Plain and Bastia. Tourist attractions include fishing, sailing, mountaineering, walking, pony-trekking, exploring the 8km circumference of the lake and skiing, 25km west of Calacuccia at Vergio (see below).

From Corte to the capital of the Niolo, Calacuccia, is 27km. Leave Corte by the N 193 going north in the direction of Bastia. Just outside the town, and immediately after the bridge over the River Orta, turn left onto the D 18 which goes up the Orta valley for 12km to Ponte Castirla (344m). Here take the D 84 road to the left and 5.5km further the road enters the *Scala di Santa Regina* (the Queen of Heaven's Ladder), the only means of communication with Corte and the east until the building of the road in 1889, originally a mule track hacked out of the granite and rising by stages. The almost purple cliffs rise sheer from the Golo torrent in the depths of the gorge and the road clings and winds its way above it, towered over by vertical cliffs on the right of the road. It is claustrophobically impressive as an approach to the Niolo and explains the region's long and almost total isolation from the rest of the island. Some idea of what this original route was like may be had from getting out at the Ponte di l'Accia over the Ruda stream which joins the Golo here and walking 150m up a track on the left bank of the stream to an old bridge, the Ponte Sottano.

Calacuccia (847m, 331 inhab.), at the north-east corner of the reservoir/lake, is a commune consisting of four hamlets grouped in the chestnut groves of the plateau. The 18C parish church of SS Peter and Paul has a 17C wooden *Christ on the Cross* in which the local sculptor represented extreme pain by the exaggeration of facial expression, muscles and bones. Many ancient and solid stone houses, one dated 1560. At the edge of the village to the right of the D 84, 1km west, the Franciscan monastery (1600) amid the chestnut trees. On 25 June 1774 French soldiers arrested 40 men, hanged 11 of them, one a boy of 15, broken on the wheel and hung from the trees by the monastery, at the same time laying waste the district and slaughtering the herds and flocks. The *François Flori museum* has a display of objects from past ways of life (to visit enquire at the monastery).

The lake is circled (8km) by the D 218. Leave south of Calacuccia by the 218 B, 3km west along the southern shore *Casamaccioli* (Casamacciuli, 868m, 91 inhab.) just off the lakeside at the foot of the wooded ridge that seals the Niolo to the south. *La Nativité* church has a wooden figure of St Roch, popular from the end of the 16C and a time of plague. The Niolin craftsman made him a mountain man with staff and small dog, his alarmed expression probably due to the bubonic lesion on his thigh. A 15C wooden figure of the Virgin is carried in procession on 8 September (Nativity of the Virgin) across the ground where the 3-day Fair of la Santa du Niolo is held. Cowled pentitents walk in the Granitola spiral (see Erbalunga, Rte 10), and on the first day of the Fair there is competition in poetic improvisation and oratory.

At Calacuccia Mérimée noted an outstanding *voceru* (see p 19) around the story of Maria Felice whose brother, a priest, was murdered in 1813. At his funeral Maria composed a *voceru* of lament and a call for vengeance. Instead of seeking out the killer, Maria's betrothed, a shepherd, left with his flock for the coastal winter pastures. When, on a premonition, he returned, he found Maria's funeral in progress. She had died of despair and shame at her fiancé's failure to conform to vendetta tradition. The shepherd killed himself at her grave.

The D 84 can be re-joined by taking the D 218 out of Casamaccioli due east

(3km). Completing the round trip east along the E 84, 3.5km to the west of Calacuccia is *Albertacce* (867m, 200 inhab.), where a small archaeological museum in an old house (open at various times in summer, ask in village) has exhibits from megalithic to Roman periods.

A. Mountain walks from Calacuccia: Monte Cinto

Monte Cinto, at 2710m, is the highest mountain in Corsica. Leave Calacuccia by the D 218 which branches north from the D 84 just west of the town. After 3km fork right on to the D 18 to reach, after 2.5km further, Lozzi (1044m, 136 inhab.). (On foot by shortcuts which are marked, 30 minutes.) From Lozzi to Cinto is a climb of 7½ hours. Allow 5 hours for coming down the same way or 4 hours down to Haut Asco (see Rte 16 and the section on the GR 20 long-distance path). It is *essential* to seek information and advice locally on conditions on this and all high mountain paths, on how to dress suitably, what to carry for eating and sleeping, the whereabouts of bergeries or similar overnight shelters and the best times to travel for physical comfort and maximum visibility. Corsicans are proud of their country and want visitors to share it with the minimum risk of danger or discomfort but personal ability must depend on each traveller's own assessment. Tackling Cinto can be tough going.

B. Le Lac de Nino

The *Lac de Nino* (1743m) is the source of the River Tavignano (80km long, with the Restonica, Vecchio, Corsigliese and Tagnone joining it as tributaries before it reaches the east coast at Aléria) and is a relatively easy and rewarding walk from Calacuccia. Take the D 84 west towards the Col de Vergio for 14km to the Chiarasghiu fountain (Funtana di u Chiarasgiu, 1129m). Just beyond the bridge take the path to the left which goes in the direction of the GR 20, leading south in 45 minutes to the *Bocca di San Petru* (1446m, Col de Saint Pierre on some maps); statue of the saint and chapel. Stay on the GR 20 going south-east from here for 1 hour to the Bocca Redda (Bocca a Reta, 1883m). This was the old mule track which followed the ridge of San Tomaghiu and of which there are traces where the stones underfoot are set in a kind of paving. The track reaches the edge of the lake in 45 minutes. The *Lac de Nino* is about 500m by 350m, well-stocked with trout and the land around the edges spongy and scored with runnels of water, rather like a Scottish peat hag but less boggy and easier walking.

There are two alternative ways down. That leading to the Maison Forestière de Popaja (or Popagghia) on the D 84 takes 85 minutes. Climb west from the lake to reach in a few minutes the Bocca di Stazzona (1762m) a great rocky shelf (legend says a herd of the devil's cattle turned to stone by St Martin) between Monte Tozzu (2007m) and la Punta Artica (2327m). A steep ravine path takes one through the forest of the Valdo Niellu (the Dark Forest). Some of the Corsican pines are centuries old and 40–50m high; in the higher reaches there are beech and birch.

The second route is to Calacuccia, about 6 hours' walk. Take the path from the north-east corner of the lake, or the GR 20 from the south shore (the tracks converge) and follow the track to the left waymarked in yellow, and not the red-and-white markings of the GR 20. It is a 1 hour walk to the Ceppu bergerie where there is a spring. You pass on the left the iron cross where the bandit Cappa was shot on 11 August 1895. Walking for half an hour brings you to the footpath which follows the left bank of the Tavignano. This steadily climbs above the valley and the beech trees of the Corte-Campotile Forest, crossing a boulder-strewn plateau and the Dinadelli stream, followed by easier walking across pastures to (2 hours) the Canalelli spring. 15 minutes further walking to the Bocca Capizolu. Footpaths on either side of this col lead down, in about 1 hour, to Casamaccioli but, if heading for Calacuccia, leave these paths on the left and take one just below the ridge going east for a few hundred metres to the Bocca a l'Arinella (1592m). From here on the way is clearly marked and it is 2 hours down to the dam and a further 10 minutes to Calacuccia village.

An 8½ hour walk through picturesque country may be taken by going up to the Bocca a l'Arinella and then following the course of the Tavignano through its gorges to Corte.

C. Other walks from Calacuccia

There is a tour of the Valdu Niellu Forest; to the Guagnerola (1837m) and Capronale (1370m) cols; to the valleys of the Tula and Viro rivers; to Capu Tafonatu (2343m), the Pierced Mountain through which the infuriated Satan hurled a broken ploughshare in the same annoying incident in which his oxen were turned to stone (see above, Bocca di Stazzona). The starting points for these, and other expeditions of varying ruggedness, are on, or easily reached from, the D 84: the Maison Forestière de Popaja (12km from Calacuccia), the Maison Ciattarinu (19km), the Maison Cantonnière de Frascaghiu (9.5km), and a number of stages on the GR 20 (see Rte 16).

At 22.5km on the D 84 from Calacuccia is the *Station de Verghio* (Verghiu, Vergiu, 1404m) 60m lower and 1.5km down the D 84 from the col. Hotel Castel de Vergio (5 teleskis, ski equipment hire) is the highest hotel in Corsica. Vergio is 18.7km from the west coast, 80km from Ajaccio and 100km from Bastia. It is a centre for alpine and cross-country skiing from December–April (depending on snow conditions) and in summer for expeditions in the surrounding mountains and the forests of Valdu Niellu and Aïtone; the GR 20 is within 2km of the Station de Ski.

From the Station the D 84 crosses the GR 20 and describes a tight horseshoe (the Fer à Cheval) before reaching the *Col de Vergio* (1464m) the highest mountain pass in Corsica that one can drive over (sometimes blocked by snow in winter and early spring, with signs 'Col ouvert' or 'Col fermé' well in advance on the D 84 approaches). 200m before the actual summit, on either side and a few metres off the road, are wide views of the surrounding peaks and mountain ranges and the valleys of the Porto to the west and the Golo to the east. A well-trodden 80m path leading up north-west from the Col brings the pierced Tafonatu summit into view. *Capo a la Cuccula* (Capu à Cuccula, 2049m) is a 2½ hour there-and-back medium easy walk from the Col. From the Cricche ridge can be seen Tafonatu to the north, Cinto to the north-east, the Niolo basin east-north-east, the

Rotondo massif to the east and south-east, and the Golfe de Porto and the Mediterranean to the west.

The D 84 for the next 10km goes through the magnificent *Forest of Aïtone*, of pine, larch, beech and ilex. Some fine specimens of Corsican pine around two centuries old and 50m high may be seen around the Maison Forestière d'Aïtone, 7.5km from the Col de Vergio and 5km from Evisa.

Evisa (850m, 248 inhab.). 36km from Calacuccia and out of the Niolo region which ends at the Col de Vergio, 23km from Porto. Situated between the Aïtone Forest and the Spelunca Gorges, Evisa has frequently been called the Pearl of Corsica. It is a very attractive place, its houses ranged steeply and tightly on the rocky spur that separates the Porto and Aïtone rivers. All around are the chestnut plantations and the darker green of Corsican pines and firs, broken up on occasion by beech groves, backed by the encircling mountain chains and peaks, broken only to the south-west where the valleys lead to the sea. The closeness to both sea and mountains make Evisa a pleasant holiday centre in all seasons, without being crowded. There are a half-dozen hotels and a *village de vacances* called the Paesolu d'Aïtone. Apart from sea-bathing and skiing, Evisa is one of the best centres in Corsica for mountain-walking with a variety to suit all capabilities, ranging from easy strolls of an hour to 5–6 hour long-distance mountain walks which, in order to avoid having to return by the same route, could be improved by the two-car arrangement if a group is walking.

To reach the *Aïtone mill and waterfall* take the D 84 in the direction of the Col de Vergio to just beyond the turning right to Vico. Then follow the first forest track to the left, 2 hours there and back.

Similarly, to reach the *Belvédère* take the D 84 for 3km in the direction of Col de Vergio. A forest path to the left winds up among the pines to the Belvédère (975m), a spur of rock jutting out over the Aïtone river with a view of jumbled red rocks and a glimpse of the sea beyond. It is 2 hours there and back.

The *Spelunca Gorge and Ota* is a walk which, taking 3 hours each way, may be better organised by having a car at Ota for the return journey. Take the D 84 in the direction of Porto. At the end of the wall around the cemetery take a footpath going down on the right towards the Aïtone ravine and then along the precipice, at the foot of which the river flows. The path corkscrews downwards to the confluence of the Aïtone and Tavulella. Cross over by the Genoese Zaglia bridge, the half-way point of the walk, after which the *cirque* and gorge of Spelunca begin. *L'Antre*, the lair, den or cavern, is an amphitheatre surrounded by steep red pinnacled rocks; this dramatic landscape can be seen from the Evisa–Porto road. Follow the track along the left bank of the river through the gorge, an old mule track with traces of rough steps that were set in the more difficult places for the pack animals. An hour's walk ends at the D 124 road, from which the D 84 is reached by turning left, 12.5km from Evisa. By carrying on along the track for another half hour the *two bridges of Ota* are reached, a double bridge across the Onca and the Aïtone which come together here to form the River Porto. There is the choice of continuing to Ota along the right bank or taking the path downstream that leads to the remains of the Genoese bridge of Pianella and joins up with the Evisa road.

Ota (335m, 460 inhab.), reached from the D 84 at 12.5km from Evisa, is the chief settlement of the commune to which it gives its name and to which Porto belongs. It is set in an amphitheatre at the foot of Capo d'Ota (1220m).

The soil of this basin is fertile and there are olive and chestnut groves, vineyards, vegetables and cereals (see Rte 6).

16 Le Parc Naturel Régional de la Corse

The Parc Naturel Régional de la Corse covers an area of 300,000 hectares, a little over a third of the island, and extends diagonally from the north-west coast, 25km south of Calvi on the D 81 to Palavèse in the south-east, 5km north-west on the D 368 from Porto Vecchio. It includes 80km of coastline and most of the central Corsican mountains, is 120km long and varies in width from 10–30km. The most northerly point is the Bocca di San Colombano on the N 179 6km to the east of Belgodère and the most southerly point the Montagne de Cagna and the D 59 10km south of Carbini.

The Parc came into being on 15 May 1972, the project having been approved on 2 February 1971 after seven years of wide-ranging scientific study. Further to the designation of an area of outstanding beauty the aim was to revitalise districts whose economy, chiefly pastoral, had declined for many reasons that included the drift of population to the towns and the transformation of traditional Eastern Plain winter pastures into farms and vineyards. In order to find alternative grazing for their flocks in autumn shepherds resorted to burning the maquis in summer and bringing down from the mountains a few months later their sheep and goats to feed on the resultant new growth of grass and brush. In an attempt to halt and reverse the rapidly disappearing long-established way of life some 200 *bergeries* were built to replace those that had fallen into ruin. These *bergeries*, sheepfolds and huts to shelter shepherds and flocks during the trans-humance, were intended to encourage the continuance of the traditional seasonal moving of livestock. Communications with the rest of the island were improved, ending the historical isolation of the mountain people from the towns and coastal population, and reorganisation of the sale of local produce was put in hand. In step with the reanimation of rural economy the region's potential for tourism, until then confined mainly to the coast, was developed. The need to reconcile all this with the traditional way of life was met in the most sensible and realistic way. A force of guides, mostly young men from villages and familiar with the hard mountain life, was recruited to explain to those affected the aims of the Parc and to allay fears of armies of tourists damaging crops and scaring stock. Tourists too had to be made aware of the mutual respect necessary to avoid friction with the local inhabitants. The setting-up had to be organised of mountain refuges, information and rescue centres for the safety and well-being of visitors. The GR 20 long-distance path through the Parc was traced and waymarked as have been two other long-distance paths since, Mare e Monti—'Between Sea and Mountain', and Mare a Mare—'From Sea to Sea', as well as shorter, mostly circular, walks of 3–5 hours' duration. Guides to the paths, books and pamphlets on flora, fauna, geology and archaeology were, and con-tinue to be, written and published (see Bibliography under the heading of Parc Naturel Régional).

The Parc is emphatically not in any way an open-air museum or a 'theme park'. Those whose homes and livelihood are there go about their daily life and work as they would anywhere else. The 83 *communes*, spread over the two départements, in which they live, are in constant touch with more than

60 Parc agents in the territory who are also ready to advise and help tourists who must, above all, remember that unauthorised camping—*le camping sauvage*—is strictly forbidden because of the danger of forest fire by which Corsica has so frequently been ravaged. Information on permitted camp sites, refuges, equipment needed, etc. is available from the central office of the Parc Naturel Régional de la Corse (address below).

One of the principal objectives of the Association des Amis du Parc, founded in 1972, is the conservation of Corsican flora and fauna, particularly of endangered species such as the *mouflon* which had been hunted almost to extinction. This is a wild sheep (Ovis musimon), about the same size as the domestic animal but whose rams are magnificently-horned. It is brownish-grey with a dark dorsal streak and in agility resembles the chamois. It is strictly protected as are, among a dozen or so other birds and mammals, the *gypaete* (Gypaetus barbatus) the bearded vulture or lammergeyer whose wingspread can attain nearly three metres, the 'royal' eagles, the fish buzzard, certain kites, cormorants and the largest surviving European bat. By 1970 the Corsican stag (*Cervus elaphus corsicanus*) had become extinct, victim of relentless hunting. But through the co-operation of Corsica's neighbouring island the stag was reintroduced from southern Sardinia in 1986 and has since been breeding actively in an enclosure near Quenza (Corse-du-Sud). At some suitable time in the future, when the herd is considered large and independent enough, the Corsican stag will once more roam freely and, it is to be hoped, safely in the Corsican mountains.

The GR 20: à travers la montagne corse de Calenzana à Conca

Since 1947 Le Comité National des Sentiers de Grande Randonnée, the CNSGR, which thirty years later became La Fédération Française de la Randonnée Pédestre—the FFRP—has been responsible for planning and organising 40,000km of *sentiers de grande randonnée*—the GR long-distance paths—in France, of which the Corsican route is the GR 20. Roughly 200km long, it runs from Calenzana, 12km inland from Calvi by the N 197 and D 151, in the north-west of the island to Conca, 22km north-west of Porto Vecchio by the N 198 and the D 168. Since 1977 the GR 20 has been *balisé*—waymarked—in the distinctive GR stripes of white above red—on boulders, rock face, tree trunks, walls and specially erected posts and cairns where necessary. The path can generally be travelled between mid-June and the beginning of November and 2–3 weeks should be allowed, according to energy, inclination, season and weather. A good standard of general fitness is needed. The GR 20 may be joined or left by a number of *bretelles*, connecting side-paths generally waymarked with a single yellow stripe, or at those points where the GR 20 crosses motor-roads, e.g. near the Col de Vergio, the Col de Verde, the Col de Bavella, and on the N 193 at 15 minutes' walk from the Gare de Vizzavona. This is the only place where the GR 20 comes close to the railway and it is roughly the half-way point between Calenzana and Conca. The former half, to the north, is higher and harder going than the southern half, by the way. The 'Topoguide GR 20', also available in English since 1990, is absolutely essential for those intending to walk all or parts of the path (see Bibliography under heading Le Parc Naturel Régional).

Mare e Monte, 'Between Sea and Mountain': Calenzana-Cargèse

This walk, to part of which there is an alternative route, is through an area classified by UNESCO in 1983 as one of the very few 'Natural Sites of World

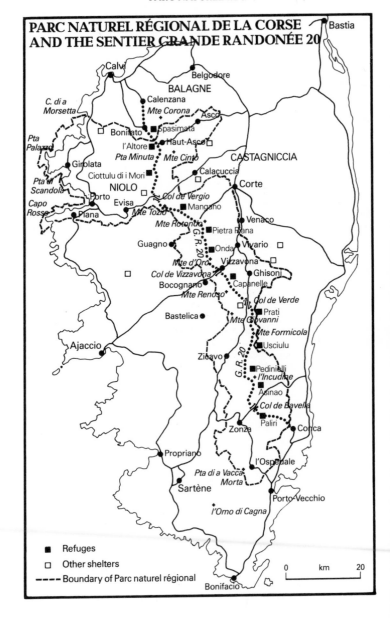

PARC NATUREL RÉGIONAL DE LA CORSE AND THE SENTIER GRANDE RANDONÉE 20

Bastia

Calvi

Belgodore

BALAGNE

Calenzana

C. di a Morsetta

Mte Corona

Asco

Bonifato

Spasmata

Pta Palazzo

l'Altore

Haut-Asco

Pta Minuta

Mte Cinto

CASTAGNICCIA

Girolata

Ciottulu di i Mori

Pta di Scandola

NIOLO

Calacuccia

Corte

Capo Rosse

Porto

Evisa

Col de Vergio

Plana

Mte Tozio

Mangano

Venaco

Mte Rotonda

Pietra Rana

Guagno

Onda

Vivario

Mte d'Oro

Vizzavona

Col de Vizzavona

Ghisoni

Bocognano

Capanelle

Mte Renoso

Col de Verde

Bastelica

Prati

Mte Giovanni

Mte Formicola

Ajaccio

Usciulu

Zicavo

Pedinielli

l'Incudine

Asinao

Col de Bavella

Zonza

Paliri

Conca

Propriano

l'Ospedale

Pta di a Vacca Morta

Sartène

Porto-Vecchio

l'Omo di Cagna

■ Refuges

□ Other shelters

--- Boundary of Parc naturel régional

0   km   20

Bonifacio

Interest'. It can be covered in 10 days throughout the greater part of the year but spring and autumn are the best season and, if travelling in summer, start in the early and cooler hours of the day. The extreme ends of the path are outside the Parc area (see Bibliography as above).

Mare a Mare, 'From Sea to Sea': east coast to west coast

There are three Mare a Mare walks: Nord, Centre and Sud.

Nord: Sermano–Corte–Cargèse. This may be walked from mid-May to November in 7 days or in 11 days taking an alternative route.

Centre: Ghisonaccia–Ajaccio. Practicable from mid May to November. In winter and early spring the pass at 1500m of the Bocca or Col de Laparo is often, but not invariably, blocked by snow. The GR 20 is crossed at this Col. Allow 7 days but the section between Cozzano and Ajaccio can be walked in all seasons in 4 days.

Sud: Porto Vecchio–Propriano. This, the furthest southern crossing of the central mountains, leaves the Tyrrhenian Sea at the Golfe de Porto Vecchio and reaches the Mediterranean at the Golfe de Valinco. It can be walked throughout the year, there being little risk of heavy snow in winter while in summer there is shade in the many pine and ilex forests crossed during the 5 days' journey. (See Bibliography as above.)

The above is the barest outline of the main Corsican long-distance paths. There are also six small regions of the Parc which have shorter walks called *Sentiers de Pays* which are waymarked in orange. For further information see the books in the Bibliography under the heading of Le Parc Naturel Régional. For precise, right up-to-date information on itineraries, walking times and distances, accommodation, equipment needed, state of the paths and weather, official publications, topoguides and other relative books, consult or visit the central office of Le Parc Naturel Régional de la Corse, rue Fiorella, BP 417, 20184 Ajaccio CEDEX, Corse-du-Sud; tel. 95 21 56 54 (see also Rte 1, Ajaccio). From June–October information is obtainable from the following Parc offices: Corte, tel. 95 46 27 44; Porto Vecchio, tel. 95 70 50 78; Zonza, tel. 95 78 66 58; Calvi, tel. 95 65 16 67.

Through the Parc Naturel Régional: from Ponte Leccia to Bocognano

ROAD (N 193) 62km.—24 Corte—34km Venaco—44km Vivario.

Much of the Parc Naturel may be seen and visited from the roads which run through, across and in and out of it, many of which feature in other sections of this Guide. Bearing in mind that the spine of the island is the mountain chain that also runs roughly down the centre of the Parc, the motor roads either lie along the valleys or are carved into the mountainside. The following is an itinerary from which much of the Parc in all its beauty and grandeur may be seen. Most of this route is followed closely by the railway from Bastia to Bocognano.

Leaving Bastia by the N 193 it is 20km south to Casamozza, then follow the N 193 west along the valley of the Golo (as does the railway). Another 18km brings one to *Ponte Nuovo* (Ponte Novu, 167m) which owes its name to the five-arched bridge built by the Genoese. It was here that the Corsicans under Paoli were defeated and massacred by the French on 8 May 1769, a battle which put a temporary stop to the campaign for Corsican independence and drove Paoli to seek refuge in England (he left Corsica on 13 June 1769). Commemorative stone at the end of the bridge.

The next Genoese bridge, in better repair, is 8km further at *Ponte Leccia*, a large village at one of Corsica's principal crossroads. Here the N 193 turns south and carries on down the valley of the Golo; the N 197 goes north by a valley route, chiefly close to the rivers Navaccia and San Colombano and the route of the railway, and eventually reaches the coast 7km to the east of l'Ile Rousse; the D 71 travels east to Morosaglia and the heart of the Castagniccia. The railway forks at Ponte Leccia too, one branch following the N 197 north until it reaches the coast, continuing to l'Ile Rousse and Calvi as 'Le Tramway de la Balagne', the other line staying close to the N 193 on its way south to Corte, Vizzavona and eventually Ajaccio.

The valley of the Asco is a comparatively short trip from Ponte Leccia (33km, returning by the same road) through magnificent scenery to one of the main centres of the Parc Naturel. Take the N 197 north for 2km then turn left on to the D 47 into the valley of the River Asco (35km long, rising at the Bocca Stranciacone, 1987m, and joining the Golo close to Ponte Leccia).

At 7.5km from Ponte Leccia a road to the right, the D 47 (the road to Asco becomes the D 147), reaches in 3km the village of *Moltifao* (Moltifau, 400m, 427 inhab.) built on the heights separating the valleys of the Asco and the Tartagine. Known for the quality of its honey, beehives are set on the terraces of fruit and olive trees. The parish church of the *Annunciation* has a fragment of a 15C interpretation of God the Father, re-used in a piece of sacristy furniture, and there is a complete wooden retable of 1545, the Crowning of the Virgin. 3km north of Moltifao is *Castifao* (Castifau, 506m, 137 inhab.), also renowned for its honey (*fau* means honeycomb) and built above the Tartagine in narrow stepped streets. There was a Franciscan monastery here, now in ruins. To the south-west are the ruins of the Chapelle de Saint Augustin (San Agostino).

At 9km from Ponte Leccia Les Gorges de l'Asco begin between mountains of 1000m. The road winds above the river whose right bank is rocky and arid while the left bank is scattered with clumps of juniper. 9.5km further is *Asco* (Ascu, 620m, 96 inhab.), its austere tall houses, outside stairs and covered passageways all recalling the isolation in which the villagers lived until the road was brought there in 1937. The settlement may have been of Ligurian origin and the present village dates from the 11C. Because of enforced self-sufficiency a specific form of local government grew up. Essential village work was organised on a community basis called *la chjamata* and decisions were taken and disputes settled by *paceri* or *sages*, presiding over assemblies of elders and widows. On the western outskirts of Asco a road to the south leads to the bank of the Asco by a single-arch Genoese bridge.

The D 147 carries on up the valley which from here on is that of the Stranciacone, soon entering the *Carozzica forest* (has suffered severely from fire) which rises to 1900m and the bare rock of the high mountains.

Haut Asco (1450m), at the end of the D 147 and 11km from Asco, was Corsica's first winter sports centre, set up in 1964. The road, with the help of the Foreign Legion, reached the plateau of Stagnu in 1968. Monte Cinto lies to the south, Capo Stranciacone to the west and La Muvrella to the north-west, with a *bretelle* to the GR 20. (There is a hotel-restaurant, open December–April for skiing, depending on state of the snow, with two ski-lifts and a number of chalets.) This is a departure point for the high ski route of Corsica and for the following mountain walks.

Monte Cinto (2706m) is a 6-hour walk up from Haut Asco and 4¼ hours down. From Haut Asco take the path going due south, waymarked in red and by numerous cairns. The route leads first through trees until the valley of the Tighjetu stream is crossed by a footbridge. The path goes up by a narrow gorge to Capu Borba (2207m) reached about 4 hours after leaving Haut Asco. From the col take the path climbing up to the left which follows glacial debris or moraine, and at the ridge take the facing slope leading to the summit (2710m), the highest point of Corsica. When the weather is good, and it is clearer in spring and winter than in summer and clearest of all at dawn, the panorama is superb. One can see to the south the mountains of Rotondo, D'Oro and Renoso with beyond them, the peaks of the Sartenais and Sardinia, to the north Calvi and the sea, to the south-west the gulfs of Ajaccio, Porto and Sagone, and to the north-east the Isle of Elba. The way down from Cinto to Calacuccia is by the south-east face and the Bergeries de Biccarello and Lozzi. Allow 5–5½ hours for the descent.

There is also a walk from Asco to Calacuccia via the *Bocca di Serra Piana* (allow 8–9 hours). The path goes by way of the bergeries of Misaldi, Pinnera and, beyond the Bocca di Serra Piana (1846m), Menta and Caracuto and the village of Corscia (837m, 156 inhab.).

A 6½–7 hours' walk from Asco, **Monte Padro** (Padru, 2393m) gives a fine view over to the north-west and l'Ile Rousse and south to Cinto. The path begins 200m beyond a small bridge 1.5km west from Asco along the Haut Asco road. Watch out for it as there is no signpost or waymark. This leads in 3 hours to the Bergeries d'Intrata. From here take the left bank of the stream leading to the right through the trees and then climb the scree to the right. In 3½ hours from Intrata one reaches the summit of Padro which forms the north-east pillar of the Cinto massif.

There are other mountain walks of varying severity and duration from both Asco and Haut Asco but one that should be mentioned here is that to the *cirque and forest of Bonifatu*, a walk of about 8½–9 hours, by way of La Muvrella (the *mouflonne*). Leave Haut Asco heading west for the trees and the path waymarked in two yellow stripes (this is a *bretelle* of the GR 20) to the Breche de Stagnu (1985m); about 2 hours' walk. The Breche de Stagnu is c 300m north of the Bocca Culaghia or Culaja where the track joins the red-and-white waymarked GR 20. The GR 20 has an offshoot here which leads to the summit of *La Muvrella* (2148m), fine view in clear weather. By following the GR 20 one passes by the foot of the mountain where in a glacial combe there is the tiny *Lac de la Muvrella*, with alders around its shore. The mountain and lake are well-named: I have both heard and seen the mouflon rattling across the mountainside scree. From the lake it is 2 hours to the Parc Régional refuge at Spasimata (1190m), surrounded by Corsican pines, a spring, and ruins of an old stone hut. The Forest of Bonifatu suffered severely from fire in 1982. There are detours down to Calenzana, for which allow 7 hours (see also Rte 5, Calvi).

Travelling south from Ponte Leccia the N 193 continues to follow the Golo valley for 9km to *Francardo* (226m) a timber-processing centre for the tree trunks brought from the Valdo-Niello forest. The D 84 leads off to the right for the Golo gorges and the Scala di Santa Regina (see Rte 15), Evisa, Porto and the west coast.

2km further on at Caporalino a turning to the left, the D 818, leads to *Omessa* (450m, 517 inhab.) in just under 2km where the *chapel of the Annunciation* has a fine marble Virgin and Child (mid 15C?). The curly hair of the Infant and the bird he holds recall the work of Donatello and later Florentine sculptors. Church of *St André*, with 15C graceful campanile, some good Italian paintings, tombs of three Colonna bishops, great patriots.

17km Col de San Quilico (559m) between the catchments of the Golo and the Tavignano; 500m beyond the D 41 leaves (left) for the villages of the Castagniccia (see Rte 12). Corte is 24km from Ponte Leccia (see Rte 14) and from Corte it is 8.5km to *Santo Pietro di Venaco* (San Petru di Venacu, 860m, 166 inhab.). This is a pleasant summer resort popular with visitors from Ajaccio and Bastia (it is linked to both by the railway) as is *Venaco* 1.5km south (Venacu, 610m, 614 inhab.) set in the middle of Corsica with Ajaccio 80km and Bastia 82km distant. There are two churches. The parish church of *St Michel* is baroque with a *trompe l'oeil* ceiling painting of Abraham and Isaac threatened by a giant sword against a Corsican landscape. The church of *St Antoine* in the hamlet of Lugo, contiguous with Venaco, has some striking modern stained-glass windows and Stations of the Cross in black-and-white mosaic by a local artist (1960). The war memorial near to the church of St Michel is a typical reminder of how much Corsican blood was shed for France in the First World War. There are the names of 77 Venacais, the dead from one average-sized village.

This is a countryside of chestnut groves, very well watered by streams, with some vineyards, orchards, meadows and pastures. The main occupation is the raising of sheep, goats and cattle. One of the many good local cheeses is le Venaco, made from ewes' milk. The district, like the inhabitants of Venaco, is called le Venacais and it offers a variety of attractions to the tourist including trout fishing in the Vecchio and other rivers and walking '*da paese a paese*' (from village to village), walking that is no more

The Altiani bridge

demanding than fell or dale rambling and offers great variety in the landscape and villages.

At 6km from Venaco by the D 43, later the D 143, is E Caselle, an hotel and bungalow complex built above the Vecchio, initially with his own hands, by Jean Pagni who returned to his native Venaco when he tired of the Sorbonne. A triumph of imagination and taste, E Caselle is a good centre for exploring the Venacais.

At the D 143 junction with the D 200 (which leads to Aléria) turn right. Close by, the Vecchio, flowing east, joins the Tavignano and near the confluence the latter is crossed by the *Pont d'Altiani*, a fine stone bridge built by the Genoese and widened this century. Locally it is called the 'Laricio bridge' because just before it was finished a great *laricio* or Corsican pine trunk was driven against it by flood waters and nearly wrecked it. At one end of the bridge, on the left bank, there is the little chapel of *San Giovanni Battista* (10C or even earlier) which has been well restored after having been used as a bergerie for a long time.

Going south from Venaco 10km down the N 193 is Vivario, 44km from Ponte Leccia. *Vivario* (Vivariu, 696m, 493 inhab.) is surrounded by the forests of Vizzavona, Cervello and Sorba. The ruins standing on a hill, overlooking the station, with the romantic name of Arabie Petrée, are relics of one of a line of forts built by the Genoese from which to 'pacify' the interior.

There are two routes to the east coast from Vivario, both of them taking time and both providing magnificent experience of the Parc. The D 343, the most northerly route, passes through *Vezzani* (800m, 336 inhab.) on the north-east outskirts of the Forest of Sorba, where there was a copper mine, no longer worked. The road from Vezzani joins the D 344 at the east end of the Défilé de l'Inzecca and continues towards Ghisonaccia and Aléria.

The D 69 leaves Vivario by the south-south-east and passes by the Col de Sorba (1311m), where there are magnificent views, to *Ghisoni* (650m, 335 inhab.; see Rte 9). Here the D 344 branches off to the east, passing through the Défilé des Strette and the Défilé de l'Inzecca to meet the road from Vezzani and continue to the east coast.

Taking the D 69 due south from Ghisoni the road runs parallel to the Fium'Orbo to the east, beyond which lie the twin peaks of Christe Eleison (1260m) and Kyrie Eleison (1535m), so named when members of the proscribed sect of the Giovannali (see Rte 9) were burned alive after being captured during the Papal crusade against them in 1362. An old priest defied the bishop by saying a Mass for the dying and at the first words of the Kyrie Eleison a white dove is said to have flown in a circle above the burning martyrs.

The Col de Verde (1289m) 17km from Ghisoni, is the pass that joins the valleys of the Fium'Orbo and the Taravo and is surrounded by beech groves. 22km south of the Col de Verde is *Zicavo* (Zicavu, 735m, 245 inhab.), set among chestnut and beech-covered mountains. This is a centre for cross-country skiing and for climbing Monte Incudine (Corsican for anvil, the shape of a rock on the ridge).

Monte Incudine (2136m) was a much longer expedition from Zicavo in the past than it is today, now that improved roads have made it easier to get to a closer starting point. Take the D 69 going south towards Bocca di a Vaccia and Aullène. Watch out for a rough forest track going left at 9.5km from Zicavo, the D 428 which crosses the beech woods of the Bosco di u Corscione (the Forêt Dominiale de Corscione), climbing through a mountain landscape where occasional fine views of the Taravo valley are glimpsed between the trees. After 7km there is a track to the right leading to the *Chapelle de Saint Pierre* (San Petru, 1360m), a small, simple building. There is a primitive sheltering place nearby which is suitable for camping (but take all the usual precautions). A few hundred metres before the chapel track the main path leads to the right towards l'Incudine, the summit of which is reached in 4½ hours. Some may choose to leave their vehicles here or near this point. It depends very much on the toughness and ground-clearance of the car. From here on for the 5km to the Bergerie de Cavallara it is rough going, with boulders on the track and streams to be forded, but the route is negotiable by sturdy vehicles. All cars must be left, further on, at the Bergerie de Cavallara from which point the forest track goes down into the valley where one picks up the red-and-white waymarks of the GR 20. Follow the GR 20 by the footbridge across the Casamintellu stream and then up its right bank through beech forests to a wide clearing and the Refuge de Pediniellu (1620m), a typical Parc refuge, this one has room for 24. From here it is 2 hours' walk following the GR 20 waymarks to the summit of Monte Incudine which is marked by a cross. View to the south of the jagged Aiguilles de Bavella, with Monte Renoso to the north, and the sea to the west and east.

From here south-west to *Quenza* (805m, 214 inhab.), starting along the GR 20, is about 5 hours. Instead of crossing the Col de Bavella fork right 2½ hours from the peak of l'Incudine, down the track past the Bergeries de Saparello and to the Zonza–Quenza D 420 road. Three hours from the summit of the mountain, on this route, there is the refuge of Asinao (1600m).

From Vivario, 44km south of Ponte Leccia, the N 193 continues south-south-west and in 2km passes the Col de la Serra (804m) and soon enters the *Forest of Vizzavona*. One of the largest and most beautiful Corsican forests, it is relieved of coniferous monotony by the mixture of beech with Corsican pine. A fork to the right, 4km beyond the Col de la Serra, loops down through the trees to the *Gare de Vizzavona* (910m, 50 inhab.). Apart from the station there is little to see except a few tree-surrounded houses of generous 19C proportions and style which were once hotels when Vizzavona-Gare was a popular summer mountain resort with those useful direct links by rail with Ajaccio and Bastia. There are still hotels and summer visitors and Vizzavona is above all a very important centre for forest walks and mountaineering.

A starting point common to a number of expeditions is the hamlet of *La Foce* (622m, 94 inhab.), 2.5km south on the N 193. From La Foce, and the GR 20 which crosses the N 193 just above the village at the Maison Forestière de Vizzavona, paths which are mostly waymarked lead to: *les Cascades des Anglais* (these waterfalls can be very small in a dry summer; the origin of the name is still a mystery); the ruined Genoese *Fort de Vizzavona*; *le chemin des Deux Ponts*; *La Madonuccia* (stones which suggest a statue of Our Lady, with fine views of the Gravona valley, the south face of Monte d'Oro and Sant'Elisio). All these walks are easy, taking no more than 2–3 hours and offering a variety of forest and mountain scenery. There is little point in giving details of itineraries as information and advice is willingly given by local people who will also help in planning expeditions to the following three of Corsica's principal mountains which can be reached from Vizzavona. (See also notes on Parc Naturel Régional information, above in this section, and Bibliography.)

*Flocks move to mountain pastures for the summer months in the
seasonal transhumance*

A. Monte Rotondo

Monte Rotondo (2822m) is the highest and furthest of the three local
mountains. Allow 6 hours or so each way whether following the valley of
the Manganello or that of the Verghello. Both valleys can be reached from
the N 193 going north towards Corte, the first by turning left to Canaglia
and driving as far as the Maison Forestière de Busso. Leave the car here
and walk on for 4km past the hamlet of Canaglia to the Tolla waterfall
where the GR 20 is joined, just before the Bergeries de Tolla (shelter
possible here at most times). Follow the GR 20 to the Bergeries de Gialgo
and then to the Refuge de Pietra Piana where one leaves the GR 20 for the
path going due north to the lake and the summit of Rotondo.

The Verghello valley route is reached by turning left at the Pont du
Vecchio further north along the N 193 and following the track around the
Bergeries de Puzzatello to a point just below the Solibello Bergerie, beyond
which is a parking place. From here it is about 5 hours' walk to Rotondo,
taking 1½ hours to the Bocca Tripoli from which, in 2 hours, the Bergeries
de Muraccioli are reached, where there is shelter for the night or in bad
weather. Usually the bergeries are occupied in late spring and summer by
shepherds and members of their families *en transhumance*. They are
helpful about camping there but remember that they are earning their
living and merit all our respect and courtesy. Just under 2 hours from the
bergeries the Lac du Monte Rotondo is reached. (For a description of the
lake and mountain, and ascent from the Restonica valley see Rte 14.)

B. Monte Renoso

There are three ways to the summit of Monte Renoso from Vizzavona. Renoso (2352m) lies between the Cols de Vizzavona and de Verde and from the Ghisoni side it is possible to drive to the ski station at the Bergeries de Capannelle (1586m) by the D 169 off the D 69 6km south of Ghisoni.

From Vizzavona it takes 8½ hours to reach Renoso by the GR 20 route that begins near the Maison Forestière de Vizzavona, following clear and well-marked forest paths to the Bocca Palmente (1645m), a walk of about 2¾ hours. At the Capannelle ski station follow a track which is cairn-marked from the top of the ski-lift west to a stony plateau (about 2.25km) and turning south climb to the summit. This is about 3 hours from Capannelle.

There are two other ways to climb Monte Renoso, one by the valley of the Gravona (5 hours) and the other by the Punta di l'Oriente (2112m; 6 hours). Seek local advice as to which of the three routes, according to prevailing weather and season, is recommended. From the summit there is a panoramic view of the whole of southern Corsica, to the sea on both west and east coasts and to the Straits of Bonifacio and Sardinia. Below to the north lies the *Lac de Bastiani* or Bastani (2090m) flanked on either side by a tiny lochan. Although for most of the year there are *neves* (blocks of crystalline ice and snow welded together by alternating frost and sun) around the shores, trout and char survive happily in the lake.

C. Monte d'Oro

Michel Fabrikant, that great authority on Corsican mountains, says that the name Monte d'Oro is a form of the old Celtic root from which are derived many names applied to water such as 'torrent', Durance and Dordogne, Monte d'Oro being the source of torrents and rivers in this region. There are several routes from Vizzavona to Monte d'Oro (2389m) and, if so inclined, a round trip may be made.

One climb of 10–11 hours starts from the hamlet of La Foce. Take the Agnone road, the one that leads to the Cascade des Anglais, and park when the road comes to an end, where the GR 20 passes. Follow the GR 20 to the Bergeries de Tortetto (1364m) which are just to the south of the GR 20 among the beeches (2 hours to here), cross the Agnone by the ford and leaving the GR 20, climb the pebbly slopes to the Col du Porc (Bocca di Porco, 2159m) by a track to the right. Another hour's climb brings you to the summit of Monte d'Oro with a view (if it is clear or sufficiently early in the morning) of Cinto and Rotondo to the north, Renoso and Sardinia to the south, to the east the sea and the Tuscan Isles, and to the west the white buildings of Ajaccio and the sea beyond. Allow about 4 hours for the return to Vizzavona by the yellow waymarked route around the northern shoulder of Monte d'Oro. In the first hour on the way down there is a tiny grassy plateau surrounded by steep escarpments and just above it the houses of Vizzavona can be seen through a gap in the rocks. This path is more a natural stairway and is aptly named La Scala. After 2 hours, and nearly half-way down, with the most difficult descent done, you reach the Berger-ies of Puzzatello (1526m). They appeared to be no longer in use when I last saw them but can provide shelter. The path continues to be clearly marked in yellow through the Corsican pine forest, traversing the Ghilareto ravine (1080m) and crossing the Tineta stream by a ford. Thence over the Agnone by bridge, and over one more bridge back into Vizzavona and the road to the railway station.

The *Col de Vizzavona* (1163m), 3km south along the N 193 beyond the turning to the village of Vizzavona is a plateau connecting the valleys of the Tavignano and the Gravona (rises in the Vizzavona massif, 44km long, reaches the west coast in the Golfe d'Ajaccio). From here it is 9km to **Bocognano** (Bucugnanu, 700m, 290 inhab.), a group of hamlets scattered through the chestnut forests that surround the main village. Next to the Post Office in the one-sided main street, is a tree-shaded terrace with benches from where one can look out over the woodlands to Monte d'Oro. A majestic fountain, built of large stones, like an up-ended cobbled street dates from 1883 and must have been constructed entirely out of civic pride because Bocognano's popularity as a summer retreat from Ajaccio had not then been established.

Bocognano possesses a bandit story as decorative as the fountain. In the early 19C a shepherd called Bonelli, who was known by the name of Bellacoscia (handsome thigh), lived in the valley of Pentica with three common-law wives, sisters, by whom he had eighteen children. Two of his sons, Antoine and Jacques, became bandits in 1848 after Antoine shot the mayor, and thenceforth the brothers ruled as undisputed masters of the Pentica gorge. Again and again the gendarmerie tried to capture them and in 1888 the Minister of War even authorised an expedition against the Bonelli bandits. They nevertheless eluded the law and remained free to entertain in their maquis hide-out aristocrats in search of a thrill, including German princesses and Prince Roland Bonaparte as well as writers like Pierre Loti, no doubt in search of copy. On 25 June 1892 Antoine, four times *in absentia* condemned to death for murder, gave himself up and was put on trial in Bastia where he was acquitted 'to a thunder of applause'. He died in his bed at Bocognano at around 100 years old in 1912. Jacques died of pneumonia in 1897 and was buried in the bed of a temporarily-dammed river, to comply with his wish that no man should walk over his grave.

Anyone in Bocagnano will tell you how to get to the old Bonelli stamping ground in the grim gorge of Pentica. But it is 4 hours' walk there and back, and the houses and site have been long abandoned.

Follow the N 193 west, closely accompanied by the railway. 9km from Bocognano, and just beyond a bridge, a path leads left and a 10-minute walk brings you to the ruins of a medieval tower, 100m beyond which is a Bronze Age *statue-menhir*, standing at the limit of the Parc Naturel. It is 30km from here to Ajaccio.

INDEX TO PEOPLE

GENERAL INDEX

2A = Corse-du-Sud   2B = Haute-Corse

The intention of the index is to lead the reader to a description or reference as quickly as possible. Corsican language and spelling do not present a major problem. For example, a mountain pass in French is the term familiar to English-speaking readers, *col*. Both *col* and the Corsican *bocca* appear on maps so they are listed here under both headings. *Lavu* appears less frequently so lakes are listed here under French lacs and bergeries, mountain sheepfolds doubling as shelters, appear under that heading.

CORSICA

	Dual carriageway
	Main road
	Secondary road
	Other motorable road
	Footpath
7	Distance in km.
	Railway
	Reg. Natural Park Boundary
✈	Airport
✈	Aerodrome
🏕	Holiday village
⚓	Yachting locality
	Wood

Scale 1:550 000

0   5   10   15   20   25km

N

Cap Corse

I. de la Giraglia

Capo Grosso
Tollare
Barcaggio
Iles Finocchiarola
Botticella
Granaggiolo
Macinaggio
Marine de Méria
Méria
Port de Centuri
Prunu
Com. de Morsiglia
Col de Sta. Lucia 1
Castellu 485
•608
•Mte.
Santa Severa
Marine de Porticciolo
Pino
Com. de Cagnano
Luri
Marine de Pietracorbara
Santa Catalina
Marine de Sisco
Erbalunga
Lavasina
Pozzo
Com. de Brando
•Cima di e Follicie 1324
D80
82
BASTIA
N193
Minervio
Marine de Giottani
Pietracorbara
Canari
Marinca
•Monte Stello 1305
40
Santa-Maria-di-Lota
Com. de
D80
Com. de Patrimonio
Col de Teghime
Furiani
20
Etang de Biguglia
Marine d'Albo
NONZA
Punta di Canelle
Punta di Migrola
Golfe de St-Florent
B. di San Bernardino
Punta di Mortella
Nebbio
S. Angelo
•Mte. 355
Patrimonio
Oletta
D82
Biguglia
SAN-MICHELE
Désert des Agriates
•Mte. Genova 421
ST-FLORENT
B. di San Pancraziu
Rapale
Santo-Pietro-di-Tenda
Urtaca
•479
B. di Vezu
Castà
D81
44
36
Ogliastro
Osticoni
Punta di l'Acciolu
Oletta
NEBB
Punta di Curza
Ostriconi
Lozari
Ile Rousse
Monticello
Sta.-Reparata-di-Balagna
Sant' Antonio
Algajola
•197 Pigna
Marine de Sant'Ambrogio
Punta di a Revellata
Golfe